CHURCH, STATE, AND STUDY

CHURCH, STATE AND STUDY

ESSAYS

BY

ERNEST BARKER

Litt.D., D.Lit., LL.D.

PROFESSOR OF POLITICAL SCIENCE
IN THE UNIVERSITY OF CAMBRIDGE

GREENWOOD PRESS, PUBLISHERS
WESTPORT, CONNECTICUT

Library of Congress Cataloging in Publication Data

Barker, Sir Ernest, 1874-1960.
Church, state, and study.

Reprint of the 1930 ed. published by Methuen,
London.
1. Church and state--Addresses, essays, lectures.
2. Political science--Addresses, essays, lectures.
3. Education--Addresses, essays, lectures.
I. Title.
JA41.B3 1974   322'.1   72-7829
ISBN 0-8371-6534-2

First published in 1930 by Methuen & Co. Ltd., London

Reprinted with the permission of Methuen & Company, Ltd.

Reprinted from an original copy in the
collections of the University of Illinois Library

Reprinted in 1974 by Greenwood Press,
a division of Williamhouse-Regency Inc.

Library of Congress Catalogue Card Number 72-7829

ISBN 0-8371-6534-2

Printed in the United States of America

PREFACE

I HAVE ventured to collect in this volume, not without some misgivings, a number of the articles I have written or the addresses I have delivered *nel mezzo del cammin di nostra vita*. Why I have done so it would be hard to say, and perhaps I need not attempt to explain. Professor Stubbs once pleaded, in a similar case, that he had a passion for correcting proofs. I confess that I have the same passion ; but I would add, in further extenuation of what I have done, that I have succeeded in rejecting much more than I have felt myself justified in collecting. Not, I would add, that there has been any massacre of innocents. I rejected only what I honestly thought, after mature reflection, to be genuinely deserving of permanent oblivion.

Three of the pieces (II, VI, and VII) belong to my Oxford days, before 1920 ; seven of them (I, V, IX–XII, and the Appendix) belong to the years which I spent in London, from the middle of 1920 to the end of 1927 ; the remainder (III, IV, and VIII) belong to the last two years, during which I have been living in Cambridge. They are the products of different places and different periods ; and I am not at all sure that they are consistent. On the other hand, I should have been surprised, and indeed alarmed, if there had been no inconsistencies. The various pieces were written during a period of remarkable change ; if most of them belong to this side of the gulf of the war, there are two or three which belong to the other side of the gulf ; and not to have changed with the changing times would only have argued a wooden sort of consistency. It is in this way that I would explain to myself, for example, the relation between II and V, and, generally, the differences of view which I seem to trace in regard to the significance of the Nation and the claims and rights of the State. But I must not argue ; and I ' put myself upon the county ' in this matter.

Nearly all the pieces (I, IV, VII, XI, and the Appendix are the only exceptions) were originally composed for delivery as addresses or ' papers ' at various meetings. The volume is thus largely a volume of lectures ; and that may give it a certain unity, at any rate of form. I have also sought, in selecting and arranging the essays, to secure some unity of the general subject-matter and, so far as I could, an ordered sequence of the particular themes. The first four essays deal with Church and State in history ; the fifth is a bridge of transition to the theory and politics of the modern State, which are treated in the three subsequent essays ; the ninth is another bridge of transition, from history and politics to education ; and the last three are concerned with different phases of that subject, in the University, the School and the area of Adult Education. All the essays may be said, in a word, to deal with the history or the theory of society.

I desire to express my sincere and cordial thanks to the publishers and editors and the various bodies who have given me permission to reprint these pieces—to the Delegates of the Clarendon Press ; the Syndics of the Cambridge University Press ; the British Association, the British Institute of Adult Education, the Burge Trustees, and the Huguenot Society of London ; and the Editors of the *Hibbert Journal*, the *English Historical Review*, *History*, the *Listener*, and the old *Political Quarterly* which appeared between 1914 and 1916.

ERNEST BARKER

Cambridge
April 1930

CONTENTS

CHURCH, STATE, AND STUDY

I

THE ROMAN CONCEPTION OF EMPIRE [1]

THE Roman Empire was born in the Eastern Mediterranean ; and it was in the Eastern Mediterranean, in the city of Constantinople, that it died. We may almost say that it was Oriental in its origin : we may at any rate affirm that it was Hellenistic ; and Hellenistic means the fusion of Greek and Oriental. The process of political development which prepared its birth began in the West, in a city on the Tiber which looked across the Tyrrhenian Sea to the setting sun ; and it was the legal genius of Roman citizens—with their conceptions of *imperium* and *provincia, potestas* and *maiestas*—which gave to the Empire the framework and structure of its institutions. But the ideas on which it rested—the ideas which made it more than a structure, and gave it a root in the minds of men—were ideas which had germinated in the East. Any permanent society must rest on a body of belief and on the social will which such a body of belief creates. It was in the East that men had learned to believe in a single universal society, and in the government of that society by a king who was ' as a god among men,' and indeed was a very god ; and it was there, in the feeling of loyalty for the person of such a monarch, and even of ' adoration ' of his divinity, that a corresponding social will had found its expression. If *imperium* was a Latin word, the idea

[1] An Essay contributed originally to] the *Legacy of Rome* (Clarendon Press, Oxford), 1923.

I

of an empire and the idea of an emperor were not of Latin origin. We must recognize in the Roman Empire the result of the fusion of Roman political development and Roman institutional structure with Hellenistic ideas.

But it would be a grave error to magnify the Hellenistic element in this fusion at the expense of the Roman ; and paradox would be wearing cap and bells if it proceeded to the proposition that the Roman Empire, if it was an empire, was not fundamentally Roman. If it was the Greek genius which, in its later days, rose to conceptions of the unity of humanity, it was the Roman genius which translated those conceptions, in themselves unsubstantial and unbodied, into an organized system of life. But the word ' translation ' fails to do justice to Rome. It implies that the Greeks first wrote an original text, of which the Romans afterwards issued an authorized version. It would be truer to say that the Romans built first—or at any rate built independently—a *de facto* empire, on which the Greeks afterwards looked, and as they looked exclaimed, ' τοῦτ' ἐκεῖνο : this is the unity of humanity of which we have been thinking all along.' From this point of view we may almost say that Hellenistic conceptions settled upon and clustered round a Roman achievement ; adorned and even modified that achievement ; but left the solid core of achievement Roman still. It is hard to weigh men of action against men of thought : it is no less difficult to weigh a people of action against a people of thought. Perhaps it is unnecessary, as it is certainly thankless, to do either ; perhaps we may avoid contention, without shirking difficulties, if we conclude by saying that Rome built an empire in a world permeated by the preparatory thought of Greece, and that Greek thought continued to permeate, and even came to cement, the empire which Rome had built.

THERE were empires before that of Alexander. There was the Egyptian Empire, which extended to the Euphrates, of Thutmos III (*c.* 1500 B.C.) and his successors ;

there were the Semitic Empires of Sargon of Accad (*c.* 2750) and Hammurabi of Babylon (*c.* 2100), of the Assyrians of Nineveh (750–606) and the Chaldeans of Babylon (606–539) ; there was the Persian Empire (organized like the Roman in provinces, and traversed like the Roman by excellent roads) which lasted from 539 to 330 B.C. The Empire of Alexander was founded upon the ruin—and also upon the tradition—of the Persian, as the Persian had been founded upon the Chaldean and the Chaldean upon the Assyrian. Whatever the inspiration of Greek ideas under which Alexander began ; whatever his original conception of a ' crusade ' and the reduction of the ' barbarians ' under the Greeks—it is certain that he came under the sway of older traditions, and embraced a different policy. Rejecting the advice offered by Aristotle in a treatise ' On Kingship,' that ' he should distinguish between Greeks and barbarians, dealing with the former as ἡγεμών and the latter as δεσπότης,' he sought to unite East and West in a common equality. He fostered intermarriage between Greeks and Persians : he received Persians into his army ; he adopted the ceremonial of the Persian court and the Persian system of provincial government. His policy was perhaps premature ; and his successors reserved the higher offices of state for Greeks and Macedonians. But the spread of a common culture achieved what policy could not directly effect ; and in the next century Eratosthenes could declare the unity of mankind, ' refusing to agree with those who divided mankind into Greeks and barbarians, and advised Alexander to treat the former as friends and the latter as foes, and declaring that it was better to divide men simply into the good and the bad.'

This meant a great revolution in thought—a revolution which was the necessary precursor of any imperial system in the Western world. Alexander had united the known world of his time (save Italy and the confines of the West) in a single society ; and he had assumed the equality of all the members of that society. He had contradicted the two axioms hitherto current in the political thought of the

Greeks — that a multiplicity of separate self-governing and self-sufficing cities was the best constitution of politics, and that differences and inequalities between the members (enfranchised and disfranchised, citizen and alien) were inevitably implied by the very genius of the city. His conquests and his policy had implied two opposite conceptions—that of a single cosmopolis of the inhabited earth, transcending cities as it transcended tribes and nations ; and that of the equality of all men, or at any rate all free men, in the life of a common humanity. These are the two fundamental conceptions which inaugurate a new epoch—an epoch which succeeds to that of the πόλις, and precedes that of the national state ; an epoch which covers the centuries that lie between Aristotle and Alexander at one end and Luther and Henry VIII at the other, and embraces in its scope the three empires of Macedon and Rome and Charlemagne. They are again the two conceptions which we find in the teaching of St. Paul, who believed in one Church of all Christians which should cover the world, and held that in that Church there was 'neither Greek nor Jew . . . barbarian, Scythian, bond nor free.'

Implicit in the achievement of Alexander there is thus the idea of the union in a single society of the peoples both of the East and the West, who had hitherto either developed in isolation, or, if they had met, had met in conflict. He united the Eastern Mediterranean with Western Asia : it remained for Rome to add the Western Mediterranean to the amalgam which he had created. But a unity such as that which Alexander had founded needed a cohesive principle : it needed a common centre of personal attachment and loyalty ; and we must therefore proceed to examine the nature of the cohesive principle which he gave to his empire, and which Rome afterwards inherited from his successors. That principle, in a word, was the deification of the ruler. The deified king could claim the universality, and receive the universal worship, of a manifest god. On this ground Greek cities and Oriental nations could unite ; and with the throne thus elevated to an altar loyalty

could become a religion.   However foreign it may seem to
the Greek idea of the state as a free association of citizens,
the conception of the deified ruler was none the less rooted in
Greek habits of thought ; and the actual deification of
Alexander may be traced among the Ionian Greeks in the
beginning of his campaign, before he touched the soil of
Egypt or of Persia.   Unlike the Semites, who fixed a great
gulf between God and man, the Greeks conceived gods in
the likeness of men, and elevated men to the ranks of gods.[1]
It was their common practice to promote founders of cities
at death to the rank of hero, and to offer them ' hero-
worship ' ; and it was only an extension of this practice
when Alexander, the first leader of a united Greece and
the greatest of all the founders of Greek cities, was even in
life conceived to be not only a hero, but a god.   But if
the deification of Alexander was in accordance with Greek
conceptions and practice, it was also aided by the conceptions
and practice of the East.   The Egyptian kings were regarded, if not as gods in themselves, at any rate as incarna-
tions of the god Ammon or Re ; and the Persian kings
claimed ' adoration ' in virtue of the *Hvareno*, a nimbus
' conceived . . . as emanating from the sun, but also as a
token of supernatural grace.'[2]   It was in the Eastern
dominions of Alexander that the worship of the deified
ruler became—what it had never been formally made by
Alexander himself—an institution of State.   The kings of
Macedonia never pretended to divinity ; and indeed as they
were the kings of a single nation there was no necessity

---

[1] Goethe's poem, *Das Göttliche*, expresses the Greek conception.

Und wir verehren	Der edle Mensch
Die Unsterblichen,	Sei hülfreich und gut !
Als wären sie Menschen,	Unermüdet schaff' er
Thäten im Grossen,	Das Nützliche, Rechte ;
Was der Beste im Kleinen	Sei uns ein Vorbild
Thut oder möchte.	Jener geahneten Wesen !

[2] See H. Stuart Jones, *The Roman Empire*, p. 217.   In this fascinating
matter of the deification of rulers I have followed A. Bauer, *Vom Griechen-
tum zum Christentum*, pp. 53–92, and P. Wendland, *Die hellenistisch-
römische Kultur*, vi. 4 and vii. 3.   See also W. Ferguson's *Greek Imperialism* ;
and Professor Murray's *Four Stages of Greek Religion*, pp. 133–41.

that they should. It was otherwise with Egypt and Asia Minor, where there was no national feeling, and where traditions of supernatural monarchy were strong. Possibly in their lifetime, and certainly after their death, Ptolemy I and Berenice were the objects of a cult : Philadelphos and Arsinoe were worshipped as θεοὶ ἀδελφοί by 270 B.C. ; and we may still read the inscription in which Ptolemy V is celebrated as ' living for ever, beloved of Ptah, God Manifest . . . son of God and Goddess, like unto Horus, son of Isis and Osiris.' In the Seleucid kingdom the two first rulers were only canonized after death ; but Antiochus II is already θεός during his life.

It would be wrong to treat these swelling titles in any cavalier spirit. In their inception, whatever they may have become when they were staled by custom, they were more than adulation. They expressed a real gratitude of the subject for peace and good governance ; they implied a serious policy of the monarch, who knew no other way of consolidating his throne or uniting his dominions. And as they accorded with old Greek conceptions, so they also agreed with the contemporary movement of religious thought. It was the age of Euhemerism, in which gods were explained as great human ' benefactors ' and ' saviours ' who had won canonization ;. and it was easy to turn a living benefactor and saviour into a present and manifest god. After all, empires have their legends. And the legend of divinity need not fear comparison with the Napoleonic legend.

GREEK philosophy was a more potent force in its decline than it was in the great days of Plato and Aristotle ; and Stoicism exerted a greater influence on the lives of men and the development of States than the Academy or the Lyceum. There is much in the philosophy of Stoicism which reflects the era of Alexander ; and it was perhaps powerful because it marched with the times. The era was one of uprooting and emigration and the mixture of peoples, in which the West moved eastwards on a steady tide, and an ebb sometimes set from the East to the West. The early Stoics came from the East, and though they might inherit Greek physics and metaphysics, they were free from the prepossessions and prejudices of Greek political thought. Zeno, the founder of the school, was a hellenized Phoenician from Cyprus : he came from that region of the Cilician gulf, fertile in its contribution to human thought, which afterwards gave to the world the hellenized Syrian, Posidonius of Apamea, and the hellenized Hebrew, Paul of Tarsus. He came to Athens at the end of the fourth century, and lived there as a resident alien. It is difficult not to believe that he was influenced in his thought by the achievement of Alexander, which must have begun its course in the days of his youth in Cyprus ; nor is it any licence of conjecture to suggest that the philosophy which he taught at Athens, at any rate on its social side, was the translation into an explicit theory of the principle implicit in that achievement.

In Stoic philosophy the whole universe is conceived as a single intelligible unity, pervaded by reason ; and the Stoic belief in a World-State is simply the political aspect of this general philosophic conception. ' The whole Universe was only one Substance, one *Physis*, in various states, and that one Substance was Reason, was God.' Reason, God, Nature (φύσις) were all synonyms—synonyms for the intelligible and homogeneous essence of the Universe. Physically, that essence was regarded as a form of matter— fire or a fiery ether—' pure and most subtil ' (as it is written in the Book of Wisdom), ' more moving than any motion,' which ' passeth and goeth through all things . . . the breath of the power of God, and a pure influence flowing from the glory of the Almighty.' In God this essential Reason was whole and pure : in man it was a fragment (ἀπό-σπασμα) ; but that fragment was ' the ruling principle ' in man, which determined the way of his life. By it, in the first place, he was knit to God and knit to his fellows ; in its virtue he was a ζῷον κοινωνικόν ; and because it was universal, the κοινωνία was universal. From it, in the second place, he derived the law of this universal κοινωνία ; for since reason was the ruling principle in each, it was the ruling principle of the society of all, and since, again, reason was the same as nature, the law of the universal society based on reason was the same as the law of nature. One universal society, one state of the whole world ; one law of nature, with which all its members must live in conformity—these are the two great tenets of Stoicism. ' He taught '—so it is recorded by Plutarch of Zeno—' that we should not live in cities and demes, each distinguished by separate rules of justice, but should regard *all* men as fellow-demesmen and fellow-citizens ; and there should be one life and order (κοσμος) as of a single flock feeding together on a common pasture (νόμος).' [1]

The teaching of Zeno had necessarily its negative aspects. He was the iconoclast of the πόλις, as he was the prophet of the World-State ; and a criticism of the institutions of the πόλις, somewhat in the vein of his predecessors the Cynics, appears more strongly in the records of his views than it does in those of his successors, who modified his asperities. We are told that he refused to admit to his ' republic ' (like Plato, he wrote a *Republic*) either temples or courts of law or currency or marriage or gymnasia or the ordinary system of education. These were perhaps the extremities of an early radicalism. More essential in his teaching was his insistence on equality. If all human beings had reason, there was a fundamental human equality ; and though one might divide the wise man from the foolish, there was no argument for distinguishing between the status of men and that of women, and little argument for distinguishing between the position of masters and that of slaves. Stoicism was thus an influence in favour of the equality of the sexes ; and if it did not make for the legal abolition of slavery, it issued in the view that slavery was an artificial institution of human law, and that in the region of the spirit all men were, or might be, equal. The graded inequality

---

[1] Plutarch, *de Alex. Fort.* i. 6. The word κόσμος means both ' order ' and ' world ' ; the word νόμος both ' law ' and ' pasture.'

of the city disappears before the solvent of this teaching ; and in it we may see the emergence of a tenet, to which the Roman lawyers gave universal currency, that ' before the law of nature all men have an equal status ' (*omnes homines natura aequales sunt*).

The vogue which S*t*oic philosophy came to enjoy at Rome, from the days of the Scipios to the days of Marcus Aurelius, is a matter known to every scholar. It imbued the Roman lawyers with their tenets of a universal law of nature and the equality of all men before that law. It carried its conception of the State of the whole world to Marcus Aurelius ; and the classical text for that conception may be found in a sentence of his *Meditations* : ' the poet saith, Dear city of Cecrops ; but thou—wilt thou not say, Dear city of God ? ' The thought on which the best of the Romans fed was a thought of the World-State, the universal law of nature, the brotherhood and the equality of men ; and thought of this nature inevitably penetrated and determined the general conception which they entertained of their empire. It is of peculiar importance, therefore, that we should understand the stage of development which Stoicism had reached, and the form of presentation which it had found, in the days of the establishment of the Roman Empire—the days, we may also add, of the beginnings of the Christian Church, which also claimed to be a universal society, and also came under the influence of Stoicism. Here we touch the name of Posidonius of Apamea, who taught in the University of Rhodes (Cicero, among others, was one of his pupils) in the last century before Christ. He was not an original thinker : he was an eclectic, who wedded Stoicism to Platonism and (it has even been held) to the religious doctrines of the East. It is his peculiar importance that ' the great body of his writings expressed with unique completeness the general mind of the Greek world at the Christian era,' [1] and that, as such a synthesis, they formed, as it were,

[1] E. Bevan, *Stoics and Sceptics*, iii. See also P. Wendland, op. cit., pp. 60 ff. and 134 ff.

the *textus receptus* of philosophic thought on which Cicero, Virgil, and many others drew.

It has been suggested by Mr. Bevan that the formula for the activity of Posidonius may be found in a simple phrase— ' to make men at home in the Universe.' In his philosophy the universe became companionable and comfortable. Above was the fiery ether ; below the world of men. At death the fiery particle of the human soul sought to rejoin its own element, and was encouraged in its upward way by the disembodied souls who had found their goal. All was ' one great city, of which gods and men were citizens . . . a compact and knowable whole.' With the whole universe thus made a companionable society, it was natural to conceive of a human society here on earth, living in sympathy with itself as it lived in sympathy with Heaven. And if the dead thus moved upward to the ether and to God, it was also natural to think of the deification of the dead. Here Posidonius found room in his philosophy for that deification of rulers which was current in the Hellenistic East. The great dead had gone home to God and joined the Godhead ; and even the great living might be regarded as sent by ' Providence ' or ' the eternal and immortal Nature of the Universe ' to be ' saviours of the community of the human race.' [1]

The philosophy of Posidonius is really of the nature of a religion : if it is based on Stoicism, it contains elements drawn, through Plato and the Pythagoreans, from the Greek mysteries ; and it may also contain elements derived from the religions of the East. It has even been suggested that Caesar may have found in the religious system of Posidonius, with its union of philosophic speculation and popular belief, the model of a religion suited to the universal empire which he would fain have built on the lines of the absolute monarchies of the East. It is at any rate probable that Caesar knew the system of Posidonius ; and without

[1] These terms may be found in two Greek inscriptions of the time of Augustus quoted in Wendland, op. cit., pp. 409–10. The language is Stoic : the reference is to Augustus himself.

subscribing to any theory of connexion between the political
ambitions of Caesar and the philosophic religion of Posidonius, we may certainly believe in a connexion between
the religious development and the political evolution of the
last three centuries before the Christian era.   We have to
remember that the ancient State was also a Church.   The
City had its civic religion, of which the civic magistrates
were priests : ' the real religion of the fifth century,' Professor Murray writes, ' was a devotion to the City itself.'
In the same way the great monarchies of the third century
had their monarchical religion ; and their real religion,
as we have seen, was a devotion to the deified king.   With
politics and religion so closely connected that they were
one, it was inevitable that, just as political movements
produced religious consequences, so religious movements
should involve political results.   Now the religious movement of the latter centuries before the birth of Christ was
towards a fusion of cults and a general belief in a single God
of the Universe.   It would be irrelevant, and it is impossible, to describe that movement here.   It is apposite,
and it is necessary, to draw attention to its political consequences.   A world with one religion will also tend to be
a world of a single State.   Granted the general conceptions
of the ancient world, we may say that the growth of mono
theism encouraged the growth of a universal monarchy.

MEANWHILE the political development of Rome itself
was moving to meet the system of thought implicit in
the Hellenistic monarchies, in the philosophy of Stoicism,
and in the religious trend.   The original City-State of Rome,
with its municipal system of magistrates, town-council
(*senatus*), and town-meeting (*comitia*), had grown to the
dimensions of a State greater than even the empire of
Alexander.   By a process of agricultural expansion, which
sowed her peasant townsmen up and down Italy, Rome
had become the mistress of the peninsula at the beginning
of the third century.   By a process of commercial expansion, which gave her trading citizens the monopoly of

Mediterranean trade at the expense of Carthage in the West and of Corinth and other centres in the East, she had become the virtual mistress of the Mediterranean littoral in the middle of the second century. There ensued a century of troubles, from the tribunate of Tiberius Gracchus to the battle of Actium, in which the municipal constitution of Rome showed itself inadequate to solve the problems or secure the allegiance of the territories which had come under its sway. Even in Rome itself, governed under an unwritten constitution which rested on understandings, the actual supremacy acquired by an aristocratic senate in the period of expansion was challenged by a popular party in the name of the formal rights of the general body of citizens. In Italy at large the inequality between allies who were really subjects and Roman citizens who acted as sovereigns produced a second and even more menacing cleavage ; and though after the Social War a remedy was sought in the grant of Roman citizenship to the allies (88 B.C.), it is obvious that a grant of citizenship which only meant inclusion in a civic assembly that they could not attend was no real bond of union between the Italians and the city of Rome, and only proved the inability of a City-State, which, with the world in its hands, remained in the sphere of civic ideas, to form even an Italian State. But it was neither the struggles in Rome nor the cleavage in Italy which in the issue subverted the civic constitution : it was the condition and the problems of the provinces of the Mediterranean littoral. Nominally protected by regulations passed by the Senate, the provinces were actually the prey of Roman governors, who in their short term of office sought to exploit their riches, and whom the constitution provided no effective means of controlling. The result was disastrous alike to the provincials, who found that their lot was not protection but pillage, and to Rome itself, where the returned governor, with his wealth, his ambitions, and his experience of absolute power, was a menace to civic ideas. And the provinces also entailed problems of defence —problems of the frontier—which could only be solved by methods which constituted a still graver menace. Armies were necessary to face the Berber tribes in the south, the Celts and Germans in the north, the kings of Pontus and Parthia in the east. The danger was constantly recurrent : the armies accordingly became standing armies, composed of professional troops, alien in spirit from the republican constitution, and a ready instrument for monarchical ambitions. With a professional army came the professional general ; and men emerged of the type of Marius and Sulla, Pompey and Caesar — masters of legions, and masters, if they would, of Rome. The dissensions in the city between the aristocratic party of the Senate and the *populares* who appealed to the masses were the opportunity of the professional generals. They threw their swords into the scale and arbitrated ; and finally the greatest and the boldest, Julius Caesar, took the sword into his hands and ruled. He had enjoyed ten years' experience of absolute power in Gaul : he was master of the finest legions of the day ; he was allied with the popular cause ; he had a genius for men and affairs.

We may define Caesarism as a form of autocracy, backed by an army, which rests formally on some manner of plebiscite and actually — so long, at any rate, as it is successful—on a measure of popular support. So defined, Caesarism is identical with Bonapartism. But there is a fundamental difference. Bonapartism showed itself personal and transitory, an ephemeral chase of flying glory : Caesarism became a permanent institution. Modified and veiled at first by the policy of Augustus, but showing itself clearly as it grew firmer and stronger, it controlled the Mediterranean world for centuries. The reasons for its permanence were partly negative and partly positive. There was no nationalism abroad to oppose a non-national State : there were only dying City-States which had lost the instinct for autonomy, and tribal formations which had not learned to cherish political ambitions. There was no democratic spirit in the air to wither an absolute government : the temper of the times was one of acquiescence, and even of gratitude. Religion and philosophy were the occupation of stirring minds : the only opposition to the Caesars came from a group of aristocratic *frondeurs*, who accumulated memories but were barren of achievements. While there was little to oppose Caesarism, there was much to support its cause. The provinces enjoyed peace : their frontiers were defended ; their governors were supervised. Their taxes were not diminished : they were even increased in order to meet the expenses of the new system of government ; but extortion ceased, and it is significant that in the new security the rate of interest sank to one-third of what it had been under the Republic. The domestic factions of Rome died. In Italy the Romans and the Italians were equally subjects of Caesar. With the head of the army at the head of the State, the peril that the army might thrust its sword into the issues of the civil State was, if not removed, at any rate diminished. A professional soldiery might still by a *coup d'épée* depose or elect a Caesar : in the third century it dominated politics for fifty troubled years ; and the military basis of the Empire was always a weakness of the emperors. But of the first two hundred years of the Empire, at any rate, we may safely say that they were years in which the civilian power was the master of the State.

If we would understand the feelings towards the Empire which were general among its subjects in the days of its foundation, we must turn to the literature and inscriptions in which they are recorded. What Rome and the Empire owed to Augustus is testified in Virgil and Horace ; and their poetry is no adulation, but the expression of a feeling as genuine as that of Tennyson for Victoria and the Victorian Age. The language of inscriptions is even more instructive testimony, because it is more direct and more naïve. We may deduct a liberal discount on the ground of conventional flattery from some of the Greek inscriptions : they still remain significant. Augustus is ' the Saviour sent to make wars cease and to order all things ' ; ' through him have come good tidings ' (εὐαγγέλια) ; ' in him Providence has not only fulfilled, but even exceeded, the prayers of all : sea and land are at peace : cities flourish in order, harmony, and prosperity : there is a height and abundance of all good things : men are filled with hopes for the future and gladness in the present.' It is impossible to doubt, as one reads these words, that the feeling of a new and better order lies behind them. A century of war, of extortion, of insecurity, of misery has come to an end. A new era is dawning. The Empire begins in hope, and continues in comfort.

> Magnus ab integro saeclorum nascitur ordo.
> iam redit et Virgo, redeunt Saturnia regna,
> iam nova progenies, caelo demittitur alto.
> . . . .
> ipsae lacte domum referent distenta capellae
> ubera, nec magnos metuent armenta leones.
> . . . .
> aspice venturo laetentur ut omnia saeclo !

THE Empire was the solution of a problem : it was even more—it was a 'salvation.' Religious feelings supported its institution and continuance ; and that religious feeling was one of adoration for a present god, sent by Providence for the ending of war and the saving of the community of the human race. Here we meet once more that idea of the deified ruler, which the Hellenistic East had known since the days of Alexander and his first successors, and which had already been moving westwards for many years before the reign of Augustus. Flamininus, the victor of Cynoscephalae, was greeted by the Greeks as deliverer and ' Saviour ' ; Chalcis decreed him divine honours ; and like the deified rulers of the East, he struck coins with his own image and superscription. This was a first burst of feeling, natural in the first formal contact of the Greeks with a grave Roman commander ; but as they realized that the Roman State had no permanent personal sovereign, they contented themselves for years to come with the worship of *Roma*. *Roma* was, however, a pale goddess : instinct, the stronger because it was now a habit, craved a personal object of devotion ; and in the first century B.C. we find provincial governors worshipped as gods in the East. As great leaders of armies rose to new eminence in Roman politics, the monarchical instinct rose to greater heights, and found a still more swelling expression. Pompey, who had given security to the Eastern Mediterranean by his campaigns against the pirates and the King of Pontus, was not only celebrated in inscriptions as the saviour who had given peace to the world : the Athenians themselves declared him a god, and joined with the ' Pompeiasts ' of Delos (the term indicates a formal cult established in his honour) in dedicating his statue to Apollo. The type and the genius of the absolute monarchies of the East became familiar to ambitious Romans ; and when they received the shadow of divine consecration, they could not but covet the substance of absolute power which cast the shadow. The foundations of imperialism are being laid when the great leaders of the standing armies of the West begin to meet in the East the type of institution and the temper of spirit which can give a concrete body to their dreams and a definite goal to their ambitions. A Roman development meets a Greek conception. That is the genesis of the conception of the Roman Empire.

It was not Pompey, in spite of his Eastern experience and honours, who was destined to Empire : it was Julius Caesar—who, if he had studied in Rhodes and heard Posidonius, had spent his political career in the West as governor first of Spain and afterwards of the two Gauls. Caesar was a scholar and a man of genius ; and he could apprehend with a rapidity and seize with a vigour denied to Pompey the chances of a fateful hour and the opportunity for founding a ' new monarchy,' which, new as it was to the West, was an ancient pattern in the East. It was not the ' restoration ' of an archaic and half-legendary municipal monarchy which Caesar planned : it was the ' translation ' to the West of that tradition of the divine monarch of a great State which lived in the East. Like Pompey, he received divine honours in the day of his success from the Greeks of the Eastern Mediterranean ; but it was a new and significant thing that he received the same honours in Rome from the Roman authorities. After the battle of Thapsus, his statue was erected by the Senate in the temple of Jupiter with the inscription *Semideo* ; after the battle of Munda, a second statue was erected, in the temple of Quirinus, with the dedication *Deo invicto*. A cult arose in his honour, with its college of *Luperci Iuliani* and its *flamen* : his image appeared on coins in token of his divinity ; his admirers crowned his statue with the white woollen fillet once worn by the Persian kings, and afterwards by Alexander and his successors ; and Shakespeare has made us all familiar with the story of Antony thrice offering him a kingly crown—which was in effect an Eastern diadem —on the feast of the Lupercalia.

The open and frank policy of translating to Rome an Eastern type of monarchy failed. It was not so much a passion for liberty, as a clinging to Roman ways and traditions in the face of a policy tending to the substitution of Oriental forms and conceptions, that inspired the opposition and dictated the murder of Caesar. Refusing to learn by the lesson of his failure, Antony—the confidant of his plans —repeated his master's attempt : taking the East for his province, and allying himself with Cleopatra, the one living representative of the divine monarchies of the East, he pretended to divinity and played the part of Hellenistic monarch. Octavian was more cautious and more ready to profit by the teaching of experience. He disarmed the opposition in Rome by disavowing any policy of adopting Oriental forms, and by professing to base his power on' old Roman conceptions of consular *imperium* and tribunician *potestas*. On this basis, which from one point of view we may almost call nationalist, as from another we may call it antiquarian, he was able to gather the Latin West to his cause, uniting under his banner both the friends and the foes of Caesar ; to discredit Antony as a representative of eastern enormities ; and, defeating his rival, to unite the East and the West under a form of government which

2

professed to be a partnership between the first magistrate of Rome and its ancient Senate.

But it was an absolutism none the less ; and it was an absolutism which from the first contained the conception and the cult of the deified ruler. At the time of the formation of the triumvirate of Octavian, Antony, and Lepidus, at the end of 43 B.C., a temple was consecrated, on the place on which his dead body had been burned, ' to the genius of *divus Iulius, pater patriae*, whom the Senate and people of Rome have received into the ranks of the Gods.' This is the worship of the dead ruler ; but, as in the Hellenistic kingdoms, the progress to a regular worship of the living ruler was rapid. Augustus, as the inscriptions which have already been quoted show, was being worshipped in the East as ' a saviour . . . through whom have come good tidings,' by the year 9 B.C. ; and even earlier (17–12 B.C.) he is described in another Greek inscription as ' God the son of God, Augustus, the Benefactor.' In Egypt he enters into the style of the Ptolemies : he is ' autocrat, Son of the Sun, Lord of the Diadem, Caesar, living for ever, beloved of Ptah and Isis.' [1] The language and practice of the East were transferred, in a modified form, to the West. Provincial *concilia*, analogous to the κοινά of Asia Minor, were associated with the imperial cult ; and in Gaul (as in Spain and also on the Rhine) representatives chosen by the different tribes annually elected a priest for the service of the *Ara Romae et Augusti*. In Rome and in Italy the worship of Augustus was nominally forbidden ; but in many of the Italian towns we may trace a cult of the emperor, with *Augustales* devoted to its service ; and in the *vici* of Rome

[1] The influence of Ptolemaic Egypt on the development of the Empire deserves notice. It had developed a remarkable system of administration (see Bauer, op. cit., pp. 33 ff.), as well as an advanced form of divine monarchy ; and both of these developments influenced the Roman emperors, the more as they treated Egypt differently from all other provinces, ruling there in their own right as successors of the Ptolemies, and not as representatives of the city of Rome. The Egyptian system of taxation influenced the financial policy of Augustus ; and it was when he became successor to the Ptolemies that he necessarily became a god.

itself we find the worship of the *Lares Compitales* combined
with that of the *genius* of Augustus.[1]   The house of Augustus
on the Palatine Hill was united with the temple of his patron
Apollo ; in his house were treasured the Sibylline oracles ;
to his house was transferred the cult of Vesta. ' The
Penates of the *gens Iulia* were united with those of the State ;
and the future and fortunes of the Roman people were
now placed in the house of Augustus.'

We must not emphasize the imperial cult unduly.
Augustus never allowed himself to be entitled openly a very
god in Rome itself, as Caesar had done : he assumed no
crown : he claimed no form of divine honour.   The poets
of his age—Propertius, Virgil, Horace, and Ovid (especially
Ovid)—may term him *Deus* : he acts as a plain Roman
citizen.   The religion which he would foster, and in the
service of which he would enlist that feeling of mingled
gratitude and hope which marks his age—as of men escaped
from shipwreck, eager to dedicate their dripping garment
to a saving deity—is the ancient religion of his country.   He
closes the temple of Janus in token of peace : he celebrates
Ludi Saeculares to purge away the sins of the past : he
dedicates an *Ara Pacis Augustae*, the crowning achievement of Augustan art.   He would associate a religious
revival with the nascent empire, and consecrate his power
by the association : he would cast round the new system
a halo, if not of the personal worship of his own divinity
(though he never frowned upon such worship), at any rate
of the religious awakening which the peace of the new system
had brought and the policy of the new monarch had fostered.
There is policy, after all, even in the religious policy which
seems least political.

The general religious reformation of the Augustan age
inspired Virgil : it had little abiding result in the mass.   But
the worship of the deified ruler continued and grew.   Cali-
gula and Nero pretended to a present divinity ; but generally the emperor was elevated to the rank of *divus*, and
made the object of a cult, after his death ; and during his

[1] H. Stuart Jones, op. cit., p. 28 ; Wendland, op. cit., pp. 146–7.

life it was his *genius* which was held to be sacred. Here
was found the basis of allegiance. The oath of officials
and soldiers was associated with the *genius* of the present
emperor and the *divi Caesares* of the past. When the new
dynasty of the Flavii succeeded to the Julian dynasty in
70 A.D., it sought to prove its legitimacy by assuming a
similar divinity. Magistrates of Roman towns in the provinces took an oath to the divinity of Augustus, Claudius,
Vespasian, and Titus : Domitian made the residence of
the Flavian family (much as Augustus had done with his
house on the Palatine) into a shrine served by a college of
Flaviales ; and, as in Egypt under the Ptolemies,[1] the
women of the family received consecration along with the
men. The deification of the emperor, and the allegiance
which he receives in virtue of his divinity, are obviously
the foundation, or at any rate the cement, of the empire.
' In this cult,' writes Wendland, ' with its peculiar mixture
of patriotic and religious feeling, there was found a common
expression, which served as a bond of union, for that membership of the empire which was shared by parts so different
in nationality and in religion : it was the token and symbol
of imperial unity.' The empire was, in effect, a politico-
ecclesiastical institution. It was a Church as well as a
State : if it had not been both, it would have been alien
from the ideas of the ancient world. A City-State entailed
a civic worship : an Empire-State entailed an empire-
worship ; and an empire-worship in turn—granted the
existence of a personal emperor, and granted, too, the need
for a personal symbol in a State so much larger and so much
less tangible than a City-State which could be personalized
itself — entailed the worship of an emperor. It is not
irrelevant or disproportionate to linger over this aspect of
the Roman Empire. If it had not shown this aspect to its
subjects, it would not have been an empire ; for it would
not have been a coherent society united by a common will.

[1] Vespasian was first proclaimed Emperor at Alexandria, while he was
in Judaea.   His first act as Emperor was to occupy Egypt ; and here he
wrought a supposed miracle of healing by the royal touch.

BUT the empire was not only a religion : it was also a citizenship ; and we have now to inquire into the development of a common imperial citizenship, with its corollary of a common imperial law.   By the end of the Republic the municipal citizenship of Rome had already developed into a State-citizenship of Italy.   Under this system, as it was inherited and developed by the early emperors, Italy was separated from and privileged above the rest of the empire ; and in other respects (no troops, for instance, were quartered in Italy, but, on the other hand, only Italians could serve in the *corps d'élite* of the praetorian cohorts) Italy enjoyed an exceptional position.   But the State-citizenship of Italy was gradually widened as colonies of Roman citizens were founded in the provinces, or provincials were admitted to Roman citizenship.   Here the army played a large part : military service conferred Roman citizenship ; and as troops were recruited mainly in the provinces, a broad highway was opened for the enfranchisement of provincials.[1] When the Emperor Claudius (who introduced Gaulish chieftains to the *cursus honorum* and the ranks of Senate) revived the office of censor and took a census, he found that the number of citizens had increased by more than a million since the end of the reign of Augustus.   The civic body had become a new thing : if it included provincials as well as Italians, it also included freedmen as well as the free-born.   It contained different nationalities and different classes ; and its growth tended to abolish both differences.

The abolition of different nationalities meant the emergence of what we may almost call a Mediterranean nationality. We may date the emergence of this new nationality from the reign of Hadrian.   He was the first emperor to diminish

---

[1] From the time of Vespasian the Italians were excused from service in the legions ; and legionaries were recruited entirely from the provinces— the eastern provinces providing troops for the East and for Africa, and the western provinces for the West.   From the time of Hadrian the legions were recruited from the various areas in which they were quartered, and recruits were thus left to serve in their native country.   Under this system a Briton recruited in Britain for service with one of the three British legions would receive Roman citizenship without leaving the island.

the peculiar privileges of Italy : he visited and adorned with buildings almost every province of the empire : he showed his cosmopolitan temper by recruiting special bodies of Oriental troops and by giving to a Greek the command of a frontier province ; and, as his predecessor Trajan had done on a still grander scale (especially in Dacia), he spread Roman colonies over the empire.[1] Half a century after the death of Hadrian the Emperor Septimius Severus, an African by birth, destitute of Hadrian's ideal of a new nationality, but practically impatient of any anomaly which interfered with military efficiency or ease of administration, abolished the military privileges of Italy and granted citizenship to many provincial towns, especially in his own native province.   It was the culmination of the policy of Hadrian and Severus, and at the same time the result of a tendency implicit in the very conception of the empire, when in 212 A.D. Caracalla promulgated the *Constitutio Antonina*, by which all free-born members of the communities of the empire were granted Roman citizenship.   With one emperor and one allegiance—an allegiance shared by all, and shared equally by all—a common citizenship naturally followed.

The edict of Caracalla not only meant the blending of nationalities in one nationality : it also meant the blending of differences of status in a common equality.   The empire had been from the first a levelling force.   Augustus had already followed the policy of opening a career to all talents : as he opened the Senate to knights, so he opened the ranks of the knights for the admission of members of the *plebs*. This is the natural policy of any absolute government : it would fain enrich its service by drawing freely on all classes, and it would set the dignity of its service, which it proclaims a dignity of desert, above any dignity based on descent. In its passion for equality—which was quite compatible

---

[1] Hadrian, like his cousin Trajan, was a provincial from Spain.   The Julian emperors were all Roman : the Flavians were Italian, of a Sabine stock.   Severus, whose family spoke Punic, and who married a Syrian wife, marks a new epoch in the principate.

with a marked preference for its own confidential servants—
imperialism came close to Stoicism, which proclaimed the
equality of citizen and alien, man and woman, bondman
and free, while it cherished a peculiar regard for the *sapiens*
who had attained to high rank in the service of Reason.
It may have been in the logic of principles other than those
of Stoicism that the Roman emperors realized the Stoic
ideal of a universal society in which all the members were
equal ; but we must remember that Stoicism influenced the
Roman lawyers' conception of a law of nature which knew
no difference of status, and that the conceptions of the
Roman lawyers influenced the policy of the Roman
emperors.

The development of a common law for the empire
accompanied, as it helped to promote, the development of a
common citizenship.   From early days, far back in the
history of the Republic, the praetors had been gradually
formulating in their edict a new procedure and system of
law, which should be generally applicable to cases in which
others than Roman citizens were concerned.   If we look
at the origin of this system, we shall call it the praetor's
law, or *ius praetorium* : if we look at the area of its application, we shall call it the general law, or *ius gentium*.   Commercial reasons dictated the growth of the new jurisprudence :
a law was needed for commercial cases, in which foreign
traders were concerned, and which grew more and more
frequent as Rome became more and more a commercial
city.   The *ius civile* of Rome, even if it had not been, as it
was, the prerogative of the Roman *civis*, was too archaic,
and too much the law of a limited agricultural community,
to suit these cases ; and the law which the praetors began
to apply, and which was thus the foundation of the *ius
gentium*, was the more modern merchant law which had
come into being, and attained a general validity, in the
Mediterranean area.   Building on this foundation, and
adding to this borrowed material a native legal genius and
grasp of legal principle, the praetors formulated in their
edict a system of law which had at once the simplicity and

the absence of archaic formalism necessary for commercial cases, and the universality of application which would suit the conditions of general Mediterranean trade. This simple and universal law, thus formulated by the praetors, became connected with the conception of a law of nature. It is quite possible that the Roman lawyers realized the ' natural ' character of the *ius gentium* even before they were imbued with Stoic philosophy : it is certain that, as they came to understand the Stoic conception of a universal law of nature, they came to regard the *ius gentium* as a close approximation to that conception ; and though it was never universally or completely identified with the law of nature, it was at any rate regarded as the concrete expression of such a law in actual human society—less perfect, in that it denied equality and recognized slavery ; but more serviceable, because it was actually formulated and administered in courts. As a school of jurisconsults arose at Rome, the practical application of the *ius gentium* in the praetor's court was supplemented by scientific inquiry ; and from the second century B.C. a body of trained jurists applied their skill to elucidate and develop its implications. The majesty of the *ius gentium* was recognized— and at the same time its growth was stopped—when Hadrian realized a plan which is said to have been entertained by Julius Caesar, and caused the jurist Salvius Julianus to codify the praetorian edict in a fixed and final form. By this time the work had been done : the city-law of Rome had been expanded to meet the needs of the new Mediterranean state : a *ius gentium,* regarded as valid for all free men *everywhere* (this is the meaning of *gentium*), and assuming an ideal aspect by its close connexion with the law of nature—a connexion which helped to ameliorate the lot even of the slave—was co-extensive with the whole empire. And if the expansion of this *ius gentium* was stopped by its codification, there was another source ready and able to provide a law no less universal. The emperors had the power of issuing ' rescripts ' in answer to any inquiry or petition ; and these rescripts, if they dealt largely with

matter of administration, were also concerned with matter of
law. The Antonines used their power to advance the
emancipation of slaves and to maintain the principle
that all accused persons must be held to be innocent until
they were proved to be guilty ; and the *constitutiones
principum*—the generic name applied to imperial rescripts,
edicts, and decrees—became a great agent of legal progress
down to the days of Justinian. Valid for the whole empire
in virtue of their origin, they continued and completed
the formation of a single law for the Mediterranean world.[1]

Along with the growth of unity in citizenship and unity
in law there went also a unification of government. We can
hardly say that the early empire possessed a unified government. The policy of Augustus was a policy of dovetailing
the new into the old and uniting the new monarchy with
the ancient Republic ; and it resulted in a partnership,
or 'dyarchy,' under which the prince divided authority
with the Senate and People—which meant, in effect, the
Senate. This dualism is most obvious in the system which
gave to the prince the frontier provinces and to the Senate
the rest ; but it is implicit in the whole structure. Dualism
could hardly have worked under any conditions : it certainly could not work when the Senate was unable to
govern, and imperfectly qualified even to oppose. The
emperors, with their trained staff of officials and their
supreme command of the army, were from the first the
superior partners ; and a zest for efficiency as well as a love
of power drove them ultimately to rule in isolation. The
process of development is slow : the struggle of the emperors
and the Senate is for long years the real content of the
political history of the empire. It is a proof of the legal

[1] It should be remarked that, great as was the legal genius of the
Romans, the development of their law owes something to Hellenistic law,
which we are gradually coming to know from papyri. We cannot, indeed,
speak of Graeco-Roman law as we speak of Graeco-Roman civilization.
But we may safely say that the Hellenistic kingdoms, with their high
civilization and intricate commerce, had developed a common jurisprudence, which affected the Roman law of mortgage and other branches
of the Roman law of contract.

genius of the Romans and their instinctive respect for precedent and constitutional tradition, that even the deified Caesars, masters of all the legions, should have respected for centuries the impotent majesty of republican forms. It may be that they were not without a suspicion that even the form of constitutionalism was better than the naked fact of a military autocracy, which might reveal to the legions only too clearly the fatal secret of their power. Whatever the reason, the fact remains that the structure of Augustus, doomed from the first to failure by its inherent flaws, was none the less slow in failing utterly. It is not until three centuries have run, and we reach the days of Aurelian and Diocletian, that we can finally detect a logical and thorough-going absolutism. To this day Roman Law preserves traces of the old dualism. If it can pronounce the emperor ' a living law on earth,' and declare him ' free from all laws,' it can also proclaim that ' it is a saying worthy of the ruler's majesty that a prince should profess himself bound by the laws.' If Ulpian enunciates the absolutist dictum, that ' the will of the prince has the force of law,' he adds at once the democratic explanation, ' because the People confers upon him and into his hands all its own sovereignty and power.' We may argue with almost equal cogency that Roman Law implies absolutism, and that it implies constitutionalism.

If the transference of plenary sovereignty to the emperor is a slow process, the process may already be traced in the reign of Hadrian. As he sought to deprive Italy of its primacy, so he began to divest the Senate of its partnership. He gave an additional importance to the knights, who constituted the civil service : it was a knight who held the only considerable command which he gave to a subject ; and knights were admitted to his *consilium* along with senators. Septimius Severus, even more inimical than Hadrian to the primacy of Italy, encroached still further on the prerogatives of the Senate. In his reign senators could no longer propose decrees : when treason was in question their dignity no longer protected them from torture ; and the

Senate ceased to exercise an influence in the apportioning of provinces or the appointing of magistrates. The system of dyarchy is dying when the Senate loses even its patronage ; but the death of the system belongs to a later epoch, and it is connected with a new ascendancy of the East and a fresh movement in the sphere of religion.

FROM the first the Roman Empire had been divided into two parts—the Hellenized East and the Roman West ; the one an amalgam of Oriental nationalities and religions, united by a general diffusion of Hellenic speech and culture, which was sometimes a veneer and sometimes a deep and genuine thing ; the other a collection of Celtic cantons, Berber tribes, and Italian townsfolk, imbued with Latin speech and pervaded by Latin traditions. It is a division which history has proved to be deep : it is a division which led to the parting of the empire into Eastern and Western halves, as it led to the schism of Christianity between Eastern and Western churches. If Julius Caesar had perhaps inclined to the East, the policy of Augustus, with its strong Latin trend, had emphasized the West, and from the beginning of his principate to the accession of Vespasian we may trace, in literature as in other directions, a dominance of Latin culture.[1] From the reign of Vespasian Greek literature begins to flourish again ; after the reign of Hadrian the centre of gravity begins to shift to the East, and the process begins which Constantine sealed by the foundation of Constantinople. What is ominous for the future is that as the East becomes more preponderant in the empire, it also becomes less Hellenic. Oriental nationalities and religions, dormant under Hellenism, but influencing Hellenism even while they were dormant, quicken to a new life ; and the Roman emperors, drawn more and more eastward by the problems of Eastern turbulence and Eastern

---

[1] Latin was the official language of the Greek East, and the Greeks used the services of interpreters. Public documents (such as the famous inscription termed the *Monumentum Ancyranum*) were bilingual ; and the imperial chancery had both a Greek and a Latin department.

frontiers, fall under the fascination of Eastern institutions and cults.

Early in the third century (227 A.D.) the Sassanids established a new Persian Empire with its capital at Ctesiphon ; and under the rule of the new dynasty, Zoroastrianism—with its cult of Ahura-mazda, the ' wise lord,' the god of heaven, who fights against Ahriman and the powers of darkness—became an official religion.[1] A form or a derivative of that religion was Mithraism. In the pure Zoroastrian faith Mithra was the god of light, the messenger of Ahura-mazda, the leader of his hosts ; but as Mithraism became an independent cult he became the supreme god, the very sun, the vivifying, penetrating, conquering ruler of the universe. Greek elements entered into Mithraism : the symbol of the god slaughtering a bull, which appears in representations of Mithra, may well be such an element. As a fusion of Persian and Hellenic elements the Mithraic religion attained a great vogue, especially. in the Roman army, and commanded the fervent allegiance of millions. The diffusion of Mithraism through the whole Roman Empire was prior to the third century ; but the rise of the Sassanid dynasty, the ardent champion of pure Zoroastrianism, and the dominance of the Roman army, with its cult of Mithra, in the troubled politics of that century, may both have contributed to the primary importance which sun-worship now assumes.

The deification of the emperor, in the form inherited by the Romans from the Hellenistic monarchies, had by the third century become a lifeless and exhausted thing. It had no longer the glamour of a new thing from the East ; and the feeling of hope and gratitude, which had inspired the worship of Augustus in the early days of the empire, was irretrievably gone. The period of the fifty tyrants (235–70 A.D.) had seen the name of emperor cheapened : it had combined civil war with foreign invasion, and exceeded the horrors of the period of slaughter which preceded

---

[1] The compilation of the Zend-avesta belongs to the period of the Sassanid dynasty.

the principate of Augustus. Some new system of government was once more needed, as it had been needed at the end of the first century B.C. : some new consecration, which would take the place of the cult of the *divi Caesares* as a bond of union and basis of allegiance, must support that system and gain it a general acceptance. Aurelian began and Diocletian completed the introduction of a new system of Oriental absolutism ; and Aurelian made an Oriental cult the religion of the empire, and bade his subjects regard him as the earthly vicar and emanation of the Unconquered Sun.

The cult of the Sun introduced by Aurelian was not in itself Mithraism, though it had its connexions with the worship of Mithra, and was calculated to attract the ready allegiance of all his worshippers. It was a Syrian form of religion, which he had come to adopt in his Eastern campaigns : it was a nature-cult, directed indeed to the worship of the brightest of the heavenly bodies, but not different in kind—except in its monotheism—from the worship of the planets and other forms of ' astral religion ' which were current in the East. What it was in itself is perhaps no great matter, and at any rate does not greatly concern us here. The fact and the consequences of the adoption of an Oriental cult are of profound importance. That adoption meant a revolution in the position of the emperor ; and it meant a revolution in the conception of the empire.

The revolution in the position of the emperor consisted in the change to an Oriental despotism. The old worship of the emperor as a god in himself may appear to us servile ; but it had been compatible with the spirit of liberty and the forms of constitutionalism. After all, the conception of the deified ruler was fundamentally Hellenic, and not Oriental ; and that conception could exist by the side of Hellenic and Roman ideas of the self-respect of the subject and the freedom of the commonwealth. When Aurelian claimed a new worship, not as a god in himself but as the incarnation or emanation of a god, he may seem to have claimed less, but he was really exacting more. He was moving in the sphere of Oriental ideas : he was asking for a blind prostration before a radiant divinity. He asserted a divine right, which could not be shared in any partnership : the Senate now lost even the formal privileges which it hitherto retained.[1] The purple, Aurelian told his troops, was the gift of God, who alone could limit His gift :

> The breath of worldly men cannot depose
> The deputy elected of the Lord.

But the emperor was more than a ' deputy ' : he was the image and epiphany of *Sol Invictus*. His was the nimbus emanating from the sun, which conferred a supernatural grace ; and if he left to the sun the title of ' Lord of the Roman Empire,' he might yet claim to be himself both ' Lord and God ' (*dominus et deus*). He wore the diadem and the great jewel-embroidered robe copied from the Sassanids : he adopted the throne and footstool, before which all subjects must prostrate themselves in adoration. All this means a new and eastern empire ; and all this passes into the system of Diocletian, which shows in the clear light of midday the results of the tendencies which dawn in the reign of Aurelian.

It was the work of Diocletian to exhibit with an exact logic the administrative consequences of the revolution in the position of the emperor which marked the end of the third and the beginning of the fourth century. He has been compared with Jeremy Bentham ; and he was certainly no less impatient of survivals and anomalies, and no less anxious to make a clean sweep and establish a new system. He made no particular profession of divinity, if he maintained the solemn state of robe and diadem and adoration ; but he pruned with a radical utilitarianism all the dead branches of the Roman past. The last trace of dyarchy disappeared, when the Senate became the municipal council of the city of Rome and its suburbs,

---

[1] Its members were excluded from military commands : it lost the old right of issuing bronze coins : the formula *Senatus Consulto* disappeared.

and a new division and regrouping obliterated any distinction between imperial and senatorial provinces. The empire became an intricate bureaucratic state, organized on a new basis of division, under which the military arm was independent of civil control, and one set of civil officials was jealously pitted against another. At the centre of the great cobweb, its ' universal spider,' the emperor held the threads and spun the filaments in a lonely absolutism. Italy ceased to enjoy any primacy, and was taxed like any other area : Rome ceased to be a capital, and the centre was shifted eastwards to Nicomedia. Losing its roots in the past, the empire became a new autocracy : severing its connexion with Rome and Italy, it found a fresh basis in the East, where it might at once feel more at home in sentiment and sit closer to its work in the details of administration.

In the conception of Diocletian the empire was still a unity : in the actual process of history the deserted West tended more and more to become a unit on its own account. Diocletian implicitly recognized, as he definitely hastened, this tendency, when he divided the empire, for convenience of administration, into an eastern and a western half by a line drawn through Illyria. The old Graeco-Roman civilization, pivoted on the middle Mediterranean, and organized on the basis of a single political community, had shown signs of fissure for the last two hundred years. After the reign of Diocletian it cracked and split. The East fell away into Byzantinism : the.West broke away into Latin Christianity. This meant a double change. The world became two instead of one (though men still clung for centuries to the conception of the one universal society) ; and in one of the two halves the Church became the basis of life in place of the State. It is the latter change which demands our attention ; for it is here that we may see a fundamental revolution in the very conception of the empire—a revolution already implied in the reign of Aurelian, but first explicit in the policy of Constantine.

WHEN Aurelian made the worship of the Sun into the religion of the empire, and himself into the earthly emanation of the Sun, he was unconsciously acknowledging a great transference in the balance of human interest. The world in which the Unconquered Sun is proclaimed ' the Lord of the Roman Empire '—in which a temple is dedicated to his majesty upon his 'birthday ' [1]—is not the world of Pericles or Alexander, of Cicero, or even of Hadrian. For many centuries — for the thousand years, we may say, from 700 B.C. to 300 A.D.—the basis of political life had been found in the political interest, and men had thought and acted as ζῷα πολιτικά. The State was the unit of life : religion was an attribute or dependency of the State. The State might be a small city—an Athens, worshipping Athene as the incarnation of itself : it might be a ' great society '— an empire, worshipping a deified emperor as the incarnate ' genius ' of its imperialism : the dominant motive in either was political, secular — a motive of this world and the life of this world. This is the essence of Graeco-Roman civiliza- tion. By the third century A.D. there comes a transfer of interest. Human life seems to swing round on a pivot : the religious motive—long growing in strength ; long spreading westward from its home in the East—acquires the dominance. For many centuries to come — for the next thousand years, we may almost say, down to 1300 A.D., when the great Church of the Middle Ages began to totter in the pontificate of Boniface VIII — the basis of human organization is the religious motive, and human society is ecclesiastical in its primary inspiration. There are still states : there is indeed still an empire. But it is the Church which counts ; and kings who are kings by the grace of God are in the last resort kings by the grace of the Church. We cannot indeed assert the proposition of the whole Mediterranean world ; but we may assert it at any rate of the West. And here we touch a paradox. The East,

---

[1] The birthday of the Sun was fixed on December 25, at the time of the winter solstice. Constantius vindicated the day for Christianity, and made it Christmas Day—the birthday of our Lord.

which gave religion and the Church to the West, fell under the control of the State. The West, which gave politics and the State to the East, came under the sovereignty of the Church. We may almost say that there was an interchange of gifts and of rôles. The western State moved into the East, to Constantinople, and subjugating the Church produced Byzantinism. The Church which arose in the East moved into the West, to Rome, and enthroning the Papacy produced Latin Christianity.

A religion which was an attribute or dependency of the State, and in the last resort a worship of the State, could never satisfy the religious instinct. The achievements of an Alexander, or the pacific triumphs of an Augustus, might create a gratitude and an adoration for the head of a State, which might last beyond the lifetime of their creator. But the State has its defeats as well as its victories ; and the abiding religious instinct, with its own aspirations towards a society and its own hope of controlling human life by its principles, stood ready to take advantage of its defeats. The religious appeal became ever stronger in the ancient world, as the process of syncretism developed and monotheism moved to victory. Christianity grew to an irresistible volume. The worship of Mithra and of Isis, the worship of the Unconquered Sun and of the great mother Cybele—with their intimate societies, their arresting rites, their consolation and their passion—all drew their votaries and kindled a deep devotion. By the time of Diocletian the State had lost its appeal and become a structure based upon fear. It was a cobweb of suspicion : its activity was an activity of extraction of taxes, relentless, remorseless, to support an army and a mass of officials : it tied the artisan to his guild, the serf to his plot, the councillor to his town, in order that each, duly penned in his place, might do his State-service and pay his State-dues. There was no spontaneous social cohesion to constitute a political community : there was no voluntary social will to support a government. In this conjuncture the religious motive entered into the foreground of life, and

3

swung forward to its triumph. The State, if it was to survive at all, could only survive by making the Church its ally, or, to speak more exactly, by becoming the ally of the Church. Thus the Roman Empire was driven in its last days by the mere instinct of self-preservation to adopt a religious creed as the basis—the only basis—on which it could still remain in existence. It sought to survive as an empire by becoming also, and indeed primarily, a Church. In the new religious temper of the times this was the only solution.

But why was the Christian Church in the issue the chosen ally of the pagan State ? The State had persecuted the Church : the Church had regarded the State as anti-Christ : on what ground could they unite ? We may meet these questions by the answer that, whatever the previous relations of the Christian Church and the Roman Empire, the peculiar conditions of the fourth century, as they have just been delineated, were such as to make an entirely new relation possible. The conflict between the two had depended on conditions which had ceased to exist. In the days in which the empire had found its basis in the worship of a deified emperor, the government had persecuted Christians because they had refused to participate in that worship; and in the Book of Revelation the Church had shown itself stung by such persecution to a passion of rebellion against the city of ' Babylon ' and the worship of the ' dragon.' But Christianity, if it protested against the persecuting State, was not in its essence opposed to the State in any of its forms or activities. St. Paul recognizes that the powers that be are ordained of God ; and prayers for the emperor and those in authority were customary among the early Christian communities. Christianity could recognize the State : what it could not recognize was the doctrine that religion was an attribute or dependency of the State ; and as long as that doctrine lasted, in the form of emperor-worship and the enforcement of emperor-worship as an essential article of citizenship, there could be no alliance between Christianity and the empire. By the end of the third century emperor-worship was passing : the empire was feeling its way towards a new form in which political unity would no longer involve a form of political religion, but community of religion would create, or at any rate sustain, political unity.   If the empire was to be united on this basis, Christianity, with its aspiration towards the Gentiles and its vision of an oecumenical Church, was ready to constitute the basis.   It offered itself as a world-religion to hold together on the ground of religious unity an empire which was doomed to dissolution if it sought to remain on the ground of political unity.   The emperors accepted the offer.   They became the powers ordained of God for the guidance of things temporal in a new empire now conceived as a Christian society.   They did not realize, nor did the Church itself realize, that as the Christian society elaborated its own principle of life, a new ecclesiastical emperor would arise in the Pope, and a new struggle of Church and State would ensue, in which secular emperors and kings would seek to vindicate an independent political sphere against the claims of a theocracy.   These results lay in the future. What happened in the reign of Constantine and his successors was that the autocratic emperors, remaining autocrats, agreed that the essential unity of the empire should henceforward be found in a common allegiance to the Christian creed.   A bureaucratic machine controlled by an Orientalized emperor was united with a religious community based on the love of God and the brethren.

It was in 312 A.D. that Constantine, about to join battle with the legions of Maxentius, fighting under the banner of the Unconquered Sun, adopted a Christian symbol as his badge and marched to victory at the battle of the Mulvian bridge.   He would oppose to the Unconquered Sun, deepseated in the allegiance of Roman legionaries, the unconquerable Christ whose votaries no persecutions could daunt, and whose coming triumph he already recognized.   His victory over the army of Maxentius was the victory of Christianity (as it were in the ordeal of battle) over Sun-worship and Mithraism and all the pagan cults.   But it

did not result in the immediate establishment of Christianity
as the religion of the State. Constantine was content to
recognize Christianity as one of the public worships of the
empire. For the next seventy years the old pagan rites
were officially performed in Rome ; and the emperor, even
while he was a Christian, and presided in Christian synods,
was also the *Pontifex maximus*. But with the emperors
confessing the Christian faith, and, still more, with the
pressing need for a unification of the empire on a common
religious basis, the establishment of Christianity as the one
acknowledged religion of the empire was inevitable. The
Emperor Gratian (375–83 A.D.) refused to wear the robes of
the *Pontifex maximus*, and abolished the official recognition
of pagan rites. The Emperor Theodosius I (379–95 A.D.),
the last creative emperor, first as the colleague and then
as the successor of Gratian, completed the work. He sum-
moned in 381 A.D. the synod of Constantinople, which ended
the Arian heresy in the empire and defined the Christian
creed ; and he prohibited pagan profession as he proscribed
heretical opinion. Behind the figures of both emperors
stands Ambrose, Bishop of Milan, who inspired the weak
Gratian as he curbed the stormy Theodosius. When in
390 A.D. Theodosius, solemnly rebuked and excluded for
months from the Church on the ground of a massacre committed by his troops at Thessalonica, divested himself at
last of the purple in Ambrose's cathedral at Milan, and after
public penance was restored to the Christian communion,
he showed not only that the empire had become a Christian
society, but also that in that society (at any rate in the
West) the officers of the Church might become the censors
of the acts of the State.

HISTORIANS have proclaimed the fall of the empire, or
at any rate of the ' Western Empire,' in the year 476
A.D. ; and we may thus be led to conclude that the empire
collapsed when it became a Christian society. Here we must
make a distinction. In one sense the empire did not and
could not fall, because it was one with Christian society,

and Christian society still stood, and grew even firmer and stronger, as it absorbed into its life the barbarian invaders from the north. It may be urged, indeed, that what remained was a Christian Church, and not a Roman Empire ; that the old universal State had gone, if a new universal Church had come ; that in place of the old universal Graeco-Roman State there were now barbaric *regna*, hardly worthy to be called states, and only loosely united by a common profession of Christianity. Such a contention rests on a false antithesis—the antithesis between Church and State, conceived as separate societies. The Christian Church had fused with the Roman State in a single society, a Christian commonwealth, which was an empire as well as a Church and a Church as well as an empire. The continuity of the Christian Church involved the continuity of the empire, because the Church and the empire were not two societies, but two aspects of a single society. It may be urged again that, if this be so, the empire only survived as an ' aspect ' —that is to say, as a mental conception—and that in the tangible world of institutions and administration it had no body and no existence. We may well admit that there is a large measure of truth in such a contention—though we may also urge that a conception which influenced the political development of Western Europe for many centuries was more than a ghost—and we must accordingly turn to consider the sense in which the empire, after all, ' fell ' in 476 A.D.

In the first place, the empire fell asunder into the two divisions of East and West. The cleavage was indeed far from being absolute, and the idea and even the form of unity long survived. So long as men cherished the idea of a single Christian society, they could hardly admit to themselves the existence of two separate societies and two separate empires. The Church of the East, though it diverged more and more from the West, especially in the days of the iconoclastic controversy (*c.* 700 A.D.), was not repudiated by the West as schismatic until the eleventh century ; and the Byzantine emperors were recognized

as emperors even in the West until the coronation of
Charlemagne, alike by barbarian kings and by the Bishop
of Rome. None the less the East had finally diverged from
the West ; and we may, if we will, date that divergence in
476 A.D. It is a matter of choice. We may equally well
date it earlier, from Diocletian's administrative division
of the empire, or from Constantine's foundation of Constantinople, or from the dynastic division of Theodosius I ;
or later, from the coronation of Charlemagne or the final
schism of the Churches. What matters is the fact that the
East had steadily withdrawn itself into its own life from
the second century of the Christian era, and that it gradually
built a polity of its own fundamentally different from that
of the West—a polity in which there was no Papacy, but
the emperor was himself the head of the Church, and the
Church was a department of the administration of the
State. This is Byzantinism ; and the essential conceptions
of Byzantinism were inherited on the one hand by the
Russian Tsars,[1] successors of the Caesars by marriage and
governors of their Church through the Holy Synod, and
on the other by the Turkish Sultan, at once Keisar-i-Rum
in virtue of Constantinople and Commander of the Faithful
in virtue of succession to the Prophet. Augustus had strange
successors. But Augustus was of the West ; and Aurelian,
son of a Pannonian peasant, and Diocletian, son of an
Illyrian freedman, both of the East and both absolute
rulers, might have recognized a closer kinship with an
Ivan or a Selim.

In the second place, the empire in the West after 476 A.D.
was in abeyance for some hundreds of years, so far as a
visible emperor, or a capital, or a system of administration

---

[1] Ivan III, who married Sophia Palaeologus, used the title of Tsar (in
old Slavonic *tsésar*) on documents and on coins : he termed himself *samod-
érzhets*, or autocrat of the Russias, in translation of the Byzantine
αὐτοκράτωρ : he adopted the Byzantine crest of the double-headed eagle.
Ivan IV was the first Russian sovereign to have himself crowned Tsar
(1547 A.D.). It was Peter the Great who finally subdued the Russian
Church to the State, and abolishing the patriarchate instituted a layman
as procurator-general of the Holy Synod to govern the Church.

was concerned.   There was no emperor to be seen, whether
at Rome or Milan or Ravenna, and there was no imperial
system of administration.[1]   The splendour of the emperor
at Constantinople might cast a shadow westwards, and men
might feel, as long as they saw the shadow, that there was
somewhere a substance of empire ; but the substance was
not in the West.   If empire means an emperor, a capital,
an administration, then Count Marcellinus was right when
he wrote of the year 476 A.D., *Hesperium gentis Romanae
imperium . . . cum hoc Augustulo periit*.   But if empire
means a society and a community, then we can only say
that the empire survived in the West ; and the whole of
mediaeval history would be unintelligible if we did not
realize that it survived.   It survived as a *respublica
Christiana*, a Christian commonwealth recognizing the
formal suzerainty of the Byzantine successors of Constantine, but gradually developing a spiritual ruler of its
own in the Bishop of Rome.

IN the *De Civitate Dei* St. Augustine faced the question
whether the empire collapsed when it became a Christian
society.   He wrote before 476 A.D., but he wrote under the
impression of the sack of Rome by Alaric ; and he sought
to meet the pagan argument that the adoption of Christianity
was the ruin of Rome.   Rome, he replies, had known vicissi-
tudes and misery even under paganism.   But this is only
a negative answer ; and Augustine quickly rises to the
height of the true Christian argument.   The love and enjoyment of God, which Christianity alone can give, are the true
happiness of humanity ; and they stand triumphant above
all the chances and calamities of temporal events.   Along
this line Augustine moves to the theme of the Two Cities,
which had already been handled by Marcus Aurelius—
the City of Rome and the City of God ; he sets one form
of social life against another, and pits the heavenly against

---

[1] Justinian reconquered Italy, and it was under Byzantine government
until 568 A.D.   Even after that date there was a Byzantine exarch at
Ravenna until 752 A.D.   But that was all.

the earthly.   He is far from identifying the heavenly city
with the community gathered in the Roman Empire ; and
we may even doubt whether he identified the *Civitas Dei*
with the visible and organized Christian Church.   Scholars
are divided on the issue : some have held that his city of
God was ' a real institution with a definite organization ' ;
others have thought that it was an unseen society, not built
with hands, a spiritual society of the predestined faithful,
distinct from the visible communion of baptized Christians.
But we are probably justified in believing that even in the
thought of St. Augustine himself, and certainly in the interpretation of later generations, the mantle of the city of God
descended upon the visible Church.   ' The conception of the
Church as a social entity wielding governing powers,' wrote
Dr. Figgis, ' owes much to St. Augustine.   He did much to
strengthen the Church as an imperial force.' [1]

The Church which could thus be conceived as a social
entity and an imperial force gradually acquired an imperial
organization.   The genius and the structure of the old
imperial system passed into the organization of the Church.
Residence in Rome, with the emperor far removed in
distant Constantinople, contributed to establish the Bishop
of Rome as the successor of the Caesars in the West ; and
the habit of looking to Rome for political guidance was
continued in the tendency, which we may trace in the Church
as early as the second century, to turn to Rome, as the
guardian of the pure apostolic tradition, for guidance in
all religious controversies.   Hobbes wrote of the Papacy
as ' the ghost of the deceased Roman Empire, sitting
crowned on the grave thereof.'   The author of the forged
Donation of Constantine (perhaps compiled in Italy, in
the latter part of the eighth century) expressed the same idea
when he made Constantine give to Sylvester I his palace,
diadem, and robes, ' with the city of Rome and all provinces, places, and cities of Italy or the western regions.'
We must not exaggerate the inheritance, or conclude that
the position of the Papacy was simply and solely the con-

[1] *The Political Aspects of St. Augustine's City of God*, pp. 71–2.

tinuance in the religious sphere of the power previously wielded by the emperor in the political. A sacramental and sacerdotal Church, such as the Latin Church of the West, demanded in its own inner logic, and apart from any inheritance, a central fountain, abounding in a *plenitudo potestatis*, from which there might emanate to the bishops, and through the bishops to their clergy, the dignity of their office, the sacramental power, and the substance of the tradition they were set to teach. But if papalism, with its sovereignty and its infallibility, was inherent in the essence of such a Church, we may still believe that tradition and environment fostered the growth of what was innate.

A city of God conceived as a visible Church, and organized as a spiritual empire, may seem to leave little room for any *terrena civitas*. But it was many centuries before the claim of ecclesiastical dominance, if it was already implicit in the Church at the end of the fourth and in the fifth century, was finally asserted. Ambrose of Milan subdued Theodosius to penitence in 390 A.D. : it was not until 1077 A.D. that Henry IV knelt in penitence before Gregory VII at Canossa. In a world of barbaric German chieftains the times were not ripe for the sway of the Church ; and during the long interval a theory of what we may call parallelism was held. There was indeed one society, men thought, and one only ; but there were two governments, each with separate powers. This is the theory expressed by Gelasius I (and scholars have accordingly termed it Gelasian) in a letter to Anastasius, the eastern emperor : ' there are two things by which this world is principally ruled—the sacred authority of the Popes and the royal power.' The one is set over things spiritual and the other over things temporal ; but the burden of the Popes is the heavier, as they must answer even for kings at the divine judgment. Two parallel sovereigns of one society, the Pope at Rome and the Emperor at Constantinople— this is the theory which is held in the West till the coronation of Charlemagne in 800 A.D. By that event a change was made, not in the relations of the two powers, but in the residence of the temporal power. There was a ' translation of the empire from the Greeks to the Germans ' (not, we may note, a division, but a transference of a single and undivided empire) ; and henceforth, till the pontificate of Gregory VII, the Pope at Rome and the Emperor at Aix-la-Chapelle are parallel rulers of the society of the western world. The East is recalcitrant. The empire has been ' translated ' ; but an East Roman Empire persists in remaining among the Greeks.

In the pontificate of Gregory VII we reach the days of ecclesiastical dominance. The system of parallelism—we may almost call it a new dyarchy, of a very different type from that devised by Augustus—is abandoned : the Church Universal, through its universal bishop, seeks to control the whole of human life : universal in extension, it would also be universal in its intensity of action. Society was recovering from the time of barbaric dispersion : trade was bringing the whole of Western Europe together : the Crusades and the spread of international orders were beginning to cement the unity. Gregorianism succeeds to Gelasianism ; and Gregorianism means a gallant attempt of the Church, through its Papacy, to bring a united Christian commonwealth, in its every reach, under the control of Christian principle. In politics and in social life, in economics and in the studies of universities, the Church would be dominant : it would control kings in their government ; by its canon law of marriage and of wills, as by its penitentiary system, it would guide the social life of the family and the individual ; it would regulate prices and prohibit usury ; it would build a great body of scholastic knowledge to satisfy every student. Gregorianism as an ideal (it could never be realized) means one universal society, which is a Church, based utterly on the law of Christ and controlled ultimately by Christ's vicar. Here the new development of the human spirit, the new trend to the religious life, which first found recognition at the end of the third and the beginning of the fourth century, attains its zenith. The combination of a religious society with an autocratic political society which we find under Constantine ; the modified form of that combination preached by Gelasius, in which the religious society acquires a religious as well as a political government—both disappear. The religious society attempts its logical complement in a theocracy.

But the political instinct of humanity is not readily quenched. The Holy Roman Empire, against which Gregorianism was pitted, was not, it is true, a strong embodiment of that instinct. A Charlemagne might have the force of a Frankish Empire at his back : the German emperors from Otto I onwards (962 A.D.) were only kings of Germany and Italy ; and while Germany was divided by tribalism and distracted by feudalism, Italy was the home of practically independent cities. Even Charlemagne, though his coins bear the inscription *Renovatio Romani Imperii*, had no tradition ; and his successors were equally destitute of any connexion with antiquity. With no root in their own realms, and no tradition for their support, the German emperors of the Middle Ages were not adequate to the struggle with the Church ; and though they might seek to vindicate an independent political sphere, they were worsted in argument and defeated in policy by the papalist forces. It was when a lay sentiment, fostered by the lawyers, arose in France, and associated itself with national feeling, that the Church found a stubborn enemy, and Boniface VIII at last met with defeat (1303 A.D.). A lay society, founded on a national basis, vanquished the conception of a universal empire in the form which that conception had more and more assumed during the thousand years since the death of Aurelian—the form of an ecclesiastical society. And the Reformation, in which the lay State, alike in England and in Germany, asserted the priority of the political motive and the supremacy of its king over all persons and in all causes as well ecclesiastical as temporal, marks the final defeat and disappearance of the conception of the Roman Empire.

I I

THE UNITY OF MEDIAEVAL CIVILIZATION [1]

Ergo humanum genus bene se habet et optime, quando secundum quod potest Deo adsimilatur. Sed genus humanum maxime Deo adsimilatur quando maxime est unum ; vera enim ratio unius in solo illo est. Propter quod scriptum est : 'Audi, Israel, Dominus Deus tuus unus est.'—DANTE, *De Monarchia*, I. viii.

I

HE who shuts his eyes to-day to make a mental picture of the world sees a globe in which the mass of Asia, the bulk of Africa, and the length of America vastly outweigh in the balance the straggling and sea-sown continent of Europe. He sees all manner of races, white and yellow, brown and black, toiling, like infinitesimal specks, in every manner of way over many thousands of miles ; and he knows that an infinite variety of creeds and civilizations, of practices and beliefs—some immemorially old, some crudely new ; some starkly savage, and some softly humane—diversify the hearts of two thousand million living beings. But if we would enter the Middle Ages, in that height and glory of their achievement which extended from the middle of the eleventh to the end of the thirteenth century, we must contract our view abruptly. The known world of the twelfth century is a very much smaller world than ours, and it is a world of a vastly greater unity. It is a Mediterranean world ; and ' Rome, the head of the world, rules the reins of the round globe.' From Rome the view may travel to the Sahara in the south ; in the east to the Euphrates, the Dniester, and the Vistula ; in the north to the Sound and the Cattegat (though some, indeed, may have

[1] A Paper read before a ' Unity ' Summer School at Birmingham in 1915.

44

heard of Iceland), and in the west to the farther shores of
Ireland and of Spain. Outside these bounds there is something, at any rate to the east, but it is something shadowy
and wavering, full of myth and fable. Inside these bounds
there is the clear light of a Christian Church, and the definite
outline of a single society, of which all are baptized members,
and by which all are knit together in a single fellowship.

Economically the world was as different from our own
as it was geographically. Money, if not unknown, was
for the most part unused. It had drifted eastwards, in
the latter days of the Roman Empire, to purchase silks
and spices ; and it had never returned. From the days of
Diocletian, society had been thrown back on an economy
in kind. Taxes took the form either of payments of personal
service or of quotas of produce : rents were paid either in
labour or in food. The presence of money means a richly
articulated society, infinitely differentiated by division of
labour, and infinitely connected by a consequent nexus of
exchange. The society of the Middle Ages was not richly
articulated. There were merchants and artisans in the
towns ; but the great bulk of the population lived in country
villages, and gained subsistence directly from the soil.
Each village was practically self-sufficing ; at the most it
imported commodities like iron and salt ; for the rest, it
drew on itself and its own resources. This produced at
once a great uniformity and a great isolation. There was
a great uniformity, because most men lived the same, grey,
quiet life of agriculture. The peasantry of Europe, in
these days when most men were peasants, lived in the same
way, under the same custom of the manor, from Berwick
to Carcassonne, and from Carcassonne to Magdeburg.
But there was also a great isolation. Men were tied to their
manors ; and the men of King's Ripton could even talk
of the ' nation ' of their village. If they were not tied by
conditions of status and the legal rights of their lord, they
were still tied, none the less, by the want of any alternative
life. There were towns indeed ; but towns were themselves
very largely agricultural—the homes of *summa rusticitas*—

and what industry and commerce they practised was the perquisite and prerogative of local guilds. Custom was king of all things, and custom had assorted men in compartments in which they generally stayed. The kaleidoscopic coming and going of a society based on monetary exchanges—its speedy riches and speedy bankruptcies, its embarrassment of alternative careers all open to talents— these were unthought and undreamed of. The same uniformity and the same isolation marked also, if in a less degree, the knightly class which followed the profession of arms. A common feudal system, if we can call that a system which was essentially unsystematic, reigned over the whole of Western Europe, and, when Western Europe went crusading into Syria, established itself in Syria. Historians have tried to establish distinctions between the feudalism of one country and that of another—between the feudalism of England, for instance, and that of France. It is generally held nowadays that they have failed to establish the distinction. A fief in England was uniform with a fief in France, as a manor in one country was uniform with manors in other countries, and a town in one country with towns in others. ' One cannot establish a line of demarcation between German and French towns,' says a famous Belgian historian, ' just as one cannot distinguish between French and German feudalism.' [1] The historian of the economic and institutional life of the Middle Ages will err unless he proceeds on the assumption of its general uniformity. But the uniformity of the fief, like that of the manor and the town, was compatible with much isolation. Each fief was a centre of local life and a home of local custom. The members of the feudal class lived, for the most part, local and isolated lives. Fighting, indeed, would bring them together ; but when the ' season ' was over, and the forty days of service were done, life ran back to its old ruts in the manor-hall, and if some of the summer was spent in company, much of the winter was spent in isolation. On a society of this

[1] Pirenne, *Revue Historique*, liii. p. 82.

order—stable, customary, uniform, with its thousands of isolated centres —the Church descended with a quickening inspiration and a permeating unity. Most of us find a large play for our minds to-day in the competition of economics or the struggles of politics. The life of the mind was opened to the Middle Ages by the hands of the Church. We may almost say that there was an exact antithesis between those days and these latter days, if it were not that exact antitheses never occur outside the world of logic. But it is as nearly true as are most antitheses that while our modern world is curiously knit together by the economic bonds of international finance, and yet sadly divided (and never more sadly than to-day) [1] by the clash of different national cultures and different creeds, the mediaeval world, sundered as it was economically into separate manors and separate towns, each leading a self-sufficing life on its own account, was yet linked together by unity of culture and unity of faith. It had a single mind, and many pockets. We have a single pocket, and many minds. That is why the wits of many nowadays will persist in going wool-gathering into the Middle Ages, to find a comfort which they cannot draw from the golden age of international finance.

But retrogression was never yet the way of progress. It is probable, for instance, that the sanitation of the Middle Ages was very inadequate, and their meals sadly indigestible ; and it would be useless to provoke a revolt of the nose and the stomach in order to satisfy a craving of the mind. An uncritical mediaevalism is the child of ignorance of the Middle Ages. Sick of vaunting national cultures, we may recur to an age in which they had not yet been born—the age of a single and international culture ; but we must remember, all the same, that the strength of the Middle Ages was rooted in weakness. They were on a low stage of economic development ; and it was pre-cisely because they were on a low stage of economic develop-

---

[1] This Paper belongs to the days of the war. I have thought it best to leave the marks of its origin.

ment that they found it so easy to believe in the unity
of civilization. Unity of a sort is easy when there are
few factors to be united ; it is more difficult, and it is
a higher thing, when it is a synthesis of many different
elements. The Middle Ages had not attained a national
economy : their economy was at the best municipal, and
for the most part only parochial. A national economy
has a higher economic value than a municipal or parochial
economy, because it means the production of a greater
number of utilities at a less cost, and a richer and fuller
life of the mind, with more varied activities and more
intricate connexions. A national economy could only
develop along with—perhaps we may say it could only
develop through—a national system of politics ; and the
national State, which is with us to-day, and with some of
whose works we are discontented, was a necessary condition
of economic progress. With the coming of the national
State the facile internationalism of the Middle Ages had
to disappear ; and as economics and politics ran into
national channels, the life of the spirit, hitherto an international life, suffered the same change, and national religions, if such a thing be not a contradiction in terms,
were duly born. But a national economy, a national
State, a national Church were all things unknown to the
Middle Ages. Its economy was a village economy : its
mental culture was an international culture bestowed
by a universal Church (a village culture there could not be,
and with a universal Church the only possible culture was
necessarily international) ; while, as for its politics, they
were something betwixt and between—sometimes parochial,
when a local feudal lord drew to himself sovereignty ;
sometimes national, when a strong king arose in Israel ;
and sometimes, under a Charlemagne, almost international.

A consideration of the linguistic factor may help to
throw light on the point in question. Here again we may
trace the same isolation and the same uniformity which
we have also seen in the world of economics. There was
an infinity of dialects, but a paucity of languages, in the

Middle Ages. One is told that to-day there are dialects in the Bight of Heligoland and among the Faroes which are peculiar to a single family. Something of the same sort must have existed in the Middle Ages. Just as there were local customs of the manor, the town, and the fief, there must have been local dialects of villages and even of hamlets. But here again isolation was compatible with uniformity. There were perhaps only two languages of any general vogue in the central epoch of the Middle Ages, and they were confined by no national frontiers. First there was Latin, the language of the Church, and since learning belonged to the Church, the language of learning. Scholars used the same language in Oxford and Prague, in Paris and Bologna ; and within the confines of Latin Christianity scholarship was an undivided unity. Besides Latin the only other language of any general vogue in the middle of the Middle Ages was vulgar Latin, or Romance. To Dante, writing at the close of the thirteenth century, Romance was still one *idioma*—even if it were *trifarium*, according as its ' yes ' was *oïl*, or *oc*, or *si*.[1] Of the three branches of this *idioma*, that of *oïl*, or Northern France, was easily predominant. The Norman conquest of England carried it to London : the Norman conquest of Sicily carried it to Palermo : the Crusades carried it to Jerusalem. With it you might have travelled most of the mediaeval world from end to end. It was the language of courts ; it was the language of chansons ; it was the language of all lay culture. It was the language of England, France, and Italy ; and St. Francis himself had delighted in his youth in the literature which it enshrined.

The linguistic basis of mediaeval civilization was thus Latin, either in its classical or in its vulgar form. There were of course other languages, and some of these had no small vogue. Just before the period of which we are treating—the period which extends from 1050 to 1300— Norse had a very wide scope. It might have been heard not only in Scandinavia and the Northern Isles, but in a

[1] *De Vulgari Eloquio*, I. viii.

4

great part of the British Islands, in Normandy, in Russia —along the river-road that ran to Constantinople—and in Constantinople itself. But the fact remains that the linguistic basis of mediaeval thought and literature was a Latin basis. The Romance University of Paris was the capital of learning : the Romance tongue of Northern France was the tongue of society. And as the linguistic basis of mediaeval civilization was Romance, so, too, was mediaeval civilization itself. The genius of Latin Christianity was the source of its inspiration : the spirit of the Romance peoples was the breath of its being. The souvenir of the old Roman Empire provided the scheme of its political ideas ; and the Holy Roman Empire, if a religious consecration had given it a new sanctity, was Roman still. Yet the irruption of the Teutons into the Empire had left its mark ; and the emperor of the Middle Ages was always of Teutonic stock. It was perhaps at this point that the unity of the mediaeval scheme betrayed a fatal flaw. It would be futile to urge that the dualism which showed itself in the struggles of papacy and empire had primarily, or even to any considerable extent, a racial basis. Those struggles are struggles of principles rather than of races ; they are contentions between a secular and a clerical view of life, rather than between the genius of Rome and the genius of Germany. Hildebrand stood for a free Church—a Church free from secular power because it was controlled by the papacy. Henry IV stood for the right of the secular power to use the clergy for purposes of secular government, and to control the episcopacy as one of the organs of secular administration. But the fact remains that a scheme which rested on a Teutonic emperor and a Roman pontiff was already a thing internally discordant, before these other and deeper dissensions appeared to increase the discord.

Such were the bases on which the unity of mediaeval civilization had to depend. There was a contracted world, which men could regard as a unity, with a single centre of coherence. There was a low stage of economic development, which on the one hand meant a general uniformity of life, in fief and manor and town, and on the other hand meant a local isolation, that needed, and in the unity of the Church found, some method of unification. With many varieties of dialect, there was yet a general identity of language, which made possible the development, and fostered the dissemination, of a single and identical culture. Nationalism, whether as an economic development, or as a way of life and a mode of the human spirit, was as yet practically unknown. Races might disagree ; classes might quarrel ; kings might fight ; there was hardly ever a national conflict in the proper sense of the word. The mediaeval lines of division, it is often said, were horizontal rather than vertical. There were different estates rather than different states. The feudal class was homogeneous throughout Western Europe ; the clerical class was a single corporation through all the extent of Latin Christianity ; and the peasantry and the townsfolk of England were very little different from the peasantry and the townsfolk of France. We have to think of a general European system of estates rather than of any balance of rival powers.

II

THE unity which rested on these bases begins to appear, as a reality and not only an idea, about the middle of the eleventh century, and it lasts till the end of the thirteenth. It was a unity, as we have seen, essentially ecclesiastical. It was the product of the Church : we may almost say that it was the Church. Before 1050 the Catholic Church, however universal in theory, had hardly been universal in fact. The period of the Frankish, the Saxon, and the early Salian emperors had been a period of what German writers call the *Landeskirche*. The power of the Bishop of Rome had not yet been fully established ; and the great churches of Reims and Mainz and Milan were practically independent centres. Independent of the papacy, they were not independent of the lay rulers within whose dominions they lay. On the contrary, their members were deeply engaged in lay activities ; they were landlords, feudatories, and officials in their various countries. In the face of these facts, the Gregorian movement of the eleventh century pursues two closely interconnected objects. It aims at asserting the universal primacy of the papacy ; it aims at vindicating the freedom of the clergy from all secular power. The one aim is a means to the other : the pope cannot be universal primate, unless the clergy he controls are free from secular control ; and the clergy cannot be free from secular control, unless the universal primacy of the papacy effects their liberation. Gregorianism wins a great if not a thorough triumph. It establishes the theory, and in a very large measure the practice, of ecclesiastical unity. The days of the *Landeskirche* are numbered : the days of the Church Universal under the universal primacy of Rome are begun. But when the universality of the Church has once been established in point of extension, it begins to be also asserted in point of intensity. Once it is ubiquitous, the papacy seeks to be omnicompetent. Depositary of the truth, and only depositary of the truth, by divine revelation, the Church, under the guidance of the papacy, seeks to realize the truth in every reach of life, and to control, in the light of Christian principle, every play of human activity. Learning and education, trade and commerce, war and peace, are all to be drawn into her orbit. By the application of Christian principle a great synthesis of human life is to be achieved, and the *lex Christi* is to be made a *lex animata in terris*.

This was the greatest ambition that has ever been cherished. It meant nothing less than the establishment of a *civitas Dei* on earth. And this kingdom of God was to be very different from that of which St. Augustine had written. His city of God was neither the actual Church nor the actual State, nor a fusion of both. It was a spiritual society of the predestined faithful, and, as such, thoroughly distinct from the State and secular society. The city of God which the great mediaeval popes were seeking to establish was a city of this world, if not of this world only. It was a fusion of the actual Church, reformed by papal direction and governed by papal control, with actual lay society, similarly reformed and similarly governed. Logically this meant a theocracy, and the bull of Boniface VIII, by which he claimed that every human creature was subject to the Roman pontiff, was its necessary outcome. But theocracy was only a means, and a means that was never greatly emphasized in the best days of the papacy. It was the end that mattered ; and the end was the moulding of human life into conformity with divine truth. The end may appear fantastic, unless one remembers the plenitude of means which stood at the command of the mediaeval Church. The seven sacraments had become the core of her organization. Central among the seven stood the sacrament of the Mass, in which bread and wine were transubstantiated into the divine body and blood of our Lord. By that sacrament man could touch God ; and by its mediation the believer met the supreme object of his belief. Only the priest could celebrate the great mystery ; and only those who were fit could be admitted by him to participation. The sacrament of penance, which became the antechamber, as it were, to the Mass, enabled the priest to determine the terms of admission. Outside the sacraments stood the Church courts, exercising a large measure of ethical and religious discipline over all Christians ; and in reserve, most terrible of all weapons, were the powers of excommunication and interdict, which could shut men and cities from the rites of the Church and the presence of the Lord. Who shall say, remembering these things, that the aims of the mediaeval Church were visionary or impracticable ?

For a time, and in some measure, they were actually accomplished. Let us look at each estate in turn, and measure the accomplishment—speaking first of the knightly world, and the Church's control of war and peace ; then of the world of the commons, and the Church's control of trade and commerce ; and last of the clerical world, and the Church's control of learning and education.

THE control of war and peace was a steady aim of the Church from the beginning of the eleventh century. The evil of feudalism was its propensity to private war. To cure that evil the Church invented the Truce of God. The Truce was a diocesan matter. The 'form' of Truce was enacted in a diocesan assembly, and the people of the diocese formed a *communitas pacis* for its enforcement. There was no attempt to put an absolute stop to private war ; the Truce was only directed to a limitation of the times and seasons in which feuds could be waged, and a definition of the persons who were to be exempted from their menace. But from seeking to limit the fighting instinct of a feudal society, the Church soon rose to the idea of enlisting that instinct under her own banner and directing it to her own ends. So arose chivalry, which, like most of the institutions of the Middle Ages, was the invention of the Church. Chivalry was the consecration of the fighting instinct to the defence of the widow, the fatherless, and the oppressed ; and by the beginning of the eleventh century liturgies already contain the form of religious service by which neophytes were initiated into knighthood. This early and religious form of chivalry (there was a later and lay form, invented by troubadour and trouvère, which was chiefly concerned with the rules for the loves of knights and ladies) culminated in the Crusades. In the Crusades we touch perhaps the most typical expression of the mediaeval spirit. Here we may see the clergy moulding into conformity with Christian principle the apparently unpromising and intractable stuff of feudal pugnacity : here we may see the papacy asserting its primacy of a united Europe by gathering Christian men together for the common purpose of carrying the flag of their faith to the grave of their Redeemer. Here the permeating influence of Christian revelation may be seen attempting to permeate even foreign policy (for what are the Crusades but the foreign policy of a Christian commonwealth controlled and directed by the papacy ?) ; and here again even the instinct for colonial expansion, so often the root of desperate wars, was brought into line with the unity of all nations in Christ, and made to serve the cause of Him ' in whom alone is to be found the true nature of the One.'

There is another aspect of the clerical control of peace and war in the interest of Christian unity which must not be forgotten. The papacy sought to become an international tribunal. The need for such a tribunal was as much a mediaeval as it is a modern commonplace. Dante, who sought to vindicate for the emperor, rather than for the pope, the position and power of an international judge, has started the argument in famous words. ' Between any two princes, of whom the one is in no way subject to the other, disputes may arise, either by their own fault, or by that of their subjects. Judgment must therefore be given between them. And since neither can have cognizance of the other, because neither is subject to the other, there must be a third of ampler jurisdiction, to control both by the ambit of his power.' [1] Such ampler jurisdiction, which might indeed be claimed for the emperor, but which he had never the power to exercise, was both claimed and exercised by the papacy. The papacy, which sought to enforce the Christian canon of conduct in every reach of life and every sphere of activity, would never admit that disputes between sovereign princes lay outside the rule of that canon. Innocent III, in a letter to the French bishops defending his claim to arbitrate between France and England, stands very far from any such admission. ' It belongs to our office,' he argues, ' to correct all Christian men for every mortal sin, and if they despise correction, to coerce them by ecclesiastical censure. And if any shall say, that kings must be treated in one way, and other men in another, we appeal in answer to the law of God, wherein it is written, " Ye shall judge the great as the small, and there shall be no acceptance of persons among you." But if it is ours to proceed against criminal sin, we are especially bound so to do when we find a sin against peace.' [2] Here,

[1] *De Monarchia*, I. x.
[2] Cf. Carlyle, *Mediaeval Political Theory in the West*, ii. 219–22.

in these words of Innocent, the clerical claim to control of peace and war touches its highest point. In the name of a Christian principle, permeating all things, and reducing all things to unity, the dread arbitrament of war is itself to be submitted to a higher and finer arbitration. The claim was too high to be sustained or translated into effect. It is not too high to be admired.

Nor was it altogether remote from the actual life of the day. Even to the laity of the Middle Ages, war was not a mere conflict of powers, in which the strongest power must necessarily prevail. It was a conflict of rights before a watching God of battles, in which the greatest right could be trusted to emerge victorious. War between States was analogous to the ordeal of battle between individuals : it was a legal way of testing rights. Now ordeal by battle was a mode of procedure in courts of law, and a mode of procedure whose conduct and control belonged to the clergy. If, therefore, war between States is analogous to ordeal, it follows, first, that it is a legal procedure which needs a high court for its interpretation (and what court could be more competent than the papal curia ?), and, next, that it is a matter which in its nature touches the clergy. Such ideas were a natural basis for the Church's attempt to control the issues of war and peace ; and if we remember these ideas, we shall acquit the Church of any impracticable quixotism.

THE attempt to control trade and commerce was no less lofty and no less arduous. It is perhaps still easier to stop war than to stop competition ; and yet the Church made the attempt. The Christian law of love was set against the economic law of demand and supply. It was canonical doctrine that the buyer should take no more, and the seller offer no less, than the just price of a commodity— a price which would in practice depend on the cost of production. The rule for prices was also the rule for wages : the just wage was the natural complement of the just price. The prohibition of usury and of the taking of

interest was another factor in the same circle of ideas.
If prices and wages are both to be returns for work done,
and returns of an exact equivalence, then, on the assumptions which the canonists made—that the usurer does no
work, and that his loan is unproductive of any new value
—it necessarily follows that no return is due, or can be
justly paid, for the use of borrowed money. Work is the
one title of all acquisition, and all acquisition should be
in exact proportion to the amount of work done. This is
the basic principle, and it is the principle of the Divine
Law : *In sudore frontis tuae comedes panem tuum.* Once
more, therefore, and once more in an unpromising and
intractable material, we find the Church seeking to enforce
the unity of the Christian principle and to reduce the Many
to the One. In the same way, and from the same motive,
that private war was to be banished from the feudal class
in the country, competition—the private war of commerce—
was to be eliminated from the trading classes in the towns.
Nor was the attack on competition, any more than the
attack on war, so much of a forlorn hope as it may seem to a
modern age. Even to-day, custom is still a force which
checks the operation of competition, and custom covered
a far greater area in the Middle Ages than it does to-day.
The rent of land, whether paid in labour or in kind, was a
customary rent ; and in every mediaeval community the
landed class was the majority. It was an easy transition
from fixed and customary rents to the fixing of just prices
for commodities and services. Lay sentiment supported
clerical principle. Guilds compelled their members to
sell commodities at a level price, and in a spirit of collec-
tivism endeavoured to prevent the making of corners and
the practice of undercutting. Governments refused to
recognize the ' laws ' of demand and supply, and sought,
by Statutes of Labourers, to force masters to give, and workmen to receive, no more and no less than a ' just ' and proper
wage.

It was not only by the regulation of trade and commerce
that the Church sought to penetrate the life of the towns.

The friars made their homes in the towns in the thirteenth century ; and the activity of the friars—Franciscan and Dominican, Austin and Carmelite—enabled the Church to exercise an influence on municipal life no less far-reaching than that which she sought to exert on the feudal classes. Towns became trustees of property for the use of the mendicant orders ; and the orders of Tertiaries, which flourished among them, enabled the townsfolk to attach themselves to religious societies without quitting the pursuits of lay life.   A mediaeval town—with its trade and commerce regulated, however imperfectly, by Christian principle ; with its town council acting as trustee for religious orders ; and with its members attached as Tertiaries to those orders—might be regarded as something of a type of Christian society ; and St. Thomas, partly under the influence of these conditions, if partly also under the influence of the Aristotelian philosophy of the πόλις, is led to find in the life of the town the closest approach to the ethics of Christianity.

THE control of learning and education by the Church is the most peculiar and essential aspect of her activity. The control of war and peace was a matter of guiding the estate of the baronage ; the control of trade and commerce was a way of directing the estate of the commons ; but the control of learning and education was nothing more nor less than the Church's guidance of herself and her direction of her own estate.   *Studium* may be distinguished from *sacerdotium* by mediaeval writers ; but the students of a mediaeval university are all ' clergy,' and the curricula of mediaeval universities are essentially clerical.   All knowledge, it is true, falls within their scope ; but every branch of knowledge, from dialectic to astronomy, is studied from the same angle, and for the same object—*ad maiorem Dei gloriam*.   Here, as elsewhere, the penetrating and assimilative genius of the Church moulded and informed a matter which was not, in its nature, easily receptive of a clerical impression.   The whole accumulated store of the

lay learning of the ages—geometry, astronomy, and natural
science ; grammar and rhetoric ; logic and metaphysics—
this was the matter to be moulded and the stuff to be permeated ; and on this stuff St. Thomas wrought the greatest
miracle of genuine alchemy which is anywhere to be found
in the annals of learning.

The learning which the Church had to transform was
essentially the learning of the Hellenic world. Created by
the centuries of nimble and inventive thought which lie
between the time of Thales and that of Hipparchus, this
learning had been systematized into a *corpus scientiae*
during that age of Greek scholasticism which generally
goes by the name of Hellenistic. In its systematized
Hellenistic form, it had been received by the Roman world,
and had become the culture of the Roman Empire. By
writers ranging from Ptolemy to Boethius the body of all
known knowledge had been arranged in a digest or series
of pandects ; and along with the legal codification of
Justinian it had been handed to the Christian Church as
the heritage of the ancient world. The attitude of the
Church to that heritage was for long unfixed and uncertain.
The logic, and still more the metaphysics, of Aristotle
were not the most comfortable of neighbours to the new
body of Christian revelation committed to the Church's
keeping. In the hands of Berengar of Tours the methods
of Greek logic proved a corrosive to the received doctrine
of the Mass. In the hands of Abelard, in the *Sic et Non*,
they served to suggest the need of criticism of the text of
Christian tradition. If unity was to be preserved, a bridge
must be built between the secular science of the Greeks
and the religious faith of the Church. In the thirteenth
century that bridge was built. Aristotle was reconciled
with St. Augustine ; the *Organon*, the *Ethics*, and the
Politics were incorporated in the body of Christian culture ;
and the mediaeval instinct for unification celebrated its
greatest and perhaps its most arduous triumph.

The thirteenth century thus witnessed a unity of
civilization alike as a structure of life and as a content of

the human mind. On the one hand, there rose a single
governing scheme of society, which culminated in the
universal primacy of Rome and the Roman pontiff. On
the other hand, set in this scheme, and contained in this
structure, there was a single stuff of thought, directed to
the manifestation of the eternal glory of God. The framework we may chiefly ascribe to Gregory VII ; the content
to St. Thomas Aquinas. But the whole resultant unity is
less the product of great personalities than of a common
instinct and a common conviction. Men saw the world
sub specie unitatis ; and its kaleidoscopic variety was insensibly focused into a single scheme under the stress of
their vision. The heavens showed forth the glory of God,
and the firmament declared His handiwork. Zoology
became, like everything else, a willing servant of Christianity ; and *bestiaria moralizata* were written to show how
all the beasts were made for an ensample, and served
for a type, of the one and only truth. All things, indeed,
were types and allegories to this way of thinking ; and just
as every text in the Bible was an allegory to mediaeval
interpretation, so all things in the world of creation, animate
and inanimate, the jewel with its ' virtue ' as well as the
beast with its ' moral,' became allegories and parables of
heavenly meanings. Thus the world of perception became
unreal, that it might be transmuted into the real world of
faith ; and symbolism like that of Hugh of St. Victor
dominated men's thought, making all things (like the Mass
itself, if in a less degree) into *signa rei sacrae.*

The unity of knowledge was thus purchased at a price.
Things must cease to be studied in themselves, and must
be allegorized into types, in order that they might be
reduced to a unity. Perhaps the purchase of unity on
terms such as these is a bad bargain ; and it is at any rate
obvious that in such an atmosphere scientific thought
will not flourish, or man learn to adjust himself readily
to the laws of his environment. From the standpoint of
natural science we may readily condemn the Middle ages
and all their works ; and we may prefer a single *Opus* of

Roger Bacon to the whole of the *Summa* of St. Thomas.
But it is necessary to judge an age which was destitute
of natural science by some other criterion than that of
science ; nor must we hasten to say that the Middle Ages
found the Universal so easily, because they ignored the
Particular so absolutely. The truth is, that though
mediaeval thinkers knew far more of the writings of Aristotle
than they did of those of Plato, they were none the less
far better Platonists than they were Aristotelians. If they
had been better Aristotelians, they would have been better
biologists ; but as they were good Platonists, they had a
conception of the purpose and system of human life in
society, which perhaps excuses all, and more than all, the
defects of their biology. Any survey, however brief, of
the political theory of the Middle Ages will show at once its
Platonic character and its incessant impulse towards the
achievement of unity.

III

TO mediaeval thought, as to Plato, the unity of society is
an organic unity, in the sense that each member of society
is an organ of the whole to which he belongs, and discharges
a function at once peculiar to himself and necessary to the
full life of the whole. Monasticism, so often misrepresented,
attains its true meaning in the light of this conception. The
monk is a necessary organ of Christian society, discharging
his function of prayer and devotion for the benefit not of
himself solely, or primarily, but rather of every member of
that society. He prays for the sins of the whole world, and
by his prayer he contributes to the realization of the end
of the world, which is the attainment of salvation. In the
same way the conception of a treasury of merits, afterwards
perverted in the system of indulgences, belongs to an
organic theory and practice of society. The merits which
Christ and the saints have accumulated are a fund for
the use of the whole of Christian society, a fund on which
any member can draw for his own salvation, just because
each is fitly 'joined and knit together with all the rest in

a single body for the attainment of a single purpose. But we need not take isolated instances of the Platonism of mediaeval thought. The whole basic conception of a system of estates, which recurs everywhere in mediaeval life, is a Platonic conception. The estates of clergy, baronage, and commons are the Platonic classes of guardians, auxiliaries, and farmers. The Platonic creed of τὸ αὐτοῦ πράττειν ('Do thine own duty') is the Christian creed of 'doing my duty in that state of life to which it shall please God to call me.' The Middle Ages are full of a spontaneous Platonism, and inspired by an *anima naturaliter Platonica*. The control which the mediaeval clergy exercised over Christian society in the light of divine revelation repeats the control which the guardians of Plato were to exercise over civic society in the light of the Idea of the Good. The communism of the mediaeval monastery is reminiscent of the communism of the Platonic barracks. And if there are differences between the society imagined by Plato and the society envisaged by the mediaeval Church, these differences only show that the mediaeval Church was trying to raise Platonism to a higher power, and to do so in the light of conceptions which were themselves Greek, though they belonged to a Greece posterior to the days of Plato. These conceptions—which were cherished by Stoic thinkers ; which penetrated into Roman Law ; and which from Roman Law flowed into the teaching and theory of the early fathers of the Church—are mainly two. One is the conception of human equality ; the other, and correlative, conception is that of a single society of all the human race. The equality of men, and the universality of the city of God in which they are all contained, are conceptions which were no less present to Marcus Aurelius than they were to St. Augustine. They are conceptions which made the instinctive Platonism of the mediaeval Church even more soaring than that of Plato. While the Republic of Plato had halted at the stage of a civic society, the *respublica Christiana* of the Middle Ages rose to the height of a single *humana civilitas*. While Plato had divided the men of his Republic into classes of gold and silver and bronze, and had reserved the ecstasy of the aspect of the divine Idea for a single class, the mediaeval Church opened the mystery of the Mass and the glory of the fruition of God to all believers, and, if she believed in three estates, nevertheless gathered the three in one around the common altar of the Redeemer. Serfdom might still remain, and find tolerance, in the economic working of society ; but in the Church herself, assembled together for the intimate purposes of her own life, there was ' neither bond nor free.'

The prevalence of Realism, which marks mediaeval metaphysics down to the end of the thirteenth century, is another Platonic inheritance, and another impulse to unity. The Universal *is*, and is a veritable thing, in which the Particular shares, and acquires its substance by its degree of sharing. The One transcends the Many ; the unity of mankind is greater than the differences between men ; and the university of mortal men, as Ockham writes, is one community. If there be thus one community, and one only, some negative results follow, which have their importance. In the first place, we can hardly say that the Middle Ages have any conception of the State. The notion of the State involves plurality ; but plurality is *ex hypothesi* not to be found. The notion of the State further involves sovereignty, in the sense of final and complete control of its members by each of a number of societies. But this, again, is *ex hypothesi* not to be found. There is one final control, and one only, in the mediaeval system—the control of Christian principle, exerted in the last resort, and exerted everywhere, without respect of persons, by the ruling vicar of Christ. But if plurality and sovereignty thus disappear from our political philosophy, we need a new orientation of all our theory. We must forget to speak of nations. We must forget, as probably many to-day would be very glad to forget, the claims of national cultures, each pretending to be a complete satisfaction and fulfilment of the national mind ; and we must remember, with Dante, that culture (which he called ' civility ') is the common possession of

Christian humanity.   We must even forget, to some extent, the existence of different national laws.   It is true that mediaeval theory admitted the fact of customary law, which varied from place to place.   But this customary law was hardly national : it varied not only from country to country, but also from fief to fief, and even from manor to manor.   It was too multiform to be national, and too infinitely various to square with political boundaries.   Nor was customary law, in mediaeval theory, anything of the nature of an ultimate command.   Transcending all customs, and supreme over all enactments, rose the sovereign majesty of natural law, which is one and indivisible, and runs through all creation.   ' All custom,' writes Gratian, the great canonist, ' and all written law, that are adverse to natural law, are to be counted null and void.' Here, in this conception of a natural law upholding all creation, we may find once more a Stoic legacy to the Christian Church.   ' We ought not to live in separate cities and demes, each distinguished by separate systems of justice '—so Zeno the Stoic had taught—' but there should be one way and order of life, like that of a single flock feeding on a common pasture.'   Zeno, like St. Paul, came from Cilicia.[1]   Like St. Paul, he taught the doctrine of the one society, in which there was neither Jew nor Gentile, neither Greek nor barbarian.   We shall not do wrong to recognize in his teaching, and in that of his school, one of the greatest influences, outside the supreme and controlling influence of the Christian principle itself, which made for the dominance of the idea of unity in mediaeval thought.

Before we proceed to draw another negative conclusion from the principle of the one community, we must enter a brief caveat in regard to the conclusion which has just been drawn.   We cannot altogether take away the State from the Middle Ages by a stroke of the pen and the sweep of a paradox.   There were states in mediaeval Europe, and there were kings who claimed and exercised *imperium*.

[1] See above, p. 8, and cf. E. R. Bevan, *Stoics and Sceptics*.

These things caused the theorists, and particularly the Roman lawyers, no little trouble. It was difficult to reconcile the unity of the *imperium* with the multiplicity of kings. Some had recourse to the theory of delegation, and this seems to be the theory of the *De Monarchia of* Dante. But there was one thinker, almost a contemporary of Dante, who said a wise thing, prophetic of the future. *Rex in regno suo*, wrote Bartolus of Sassoferrato, *est Imperator regni sui*.[1] In that sentence we may hear the cracking of the Middle Ages. When kings become ' entire emperors of their realms ' (the phrase was used in England by Richard II, and the imperial style was affected by Henry VIII), unity soon prepares to fly out of the window. But she never entirely took flight until the Reformation shattered the fabric of the Church, and made kings into popes as well as emperors in their dominions.

We may now turn to draw another conclusion from the mediaeval principle of unity. To-day the world recognizes, and has recognized for over three centuries, not only a distinction between States, but also a distinction between two societies in each State—the secular and the religious. These two societies may have different laws (for instance, in the matter of marriage), and conflicts of duties and of jurisdictions may easily arise in consequence. The State may permit what the Church forbids ; and in that case the citizen who is also a churchman must necessarily revolt against one or other of the societies to which he belongs. The conflict between the two societies and the different obligations which they impose was a conflict unknown to the Middle Ages. Kings might indeed be excommunicated, and in that event their subjects would be compelled to decide whether they should disobey excommunicated king or excommunicating pope. But that was only a conflict between two different allegiances to two different authorities ; it was not a conflict between two different memberships of two different societies. The conflict

---

[1] The dictum is not original in Bartolus (cf. C. N. S. Woolf's book on Bartolus, p. 380). But it attained vogue through his writings.

between the two societies—Church and State—was one
which could hardly arise in the Middle Ages, because there
was only a single society, an undivided Christian commonwealth, which was at one and the same time both Church
and State. Because there was only one society, baptism
counted as admission both to churchmanship and to
citizenship, which were one thing, and one only, in the
Christian commonwealth ; and for the same reason excommunication, which shut the offender from all religious
life, excluded him equally and by the same act from every
civil right. The excommunicated person could not enter
either the Church or the law court ; could not receive
either the eucharist or a legacy ; could not own either a
cure of souls or an acre of soil. Civil right and religious
status implied one another ; and not only was *extra ecclesiam nulla salus* a true saying, but *extra ecclesiam nullum
ius* would also be very near the truth. Here again is a
reason for saying that the State as such can hardly be
traced in the Middle Ages. The State is an organization of
secular life. Even if it goes beyond its elementary purpose
of security for person and property, and devotes itself
to spiritual purposes, it is concerned with the development of the spirit in its mortal existence, and confined to
the expansion of the mind in the bounds of a mortal society.
The Middle Ages thought more of salvation than of security,
and more of the eternal society of all the faithful, united
together in Christ their Head, than of any passing society
of this world only. They could recognize kings, who bore
the sword for the sake of security, and did justice in virtue
of their anointing. But kings were not, to their thinking,
the heads of secular societies. They were agents of the
one divine commonwealth—defenders of the Faith, who
wielded the secular sword for the furtherance of the purposes
of God. Thus there was one society, if there were two
orders of ministering agents ; and thus, though *regnum*
and *sacerdotium* might be distinguished, the State and the
Church could not be divided. Stephen of Tournai, a
canonist of the twelfth century, recognizes the two powers ;

but he only knows one society, under one king. That society is the Church : the king is Christ.

Under conditions such as these—with the plurality of States unrecognized by theory, even if it existed in practice, and with distinction between State and Church unknown and unenforced—we may truly say with a German writer, whose name I should like to mention *honoris causa*, Professor Tröltsch, that ' there was no feeling for the State ; no common and uniform dependence on a central power ; no omnipotent sovereignty ; no equal pressure of a public civil law ; no abstract basis of association in formal and legal rules—or at any rate, so far as anything of the sort was present, it was a matter only for the Church, and in no wise for the State.' [1] So far as social life was consciously articulated in a scheme, the achievement was that of the clergy, and the scheme was that of the Church. The interdependencies and associations of lay life—kingdoms and fiefs and manors—were only personal groupings, based on personal sentiments of loyalty and unconscious elements of custom. A mixture of uniformity and isolation, as we have seen, was the characteristic of these groupings : they were at once very like one another, throughout the extent of Western Europe, and (except for their connexion in a common membership of the Church Universal) very much separated from one another. But with one at any rate of these groupings—the kingdom, which in its day was to become the modern State—the future lay ; and we shall perhaps end our inquiry most fitly by a brief review of the lines of its future development.

IV

THE development of the kingdom into the State was largely the work of the lawyers. The law is a tenacious profession, and in England at any rate its members have exercised a large influence on politics from the twelfth to the twentieth century—from the days of Glanville, the

[1] *Die Soziallehren der christlichen Kirchen*, p. 242.

justiciar of Henry II, to the days of Mr. Asquith, the prime minister of George V. It is perhaps in England that we may first see the germs of the modern State emerging to light under the fostering care of the royal judges. Henry II is something of a sovereign : his judges formulate a series of commands, largely in the shape of writs, which became the common law of the land ; and in the Constitutions of Clarendon we may already see the distinction between Church and State beginning to be attempted. With a sovereign, a law, and a secular policy all present, we may begin to suspect the presence of a State. In France also a similar development, if somewhat later than the English, occurs at a comparatively early date. By the end of the thirteenth century the legists of Philippe le Bel have created something of *étatisme* in their master's dominions. The king's court begins to rule the land ; and proud of its young strength it enters the lists against Boniface VIII, the great prophet of the Church Universal, who proclaimed that every human creature was subject to the Roman pontiff. The collapse of Boniface at Anagni in 1303 is the traditional date of the final defeat of the mediaeval papacy. Everywhere, indeed, the tide seemed on the turn at the close of the thirteenth century. The Crusades ended with the fall of Acre in 1291. The suppression of the great international order of the Templars twenty years later marked a new leap of the encroaching waves. The new era of the modern national State might seem already to have begun.

But tides move slowly and by gradual inches. It needed two centuries more before the conditions in which the modern State could flourish had been fully and finally established. Economic conditions had to change—a process always gradual and slow ; and a national economy based on money had to replace the old local economy based on kind. Languages had to be formed, and local dialects had to be transformed into national and literary forms, before national States could find the means of utterance. The revival of learning had to challenge the old clerical structure of knowledge, and to set free the progress of secular science, before the minds of men could be readily receptive of new forms of social structure and new modes of human activity. But by 1500 the work of preparation had been largely accomplished. The progress of discovery had enlarged the world immeasurably. The addition of America to the map had spiritual effects which it is difficult to estimate in any proper terms. If the old world of the Mediterranean regions could be thought into a unity, it was more difficult to reduce to the One the new world which swam into men's ken. Still more burdened with fate for the future generations was the vast volume of commerce, necessarily conducted on a national basis, which the age of discoveries went to swell. Meanwhile, men had begun to think and to write in national languages. Already by the reign of Richard II the dialect of the East Midlands, which was spoken in the capital and the universities, had become a literary language in which Chaucer and Wyclif had spoken to all the nation. Still earlier had come the development of Italian, and a little more than a century after the days of Wyclif Luther was to give to Germany a common speech and a common Bible. It was little wonder that in such times the old unity of the Christian commonwealth of the Middle Ages shivered into fragments, or that, side by side with a national language, there developed—at any rate in England and in Germany —a national Church. The unity of a common Roman Church and a common Romance culture was gone. *Cuius regio eius religio.* To each region its religion ; and to each nation, we may add, its national culture. The Renaissance may have begun as a cosmopolitan movement, and have found in Erasmus a cosmopolitan representative. It ended in national literatures ; and a hundred years after Erasmus, Shakespeare was writing in England, Ariosto in Italy, and Lope de Vega in Spain.

In the sixteenth century the State was active and doing after its kind. It was engaged in war. France was fighting Spain : England was seeking to maintain the balance :

Turkey was engaged in the struggle. It is a world with
which we are familiar—a world of national languages,
national religions, national cultures, national wars, with
the national State behind all, upholding and sustaining
every form of national activity.   But unity was not entirely
dead.   Science might still transcend the bounds of nations,
and a Grotius or Descartes, a Spinoza or a Leibniz, fill
the European stage.   Religion, which divided, might also
unite ; and a common Calvinism might bind together the
Magyars of Hungary and the French of Geneva, the Dutch-
man and the Scot.   Leyden in the seventeenth century
could still serve as a meeting ground of the nations ;
it could play the part of an international university, and
provide a common centre of medical science and classical
culture.   But the old unity of the Middle Ages was
gone—gone past recall.   Between those days and the new
days lay a gulf across which no voice or language could
carry.   Much was lost that could never be recovered ;
and if new gold was added to the currency of the spirit,
new alloys were wrought into its substance.   It would be
a hard thing to find an agreed standard of measurement,
which should cast the balance of our gain and loss, or
determine whether the new world was a better thing than
the old.   One will cry that the old world was the home of
clericalism and obscurantism ; and another will say in his
bitterness that the new world is the abode of two other
evil spirits—nationalism and commercialism.   One thing
is perhaps certain.   We cannot, as far as human sight
can discern, ever hope to reconstruct unity on the old basis
of the Christian commonwealth of the Middle Ages.   Yet
need is upon us still—need urgent and importunate—to
find some unity of the spirit in which we can all dwell
together in peace.   Some have hoped for unity in the sphere
of economics, and have thought that international industry
and commerce would build the foundations of an international polity.   Their hopes have had to sleep, and years
of war have shown that ' a synchronized bank-rate and
reacting bourses ' imply no further unity.   Some again

may hope for unity in the field of science, and may trust that the collaboration of the nations in the building of the common house of knowledge will lead to co-operation in the building of a greater mansion for the common society of civilized mankind. But nationalism can pervert even knowledge to its own ends, turning anthropology to politics, and chemistry to war. There remains a last hope—the hope of a common ethical unity, which, as moral convictions slowly settle into law, may gradually grow concrete in a common public law of the world. Even this hope can only be modest, but it is perhaps the wisest and the surest of all our hopes. *Idem scire* is a good thing ; but men of all nations may know the same thing, and yet remain strangers one to another. *Idem velle idem nolle in re publica, ea demum firma amicitia est.* The nations will at last attain firm friendship one with another in the day when a common moral will controls the scope of public things. And when they have attained this friendship, then—on a far higher level of economic development and with an improvement by each nation of its talent which is almost entirely new—they will have found again, if in a different medium, something of the unity of mediaeval civilization.

III

A HUGUENOT THEORY OF POLITICS: THE *VINDICIAE CONTRA TYRANNOS* [1]

IN 1559 France was plunged into the melting-pot, and she remained there for the next forty years, until 1598, when a new Bourbon France emerged with the ending of the war against Spain and the issue of the Edict of Nantes. Two things had happened in 1559. In the first place, there had come to an end a long series of foreign wars, almost continuous since the French invasion of Italy in 1494. That raised a serious question of unemployment. What was to be done with a nobility which for over sixty years had found both distraction and occupation in war, and now had idle hands and empty pockets ? Here was a chance for Satan to find some mischief. In the second place, there had died the last strong king of the House of Valois, Henry II, leaving behind him a widow (who was a Florentine of the house of the Medici) and a young family of four sons and three daughters. That raised a serious problem of government. It is written in the Book of Ecclesiastes, ' Woe to thee, O land, when thy king is a child.' I have more than once thought, in my reading of history, that the words might be added, ' And woe to thee even more when thy regent is a woman, and woe above all when she is a foreigner.' Here indeed was a chance for Satan, when an Italian queen dowager, brooding with fierce eyes over a young family, confronted an unemployed nobility—and, in addition, as if that were not enough, a body of ambitious Princes of the Blood who were only agreed in a common desire to relieve her of her tutelary care.

[1] Based upon a Paper read to the Huguenot Society of London in January 1930.

Could France, under these conditions, remain a unitary State, controlled by a single and effective sovereignty? The prospect seemed dubious. Apart from the immediate questions of aristocratic unemployment and royal government, there was a more permanent and general problem. France was still a congeries of annexed provinces, united only in the person and office of the monarchy which had made the annexations. The 'spirit of the province' was still strong in Dauphiné, Brittany, Gascony, Provence. Provinces had their own 'liberties,' their own provincial assemblies of Estates, their own provincial bodies of law. Nor was this all. Within the province itself there was the fief and the municipality. Besides the localism of the province there was also that of the feudatory, anxious to be Seigneur over his fief; there was also that of the city, resolute to be master within its walls. Add feudalism and municipalism to provincialism, and the result is a triad of localisms, accumulating an almost intolerable load of stresses and strains upon the arch of the monarchy. Could it carry the load? Or would France disintegrate under the pressure into a loose federation on the model of contemporary Germany? Looking back over the centuries, we can easily give an answer in the first sense. We can see that there was in France an indomitable instinct of political unity—whether inherited from the centralization of ancient Rome, or rooted still deeper in a common passion for French soil and a common feeling of French blood and culture—which would successfully thwart every tendency towards disintegration. But to those living at the time an answer was far less easy; and the odds might well seem to be in favour of a collapse. The practical example of Germany, which was now a loose confederation, offered a standing invitation to the separatist instincts of provinces, princes and towns. Nor was the theory of unitary monarchy as yet established in European thought. Machiavelli, indeed, had preached the Prince one and irresistible, the State one and indivisible; but the name of the great Florentine was not a name by which men could conjure, least of all in

France, in the days of the Florentine woman Catherine de
Medici.   The French jurist Bodin was to establish a theory
of sovereignty in his *Six Books of the Republic* : but that
massive work did not appear until 1576, and years had to
pass before its teaching could sink deeply into men's minds.
Meanwhile the theory of politics was still largely in the
hands of civilians trained in the Roman law ; and among
them the great name was still that of Bartolus, a jurist who
had taught and written in Perugia in the first half of the
fourteenth century.   Now Bartolus was an apostle of
federalism rather than of unity—of liberty rather than of
sovereignty.   Living among Italian City States, he had
sought to defend in theory the independence which they
had attained in practice, and he had evolved the doctrine
of the *civitas sibi princeps* — the city which is Prince for
itself.   That is a theory which looks towards federalism.
Living, again, at a time when tyrants were arising in the
city-states, he had sought to find a juristic basis for the
right of civic self-government ; and his treatise *De Tyrannia*
was a mediaeval counterpart (still known and cherished in
the latter half of the sixteenth century) to Mill's Essays
on *Liberty* and *Representative Government.*   If political
theory affects political practice (and that is perhaps a large
assumption), we may say that the political theory current
in 1559 boded ill for the unity of France.

IN this conjuncture of the stars of France there swung
into the sky the meteor of religion, the army of French
Calvinism, the ranks of the Huguenots.   It was one of the
noblest movements of thought in a country ever fertile
and ever generous in such movements ; and even to think
of it now, after all these years, still stirs the blood.   They
who were ' of the religion ' were gallant men : they fought
a good fight : they endured tribulations : they are counted
among the salt of the earth.   But what did they mean for
France ; and what was their contribution to the problem of
French unity—or French disintegration ?   That is the question
we have to face.   What is the answer which we must give ?

If the Huguenots could have brought the monarchy over to their side ; if Charles IX, the second of the sons of Henry II, who reigned from 1560 to 1574, had joined their cause ; and if, through that junction, their cause had become successful—then, and on that large assumption, we may say that the Huguenots would have been a force making for the unity of France, on a constitutional and Protestant basis. In that case France would have undergone, somewhere about 1572, a revolution comparable to our own Whig Revolution of 1688—our own Revolution of which, I should like to say in passing, I believe that the Huguenots, even in their failure, and perhaps because of their failure, and owing to the Whig doctrines of resistance produced by their failure, may be accounted the spiritual ancestors.   We may even imagine, on this basis of hypothesis, a Huguenot France which pushed unity to excess, insisting in its hour of triumph upon unity of religion no less rigorously than the Puritans of Massachusetts, in the days of their triumph, insisted upon a similar unity between 1630 and 1690.   In any case I should contend that Huguenotism was not, in its essence, inimical to the unity of France—in its essence, I repeat ; in its pure logic ; in the form which it would have taken if only it could have worked out freely its immanent potentiality.   *Per accidens*, it is true, it did become inimical : time and contingency made it a minority ; and, as a minority, it was forced to struggle against a scheme of compulsory unity.   But its original and native instinct was towards the monarchy, the unity of France, the great-ness of France.   It was the policy of Coligny, one of the greatest of the Huguenots, to capture the mind of Charles IX : to turn France towards hostilities against Philip of Spain in the Netherlands : to bring a united France to aid the cause of liberty and religion on her northern frontier, and to cement her unity by common effort in a common cause.   The policy failed ; and the day of its failure was St. Bartholomew's Day, August 24, 1572.   Massacre was the answer to Coligny ; and all hope of the Huguenots guiding France died with the massacre.   Perhaps there never had been any hope : perhaps there never could have been any hope. For the massacre was no mere move on the part of the queen-mother, resolved, at any price, to prevent her son from escaping from her tutelage and falling into the arms of Coligny. It was a popular massacre : we may even say that it was a national massacre. It was popular, because the people at large threw themselves into it heart and soul. After all, the Huguenots were an *élite*— an aristocratic *élite* : a civic *élite*—and the people had no liking for the *élite*. Again, it was national, as well as popular : it raged all over France : it made Lyons a shambles as well as Paris. Thirty thousand were killed. It is, says a German scholar, ‘ as if we might detect in this terror the will to unity of the French people, which can suffer no foreign bodies, no disunion.’ [1] One remembers a similar terror and a similar will to unity in 1793.

After that ‘ day ’ in 1572 the Huguenots were a minority, and, for the moment, a scattered minority. Mornay—whose wife’s memoirs of his life, published in the Broadway Series of Translations under the title of *A Huguenot Family in the Sixteenth Century*, are a precious mine—fled overseas to England. Others escaped to Geneva, where the Frenchman Beza was now the head of Calvin’s Church : others found a refuge in Germany and the Netherlands. What remained to this scattered minority ? What remains to a minority always, and that is—thought, and the appeal to thought. The Huguenots sat down by their waters of Babylon, and they thought—thought and wrote. They recited their history : they published their philosophy ; and by that history and philosophy they appealed to Caesar—to the conscience of Christian Europe. There is a series of writings in the seven years that followed St. Bartholomew’s Day, 1572–9, which should never be forgotten by any who confess the cause of liberty, civil and religious. The great Beza himself published anonymously, about 1574, a treatise *De jure magistratuum*. Not only had he to publish it

[1] Elkan, *Die Publizistik der Bartholomäusnacht*, p. 16.

anonymously : he had even to suggest on the title-page that
it was only an amplified edition of a previous work, by
' those of Magdeburg,' of the year 1550 ; and even so he
was driven from pillar to post to find a printer.   Hotman,
professor of law in the University of Geneva founded by
Calvin, published at Geneva in 1573 his *Franco-Gallia*, which
sought to vindicate the ancient constitutional liberties of
France.   It was a work destined to a large vogue : it
crossed the seas to England : it became one of the inspirations of English Whigs who also sought to vindicate the
ancient constitutional liberties of *their* country.   Three
other works also deserve mention, both in themselves and
because they are all linked together by a curious tie.   One
is a treatise of the year 1573, *de furoribus Gallicis*, an
account of the massacre, said to be written by one Ricaud,
a preacher of Lyons, who entitles himself on his title-page
by the name of Ernestus Varamundus Frisius.   A second
is two dialogues, in which Hotman may have had a hand,
published together in 1574 under the title of the *Réveille
Matin* (a trumpet to call ' the French and their neighbours '
to arms against the murderers of the Huguenots), and professing to be written by one Eusebius Philadelphus Cosmo-
polita.   A third is the *Vindiciae Contra Tyrannos* of the
year 1579, whose anonymous author entitled himself
Stephanus Junius Brutus Celta, and which contains a
philosophy of liberty in Church and State.   The curious
tie that unites all three is that they are all stated on their
title-pages to have been printed at Edinburgh.[1]   None of
them were, but the actual press had to be hidden ; Edinburgh was a far cry and a safe attribution ; moreover it
was a home of Calvinism and the residence of George
Buchanan, a Scottish scholar well known to many friends
in France, who wrote a radical treatise *de Jure Regni
apud Scotos*, which actually *was* printed at Edinburgh in
1579.

[1] On the title-page of the *Réveille Matin* the name of the printer is
given.   It is *Jaques James*.   The words ' avec permission ' are added by
way of an additional witticism.

OF all these writings I can deal here only with one—the *Vindiciae contra Tyrannos.* It is the most famous ; it had the deepest influence, especially in England ; I am inclined to think it the most profound ; and in any case it suffices abundantly to show the temper and the philosophy of the Huguenots after the massacre, in the middle of those forty years during which, as I have said, France was plunged into the melting-pot. But there is a preliminary question, which I confess is a matter of caviare, but about which I feel bound to say one word. It is the question of the authorship of the *Vindiciae.* For the last forty years, since a German scholar called Lossen wrote a paper on the subject in 1887, it has been customary to say that Mornay, the Huguenot I have already mentioned, who afterwards served Henry of Navarre and wrote a number of theological treatises, was the man who called himself Stephanus Junius Brutus. The more I have looked into the matter, the less I believe that he was. It is true that his wife records that in 1574 he wrote upon ' the lawful power of a prince over his people ' (a phrase which corresponds to part of the sub-title of the *Vindiciae* [1]), and that what he wrote was ' afterwards printed and published, but without its being widely known that he was the author.' Mornay may well have written on so obvious a topic ; but this does not prove that he wrote the 240 Latin pages of the *Vindiciae,* packed with legal learning and backed by an armoury of references, which appeared in 1579. I do not see how he could possibly have done so, even on the mere ground of time, during that brief breathing-space among forays and excursions which he spent at Jametz in the early half of 1574 (and to which his wife

---

[1] The full sub-title runs ' Concerning the lawful power of a prince over his people and of a people over its prince.' There is certainly a parallel between Madame Mornay's phrase and the first part of the sub-title. But the phrase was a commonplace. The full title of Beza's *De jure Magistratuum* is ' concerning the right of magistrates over subjects and the duty of subjects towards magistrates.' Again, the *Dialogue d'Archon et de Politie,* published in 1576, has the sub-title ' Concerning the authority of princes and the liberty of peoples.' Madame de Mornay's phrase might apply to either of these as well as to the *Vindiciae.*

refers his essay on the lawful power of a prince) ; and I become the more sceptical when I reflect that he was falling in love about this time. In any case, I cannot but feel that Mornay's legal scholarship was not equal to the task : that his real interest was in theology rather than in political philosophy : that his recorded views on politics do not square with those of the *Vindiciae* [1] : that he was too young a man in 1574 (for he was then only in his twenty-fifth year) to have written a treatise such as the *Vindiciae* ; and that it is difficult to see why a work composed in 1574 should never have seen the light until 1579. I put Mornay therefore on one side, for these and for many other reasons which I must forbear to mention ; and I turn to another possible author, for whom the *Vindiciae* was vindicated by the great Bayle about 1690, and to whom it was steadily ascribed by scholars for nearly two hundred years. This is Hubert Languet, a Burgundian, born in 1519 (and therefore thirty years older than Mornay), who lived for much of his life in Germany. He was a lawyer so distinguished as twice to have been offered chairs of law in German Universities ; he was a scholar who had lived for years with Melanchthon ; he was a traveller and a diplomat who knew the cities and the minds of men from Lapland and Stockholm to Vienna and Padua ; and he was a man of affairs, who spent the last four years of his life, from 1577 to 1581, in the service and friendship of William of Orange. His life, his attainments, his opinions, all square with the *Vindiciae*. He knew law ; and it is full of legal knowledge. He knew the history and conditions of most European countries ; and it is full of references to their history and conditions. Nor is this all. The *Vindiciae* has close analogies with the *Apology* for his actions published on behalf of William of Orange in 1580. Good testimony ascribes the composition of that *Apology* to Languet ; [2]

---

[1] His wife records that in 1576 he was ' exposing the worthlessness of all Estates, whether provincial or general.' The argument of the *Vindiciae* is directed to establishing the value of both.

[2] The author of the *Vita Huberti Langueti* (Philibert de Marre, who, by

and this suggests that he also composed the.*Vindiciae*, which it resembles. Again, the *Vindiciae* is quoted repeatedly in the annotations to the *Acta* of a congress held at Cologne for the purpose of mediating between the Netherlands and Philip of Spain, at the end of 1579. Languet was present as an envoy at that congress ; and his book may well have glided into the notes appended to the record of its acts. The more I think about the matter, the more I am inclined to say ' aut Languet aut diabolus.' But I confess that I may be mistaken, and the real author may be neither. I will only add that Languet died in 1581, two years after the publication of the *Vindicae*. If he wrote it, he carried the secret with him to the grave. Mornay lived for over forty years after the publication of the *Vindiciae*. If he wrote it, he kept the secret for a long time. . . .[1] And he was not a secretive man.

I turn to the substance of the *Vindiciae*. I will ask you to imagine a man sitting down, some three hundred and fifty years ago, to write on the vital problems of contemporary politics. The year is somewhere about 1579 ; the place is possibly Antwerp. In France, since the Treaty of Bergerac

the way, attributes the *Vindiciae* to Languet) states that he had heard from Languet's heirs that, a few days before his death, he sent to each of them a copy of the *Apology, quasi a se exaratus.*, I noted lately, in reading Irving's *Memoirs of Buchanan*, that in 1581 Languet wrote to Buchanan (now well known abroad for his *de jure Regni*), reminding him that they had met in Paris about twenty years ago, and enclosing a copy of the *Apology*. It seems unlikely that Languet should have written to recall his existence after so many years, and to enclose a pamphlet, unless the pamphlet he enclosed was of his own composition. That is the way of authors.

[1] There is a story, coming from the middle of the seventeenth century, that a certain Daillé, who lived with Mornay for seven years, was regularly sent by him, when visitors came to inspect his library, to remove a copy of the *Vindiciae* from a cupboard in which he kept together copies of his own writings. This seems to suggest that Mornay *had* written the *Vindiciae*, and was troubled by the secret. But all that the story proves, if it be true, is that Mornay had some sort of a connexion with the *Vindiciae*, which led him to keep a copy of it among his own writings. He was a friend of Languet. He may have written some of the Latin verses attached to the *Vindiciae*. He may, again, have been responsible for the French translation of the *Vindiciae*, which appeared in 1581. See p. 108, below *infra*.

in 1577, which was tolerably favourable to the Huguenots, there is now comparative peace ; and that peace is destined to continue, except for a short war in 1580, until 1585. In the Netherlands, on the other hand, everything is marching to a crisis. The man who sits down to write is a Frenchman, and France is his exemplar (*in quo, tanquam caeterorum exemplari, diutius haereo*) ; but he has surveyed the world, and he has a full mind. You must imagine that he knows the Bible thoroughly, but that, with a lawyer's training, he throws a legal colour over its records and texts. In law he is thoroughly steeped : he knows the *Digest* of Justinian : he knows the writings of the great Bartolus and his theories of the *civitas sibi princeps* and the nature of tyranny. He is a classical scholar to his finger-tips : he quotes Greek — and rare Greek at that, such as only an accomplished scholar would know — with facility : he knows the *Politics* of Aristotle, the *Cyropaedia* of Xenophon, the *Republic* of Plato : he knows his Latin authors, and not least Seneca's letters and Cicero's *de Officiis*. He had obviously read, though he never quotes, the passage of Calvin's *Institutes* which deals with the State : he has read and he quotes St. Augustine ' On the City of God ' ; he has also read, and he also quotes, the *Summa* of St. Thomas Aquinas. He knows a good deal about German history, a good deal about French, and something about English, Scottish, and Scandinavian history : he is tolerably versed in Polish affairs : he can quote the *Sachsenspiegel* of Germany, the *Liber Feudorum* of Lombardy, and what he calls the ' Spanish Code.' He has probably read Beza's *De jure magistraruum* : he has almost certainly read Hotman's *Franco-Gallia* ; perhaps he knows something about Bodin's *Six Books on the Republic* : he may also have read the work of Salamonius, *De Principatu*, just republished in France in 1578, and he may have digested its theory of a social contract. Anyhow, he has material enough : he has passion : he has a clear incisive style, sometimes rising to eloquence, sometimes adorned with picturesque images ; [1] and he has a singular

[1] On the style of the *Vindiciae*, see Note A, at the end of this Essay.

6

gift of logic, which makes him resolved, ' in the manner of a geometer ' (as it is written in the Preface) to discover the axioms and to deduce the propositions of politics.   He writes his work, in its four parts : he entitles himself Stephanus, in memory, perhaps, of the first martyr ; Junius Brutus, in memory of the protagonist of Roman liberty ; and Celta, to show that he is French : he adorns his work, or gets it adorned by another (the style is certainly different), with a preface professing to be written by a Gascon : he adorns it further with a prefatory poem masquerading as the work of a Belgian, and with a final poem disguised as the composition of a Spaniard from Tarragona.   He has, you will see, wrapped up political science in a mystery.   I doubt if we shall ever penetrate some of the mystery, or know who wrote the preface or the poems ; and I doubt if we shall ever be quite sure who wrote the main work itself. . . . But Mornay was a young friend of Languet.   He was living in Antwerp about the same time.   He liked to write Latin verses—and possibly prefaces.   That is all I can say.

THE serious matter, however, is not who said what, but what was actually said.   We must abjure the scholar's temptation to play with riddles of authorship, and we must face the scholar's real task, which is that of recovering and understanding an author's thought.   The author of the *Vindiciae* had two problems to face.   One was the problem of the duty of the individual when confronted with a State which commands him to do or believe what he cannot do or believe.   It is the problem of Antigone face to face with Creon : it is the problem of the conscientious objector face to face with the law of conscription : it is the problem of English Nonconformity, the Antigone of our national history, confronted by penal statutes.   Here the author of the *Vindiciae* had before him the doctrine of the *Institutes* of Calvin, in the twentieth chapter of Book IV ; and that was a doctrine of non-resistance.   The powers that be are ordained of God ; and the duty of obedience to those powers is a divine imperative.   Whatever they command

we are bound to obey ; and if they command evil, our only
remedy is patience and prayer.   The author of the *Vindiciae*
follows the master.   Private persons cannot resist the
public authority.   They have no commission from God.
To plead the right of private conscience in this matter is
dangerous.   'If any man arrogate that authority to
himself, as though he were one breathed upon by the Holy
Spirit, let him beware that he be not puffed up by arrogance,
that he be not a god to himself, that he be not himself
assuming for himself these great spiritual motions, that he
be not conceiving vanity and bringing forth a lie.' [1]   What
then remains ?   Two choices.   First, to do as our Lord
said : 'When they persecute you in this city, flee ye into
another.'   Next, and if it be not given to flee elsewhere,
'to renounce life rather than God, and to be crucified
rather than crucify Christ afresh.' [2]   Exile or death—
that is the choice for the private person when he stands
face to face with the will of an ungodly State.   It was the
choice which thousands of Huguenots made.   We know
from the records of history how they accepted the saying
of Jesus, and fled into another city, accepting dispersion
among the nations, and fructifying the cities among which
they were dispersed.   The cities of London and Canterbury :
the cities of Switzerland, Germany, and the Netherlands—
all these received them.   Across the Atlantic, in the far
country of South Carolina, after the revocation of the Edict
of Nantes, the city of Charleston—at that time one of the
greatest of American cities—also received them.   'Commerce is of noble origin in South Carolina,' wrote its first
historian.   Is it fanciful to ascribe to this Huguenot recep-

---

[1] *Vindiciae*, pp. 68–9 (edition 1579).

[2] Ibid., p. 67.   Here the author is discussing the rights of private
resistance on religious grounds.   But he is equally opposed to private
resistance on political grounds ; and in the face of political oppression
he bids the people beware that 'in seeking to cross the sea dry-shod under
the guidance of some impostor, it fall not headlong into the abyss ; in
seeking a *vindex* for tyranny, it follow not one who may transfer tyranny
to himself, after the tyrant has been expelled : in seeking to serve the
commonwealth, it aid not the private greed of a person ' (p. 214).

tion the fact, remarked by the latest historian of the United States, that ' in 1920 Charleston had only 68,000 inhabitants, but more distinction and flavour than any one of the hundred American cities that exceeded it in size ' ? [1]

But there was another problem, and for our purposes a profounder problem, which the author of the *Vindiciae* had to face. Private resistance may be impossible. But what is to be said of public resistance ? Let us suppose that the king has become a tyrant, and a persecutor of ' the religion.' Is there no resource ? If individuals are powerless, what is to be said of the people as a body, a corporation, *non ut singuli, sed ut universi* ? What is to be said of parliaments, or meetings of the three Estates, which represent the people as an epitome ? What is to be said of the public authorities, central and local, which are connected with the people, represent the people, and may act on the people's behalf ? Here the author of the *Vindiciae* had another passage in the *Institutes*, from a later section of the same chapter of the same book, to give him guidance. ' If there be magistrates constituted for the defence of the people, to bridle the excessive cupidity and licence of kings, such as the Ephors in Sparta,[2] the tribunes at Rome . . . and to-day, it may be, in each kingdom the Three Estates assembled ; they have not only the right, but the duty, to oppose and resist the intemperance of kings, according to the obligation of their office ; and they may even be accused as guilty of perjury by reason of any deception, whereby treacherously they betray the liberty of the people, of which they ought to recognize themselves as ordained trustees (*tutores*) by the will of God.' I am inclined to think that Book IV, chapter xx, section 31 of the *Institutes* is one of the seed-beds of modern liberty. It passed into the Huguenot

---

[1] S. E. Morison, *Oxford History of the United States*, i. p. 35.

[2] This would seem to be the origin of what we may call ' the doctrine of the Ephorate.' It is adopted not only in the *Vindiciae*, but also in other Huguenot writings and in the *Politica* of Althusius (c. xviii. §§ 48 sqq.). The author of the *Vindiciae* takes as one of the two mottoes of his book a passage from Justin, *de Lycurgo Legislatore*, which naturally carries our thoughts to Sparta and its legislator and Ephors.

writings of the years 1572–9, and particularly into the argument of the *Vindiciae*. Through them it passed into the
Dutch Declaration of Independence, or Act of Abjuration,
of 1581, which breathes ideas I cannot but believe to have
been inspired by Huguenots then living and working in the
Netherlands. Through them, again, it passed, by ways
I shall endeavour to trace, into the English Revolution
and Bill of Rights of the year 1689 ; and it continued there-
after to be a source—little known and yet active—of the
principles of the great Whig party.

The passage which I have quoted from Calvin under-
went a great development in the hands of the writer of the
Vindiciae. Briefly, I should summarize that development
by saying that he made explicit, singularly explicit, the
notion of the sovereignty of the people implied by Calvin ;
that he connected with that notion, as corollaries, the three
ideas of contract, trusteeship, and resistance, which were
all to acquire a universal vogue ; and that he also connected
with it, as a peculiar corollary, an idea of federalism, which,
it is true, appeared, and was even extended, in the thought
of Althusius and in connexion with the federation of the
United Provinces of the Dutch, but which never attained
the general vogue of the other three ideas.

THE people and its sovereignty are facts which appear
to be simply assumed. We are not told, so far as I can
see, how a *populus* comes into existence, or how it acquires
sovereignty, or indeed what it is.[1] The author seems to

---

[1] The author explains, in an interesting passage which has some
affinities with Locke's second *Treatise*, why the people turns itself into
a State by creating a government and instituting a king (pp. 107–9).
What he does not explain is the origin of the people and the reason for its
sovereignty. He simply assumes, as the basis of his argument, (1) that
the people exists *per se*, whereas the king can only exist *per populum*, and
that it is therefore prior to the king (p. 82) ; (2) that the people, being as
it is prior, and instituting as it does the government, is also *potior* (p. 85) ;
and (3) that the people, existing *a se*, and possessing priority and superiority,
has imprescriptible rights, inherent in its nature as an immortal corporation or *Universitas* (p. 104). ' As the Rhine, the Seine, and the Tiber
are the same as they were a thousand years ago, so the German, the Gallic,

assume the given fact of the existence of what he calls the
populus ; and he seems to assume that by what we should
call natural law ' the people ' has sovereignty.   In this
sense he is one of the founders of that school of natural law
which extends through Grotius, and Puffendorf, and Locke,
in the seventeenth century, to the American Declaration
of Independence in 1776, with its reference to ' the laws of
Nature and of Nature's God,' and to Tom Paine's *Rights
of Man* in 1791.   But we must add that the writer of the
Vindiciae also feels that the divine law of the Scriptures,
no less than natural law, will justify the sovereignty of the
people ; and he quotes the Old Testament again and again
to prove the rights of the people of God in ancient Israel.
This addition may lead us to another reflection.   The
populus of the author of the *Vindiciae* is really two things,
though the author never makes the distinction clear.
In the first place, it is a people of God : it is the people
sub specie religionis : it was what we may call a Church—
an *ecclesia*.   This is a difficult saying when we reflect that
the Huguenots, for whom the author is speaking, were by no
means co-extensive with the people of France, and indeed,
on the contrary, were only a small minority of that people.
None the less, it is a saying which is implied in the argument
of the *Vindiciae* ; and it must even be considered as an
integral part of the argument.   But in the second place, the
people is also what we may call a natural people, with the
rights of natural law ; or again we may say that it is a
political people, with the political right of sovereignty ;
or again, and more simply, we may say that it is a State.
Populus and Respublica are thus one : l'Etat, c'est le
peuple.   We may add that if populus is thus respublica
as well as ecclesia, if the people is the State as well as the
Church, it also follows that State and Church are one.
L'Eglise, c'est l'Etat : l'Etat, c'est l'Eglise.[1]

or the Roman people is the same ; nor can their rights be changed one
jot or tittle either, by the flow of their waters, or by the alteration of their
individual members.'
      [1] The co-extension (identification is perhaps too strong a word) of

WE may now turn to the notion of Contract. This is the specific contribution of the author of the *Vindiciae*. True, the idea of a political contract had appeared in the Middle Ages : it is as old as St. Thomas, and even older : true, again, it had been used in recent times by Salamonius. It none the less remains also true that the idea of the ' original contract,' which served such solemn uses in our own Revolution Settlement, starts on its modern history with the publication of the *Vindiciae* in 1579. The author is very clear about contract, and indeed about *two* contracts which correspond to the two senses in which we may understand the ' people.' In the first place, the people as the people of God makes a covenant with God, that ' it will be and will remain the people of God.' This comes straight from the Old Testament and its covenant. Indeed, what is Vetus Testamentum but παλαιὰ διαθήκη, and what is διαθήκη but covenant or contract ? We cannot speak of the Old Testament without speaking also of covenant— the covenant of El, who is God, with Isra-el, ' the warriors of

people and Church is an assumption common to Lutherans, Calvinists, and Anglicans in the sixteenth century. It is only in the theory of the seventeenth century (among the Jesuits and in Calvinist writers such as Voetius) that we find the idea of the Church as a society separate from and not necessarily co-extensive with the people. There is a phrase in the schedule to the Church of Scotland Act of 1921 which recalls the ideas of the sixteenth century—a phrase in which the Church of Scotland is described as ' a national church representative of the Christian faith of the Scottish people.' In this phrase the Church of Scotland and the Scottish people seem to be co-extensive and even identical. Gierke, in the fourth volume of his *Genossenschaftsrecht* (especially pp. 363–71), throws light on the whole matter.

It must be added that in his fourth ' question,' when he is discussing the problem ' whether neighbouring princes may aid the subjects of a prince afflicted by reason of the pure religion,' the author of the *Vindiciae* alters his ground. He has to argue that such princes are bound to protect the one pure religion wherever it be, and that the pure religion is a single Church, irrespective of boundaries and peoples, which must be protected in all places and among all peoples. Here, therefore, he distinguishes Ecclesia, *quae una omnium est, quae una universaque singulis commissa est* and Respublica, *quae alia aliorum esse potest, alia aliis . . . commendata est* (p. 229). Here the identity of Populus with Ecclesia and Respublica, and therefore of Respublica with Ecclesia, disappears.

God.' The author of the *Vindiciae* adds a refinement to this covenant, which he gathers from the Scriptures. When kings arose in Israel, the covenant or contract altered its character : it ceased to be simply an agreement between God and the people : it became an agreement between God on the one side, and the people *and* the king on the other. People and king are thus *copromissores* ; and it follows, on the logic of *copromissio*, that if the king violates his promise and obligation by departing from God, the people are bound, for the sake of keeping their promise and obligation, to resist or constrain or even depose the king. What was true for Israel of old is true for all peoples to-day ; for the polity of Israel was an ideal polity, proceeding 'not from Plato and Aristotle,' but from God. Here is a first ground laid for resistance ; but it is not the only ground. There is a second contract to be considered. The people, besides making a covenant with God, in its religious capacity, also makes a covenant with the king in its natural or political capacity—a covenant 'to obey the king truly while he rules truly.' This is a covenant also expressed in the Scriptures, where we are told that the kings of Israel made covenants with Israel : it is a covenant which is moreover implied in the coronation ceremony of contemporary kingdoms, where the king promises to rule truly, and the people promises to obey truly in return ; it is a covenant to which the example of Aragon explicitly testifies.[1]   It follows on this covenant, once more, that if the king violates his obligation by infringing its terms, the people may resist or constrain or even depose the king. There is, however, a difficulty in this second or political contract, which escapes the author of the *Vindiciae*, but is inherent in all theories of a contract between king and people. Parties to a contract are separate and independent parties. If you make

[1] The author of the *Vindiciae* (quoting, I think, from the *Franco-Gallia*, where the original Spanish is cited) twice refers to the proud claim of the Aragonese nobles : ' We, who have as much worth as you, and more power than you, elect you king, *on such and such conditions.*' Bodin (pp. 131–2 of the Frankfort edition of 1594) refers to the Aragonese custom, but refuses to admit its application.

king and people contractors, you make king and people
separate and independent parties. The people ceases to be
identical with the State, and the State is split into a duality
of king and people.   Unity is lost ; and as long as you talk
in terms of a contract of king and people it will never be
recovered.   It is a better thing to talk of a contract, not
between king and people, but between the members of the
people, one with another, for the purpose of forming a
body politic.   On that basis you may say that the body
politic so formed proceeds to delegate powers to a king, who
is thus a delegate or trustee, but not a contractor.   On
the same basis you may further say that the body politic
also, and *pari passu*, delegates powers to other public
authorities as well as the king, and that these bodies stand
by the side of the king in the same capacity of delegates or
trustees.   I believe that this is what Locke said, or tried
to say, in 1689; and I am sure that it is what Burke was
saying in 1770, in the *Thoughts on the Causes of the Present
Discontents*.   Both Locke and Burke believed in a contract
of the sort which constitutes the people a body politic, and
both of them regarded political power as a delegation or
trust proceeding from that body politic.   The author of the
Vindiciae follows a different and less consistent theory.
His people is an unexplained body politic. *His* king is a
separate contractor with that unexplained body politic.
And yet his king, and other public magistrates also, are
somehow, at the same time, no more than trustees or
delegates.

WE are thus brought to another idea which appears
in the *Vindiciae* ; and that is the idea of trusteeship.
I cannot see that it goes logically with the idea of contract
between king and people.   I cannot see that the king can
be at one and the same time a separate and independent
contractor and a delegate or trustee.   But that is what he
is, according to the theory of the *Vindiciae*.   Along with the
argument about contract, there is also an argument that
the king is a *tutor*, which is the word that Calvin had used

and which in Roman law approximates, I suppose, to our English word trustee. Having used this word, the author dilates, with a good deal of lore drawn from Roman law, on the origin and duties of the *tutor*—on his origin, in the choice and designation of the people ; [1] on his duties, in virtue of his mandate or trust. He goes further. He argues that the king is not the only authority in the State vested with this capacity. Calvin's hint about ephors in ancient times and the three Estates in modern kingdoms receives a large development. There are two sorts of public authorities, according to the author of the *Vindiciae*, which must be considered as parallel with the king. In the first place there are the *officiarii regni*, as distinct from the *officiarii regis*. These are the great public officers, such as the Constable : they draw their authority from the people, like the king himself, and not (like the king's private officers) from the king : they are ' assessors and consorts ' of the king : collectively they are even greater than the king ; and if they are true to the tutorial authority vested in them by the people, they will, as is their bounden duty, restrain a king who infringes the terms of his trusteeship. All this may well remind us of the position assumed by the great Whig magnates after the Revolution of 1688. In the second place, there are the delegates of the orders, the representatives of the three Estates, or, as we should say, the Parliament of the realm The Estates General of France, intermitted for many years before 1559, had been resumed during the troubles which followed ; and the author of the *Vindiciae* is clear that the Estates are a

---

[1] Strictly speaking, kingship proceeds both from God and the people. As St. Thomas had taught, and Burke long afterwards repeats, God gives the *principium* of political authority, but the people determines the *modus* (or form of government), and attributes the *exercitium* (or actual exercise of authority) to a definite person or body of persons. In the same sense the author of the *Vindiciae*, who had read and twice quotes the *Summa* of St. Thomas, holds that kings rule *a Deo quidem, sed per populum et propter populum* (p. 79). In the same sense Burke writes, ' although government certainly is an institution of divine authority, yet its forms, and the persons who administer it, all originate from the people ' (*Thoughts on the Causes of the Present Discontents*).

representation of the people, an epitome of the people, vested by it with authority to give consent on all great issues, to rebuke the king, and even to change the succession to the Crown. This emphasis on the Estates has equally its affinities with the Whig Parliamentarianism of our eighteenth century.

WE may now turn to the third of the ideas which we ascribed to the author of the *Vindiciae*—the idea of resistance. It follows from what has been said about contract that the people may resist the king on the ground of breach of contract. It follows on what has been said about the trusteeship of *officiarii*, and the representative position of the Estates, that both of these *can* resist, and both indeed *must* resist, if the king violates his trusteeship and delegation, since otherwise they will be failing in their own trusteeship and representation. The right of public resistance runs through the whole argument—resistance of the people of God, for breach of the first contract ; resistance of the political people, for breach of the second ; resistance of officers of State and the three Estates, on grounds of public trusteeship and representation. By resistance kings must be kept within the divine law of the word of God ; and by it they must be kept within the law of the land—a law not of their making, even if they have concurred in its making, a law according to which they have sworn at their coronation to rule, a law of which they are only the servants.[1] Such resistance may go to the length of deposition ; and shall we not say, considering this zeal of popular liberty and popular vigilance, that kings have become a little thing, and no more than dust in the balance ? If kingship was necessary to maintain the unity of France, the author of the *Vindiciae* leaves very little kingship to

---

[1] The idea of the sovereignty of law over the ruler is strongly enforced by the author of the *Vindiciae*. One of his two mottoes is the famous passage from the Codex Theodosianus, *Digna vox est majestate regnantis legibus alligatum se principem profiteri*. See Note B at the end of this essay.

maintain that unity.   Yet we must beware of exaggerating
the amount of popular liberty which he vindicates.   We have
to look carefully into the meaning of the word ' people '
in the *Vindiciae*.   The author is not, after all, a democrat.
He is really, we soon discover, an aristocrat.   This becomes
plain in an early part of his argument.   Can the people,
he imagines some doubter asking, really resist—the people
in the sense of the universal multitude, that beast of innumerable heads ?   He replies, ' When we speak of the
universus populus, we mean those who have authority from
the people—the magistrates . . . chosen by the people . . .
consorts, as it were, of sovereignty and ephors (or over-seers)
over monarchs.   We mean also assemblies, which are
nothing else but epitomes of the people. . . . In a word,
whatever we have said to be conceded or committed to the
whole people, belongs to its *officiarii* ;   whatever to Israel,
belongs to the Princes and Elders of Israel.' [1]   This argument, in its aristocratic implication, consorts with the
genius of Calvinism.   Calvinism was not democratic, but
aristocratic : it was government not by the congregation,
but by the presbyter and elders of the congregation.   It
consorts again with the Whiggism of the eighteenth century,
which was aristocratic liberalism.   That is the worst of the
conception of trusteeship in its application to politics.   The
political trustee is apt to regard himself as acting from above,
on behalf of beneficiaries who are always below and always
in a minority.   The *curator* or *tutor,* to use the language of
the *Vindiciae,* has a perpetual tutelage of his *pupilli.* [2]

THERE remains to be mentioned, in conclusion, the
fourth and last idea of the author of the *Vindiciae*—the
idea of federalism.   Federalism, again, is perhaps an idea

[1] *Vindiciae,* pp. 46–8.
[2] Bodin, on the other hand, regards the conception of *curator* or *tutor*
as derogating from the sovereignty of the true king.   In a passage which
seems like a rebuke to the argument of the *Vindiciae,* he contends that
any one using *aliena potestas* either by way of *curatio* or by mere right
of magistracy, whether for a time or in perpetuity, has no sovereignty
(p. 119).

natural to Calvinism, which unites congregations in presbyteries, presbyteries in synods, and synods in a general assembly.   But it was an idea which meant life and death to the Calvinists of France.   It was all very well to talk of the *universus populus*, but the Huguenots were not the universal people of France.   They might indeed form the *populus* of a seignory under a Huguenot noble : they might again form the *populus* of an *urbs* or *civitas* which had embraced the religion of Calvinism.   Even so, they were only a *populus* within the *populus* : they were what we may call a *sub-populus*.   Some way must be found of vindicating the position of such a *sub-populus*.   The author of the *Vindiciae* attempts a way, perhaps remembering Bartolus' doctrine of the Italian *civitas sibi princeps*.   He would make French cities, at any rate those of ' the religion,' as independent of the French monarchy as Bartolus had made the Italian cities independent of the Empire : and he would thus turn France into a sort of Germany.   This was the danger of Huguenotism—the danger which made the political unitarianism of France turn upon it under Richelieu, and, more drastically still, under Louis XIV. The argument of the *Vindiciae* is significant on this point. Not only has the *universus populus* made a double compact: the *populus* of a city—for a city is a people, and not a place or ' a heap of stones ' [1]—has also made *its* double compact.   *It* must keep its heavenly compact with God, and may resist the king in the strength thereof ; and *it* may insist that the king shall keep his earthly pact with it, and observe the municipal conventions to which he has sworn.   This postulates a multitude of pacts, or at any rate two sorts of pacts, each of them double—the double central pact of the *universus populus*, and the double local pacts of the provinces and cities, pacts as many in number as there are provinces and cities concerned.   And it is to be noticed that both sorts seem to be of equal validity with one another.   In the light of such arguments the question may be raised whether we are justified in applying

[1] *Vindiciae*, p. 58.

even the term 'federalist' to the theory of the *Vindiciae*.
Is not the term pitched too high ?   Are we not confronted
by something lower than federalism—something of the
nature of a loose confederation—something like what
Germany was already becoming, and was formally recognized as being by the Treaty of Westphalia in 1648 ?
Or shall we rather compare the theory of the *Vindiciae*
with the federal form which the Seven United Provinces
were soon afterwards to assume ?   If we do so, we shall be
led to notice a matter of some importance ; and that is the
similarity between the federal theory of the State in the
Vindiciae and the similar theory of the State in the work of
Althusius, *Politica methodice digesta* (published in 1603)—
a work which seems to owe much of its inspiration to a study
of Dutch conditions.   The *Vindiciae* (we may then say),
if it looks back to Bartolus and his theory of the *Civitas
sibi princeps*, looks also forward to Althusius, and anticipates
his theory of the State as an association composed of provinces and cities, each of which may retain its own 'majesty,'
or (as we should say) its sovereignty, and so be a 'prince for
itself.'

IF time and space had sufficed, some words might have
been said at this point in regard to the influence of the
general theory of the *Vindiciae* upon the course of the
Dutch war of independence.   I can only say, without proof
of my guesses, that I would venture three conjectures in
this connexion.   First, I am inclined to believe, as I have
already had occasion to observe, that the famous *Apology*
of the Prince of Orange, issued in 1580 in answer to the
ban pronounced by Philip II of Spain, was largely drafted
by Languet, who, as I have attempted to argue, was probably
the author of the *Vindiciae*.   Secondly, I am inclined to
think that the Dutch Act of Abjuration of 1581—an Act
as solemn as the Declaration of Independence of 1776—
owed something to the same inspiration.   Thirdly, I suspect
that the instructions given by the Dutch 'States' to the
envoys who were to justify the Abjuration before the Diet

of the Empire (of which they were still nominally a part), in 1582, were also indebted to that inspiration.   Contract was the basis of these instructions—contract and again contract.   ' The contracts which the king has broken,' the envoys said, ' are no pedantic fantasies.'   I would add that the contracts of which the author of the *Vindiciae* spoke were also more than pedantic fantasies.   They helped, I think, to make history—both in the age in which they were first put forward, and in succeeding ages.

The *Vindiciae* was a popular book.   There were six Latin editions between 1579 and 1599, and six more before the Peace of Westphalia in 1648—some printed in one place and some in another, from which we may guess the general vogue of the work.   It was often printed along with the *Prince* of Machiavelli, by way (I suppose) of a corrective.[1] The first French translation was printed at Geneva, as early as 1581 ; and there was another published in 1615. English translations also began to appear.   The first of which I know was a translation only of a small part—the part which deals with the question whether neighbouring princes may aid the subjects of another prince suffering from persecution or tyranny ; but this was exactly the part which had a lively interest for the England of Elizabeth, confronted as it was with that very question in France and in Holland.   The translation appeared in London in 1588, under the title of *A Short Apology for Christian*

---

[1] Generally the *Vindiciae* appeared as a sequel to the *Prince*.   In one instance, however, the *Prince* (in Latin) appears as a sequel to the *Vindiciae* (E. Armstrong, *Eng. Hist. Rev.*, iv. p. 17).   The Huguenots naturally professed to be anti-Machiavellian, in order to throw odium on Machiavelli's countrywoman, Catharine de Medici.   In the preface to the *Vindiciae* much is made of the fact that the book is diametrically opposed to the evil arts, the wicked counsels, and the false and pestiferous doctrine of the *Prince*.   The prefatory poem also begins with a denunciation of that *contemptor superûm* who is *nomine notus Maculosi Velleris*— a curious pun.   Actually I have only noted one explicit reference to Machiavelli (p. 176) ; and against that I would set the fact that there is also a reference (not indeed *nominatim*) to Ariosto and Tasso (pp. 196–7). The *Vindiciae* is not written to controvert the *Prince*, and its argument would have been just the same if the *Prince* had never been written.

Soldiers. More important is the translation of the whole of the *Vindiciae* which appeared in London in 1648, and was reprinted again in London in 1689. It is a striking fact that this translation should first have appeared in the year before the execution of Charles I, and that it should have been reprinted in the year of the deposition of James II.

The history of the book in England, whether in the original or in translations, is curious. In the early part of the seventeenth century the book was ascribed in England to the Jesuits. This may seem paradoxical ; but the reason is simple. The book was anti-monarchical : the Jesuits in England were anti-monarchical ; therefore the book was written by a Jesuit. James I spoke of its author as ' an anonymous writer, perhaps an emissary of Roman Church, anxious by its means to cause a dislike for the Reformed Religion among princes.' A common report assigned the authorship to the Jesuit Parsons. The Puritans of England must have known better. They must have guessed that the book came from the ranks of the reformed religion for which they fought ; and it must have been from some Puritan source that the translation of 1648 was derived.

That translation was made by a certain William Walker. Thomas Hollis, a famous antiquarian and Radical of the eighteenth century, to whom I shall recur, possessed a copy of the original Latin edition of 1579, on a blank page of which was written the motto, ' Will and Walke aright,' with the name of William Walker underneath ; and Hollis believed that it was from this copy that Walker had made his translation. There is a story about this William Walker that he came from Darnal, near Sheffield, and that he was the man who cut off the head of Charles I. The story appears in a note, written by some owner, in a copy of Walker's translation of the *Vindiciae* now in the British Museum ; and there was a discussion of the story in the *Gentleman's Magazine* for November 1767. I should be inclined to guess that an ingenious guesser jumped to the conclusion that the translator of the *Vindiciae contra Tyrannos* must himself have committed tyrannicide. A truer light is thrown on Walker, and the circumstances of his translating the *Vindiciae*, in an account which is given in Blackburne's *Memorials of Thomas Hollis*. In 1649, we are told, the Presbyterian ministers had to defend themselves against an imputation of anti-monarchical principles, which their adversary, a Catholic priest, declared them to have drawn from Beza, the author of the *Vindiciae*. (Beza, along with Hotman and George Buchanan, was one of its many supposed authors : and as late as 1660 an edition appeared at Amsterdam with the imprint, *Stephano Junio Bruto sive ut putatur Theodoro Beza auctore.*)   The ministers replied that the *Vindiciae* was written by Parsons the Jesuit. They added (somewhat inconsistently, one cannot but feel) that a member of Parliament now sitting in the House had caused the *Vindiciae* to be translated into English by the same Walker who had written the *Monthly Mercuries*. Walker, it would appear, was a journalist rather than a tyrannicide ; and it was an English journalist, acting on the suggestion of an English M.P., who gave to his countrymen a full-dress presentation of a current and standard defence of religious and civil liberty.

The *Vindiciae* was obviously a live book in England in the first half of the seventeenth century. It continued to live in the latter half. In 1683, during the period of Tory reaction at the end of the reign of Charles II, the University of Oxford passed in its Convocation ' a judgment and decree against certain pernicious books and damnable doctrines, destructive to the sacred persons of princes, their State and Government, and of all human society.' Damning *imprimis* the doctrine that ' all civil authority is derived from the people,' the University consigned to the flames, in the Bodleian quadrangle, the *Vindiciae contra Tyrannos*, along with George Buchanan's *De jure regni apud Scotos* and Milton's *Defensio pro populo Anglicano*. The decree was passed, and the bonfire lit, on the day on which Russel was executed. A graduate of Christ Church wrote a copy of Latin hexameters in celebration of the *flammae ultrices*, and the decree was presented to Charles II. It is perhaps worth

7

mentioning that in 1710 the decree, by order of the House of Lords, was publicly burned along with Sacheverel's sermon.

Between the burning of books by the Oxford decree and the burning of the Oxford decree by order of the House of Lords, there had intervened the Revolution of 1688.[1] That Revolution was in itself a solemn enactment of the principles for which the author of the *Vindiciae* had contended—principles which had now entered into English thought, and were backed by the memory of the Long Parliament and the policy of the Whig party. These principles found a new formulation in 1690 in Locke's *Two Treatises of Government*, which henceforth became the Bible of the Whigs. The similarity of the principles of Locke to those of the author of the *Vindiciae* is obvious. The basis of natural law ; the assumption of the ultimate sovereignty of the people ; the theory of contract (if in a different form) ; the doctrine of the people's right to institute, to oppose, and even to depose, kings ; above all, the idea of political trusteeship (which is fundamentally important in Locke's *Treatises*, as it also bulks largely in the *Vindiciae*)—all these are common to Locke with his forerunner. It does not follow that Locke borrowed directly from the *Vindiciae*. The essence of its argument—an argument which also appears, if less fully and trenchantly stated, in the works of other Huguenot and Calvinist writers after 1572—had been wrought into the general substance of what we may call progressive political thought ; and Locke would readily find what was now universally current. But there can be no doubt that Locke knew the *Vindiciae*. It is true that he does not expressly refer to the book. He was a shrewd man, and in his shrewd way he preferred to cite conservative writers in order to justify

---

[1] It is only fair to Oxford to say that its heart had been changed, by events at Magdalen College and elsewhere, as early as 1688. While the Prince of Orange was still in the far West, after his landing at Torbay, some of the Heads of the Colleges sent the Warden of All Souls to meet him, ' assuring him that they would declare for him, and inviting him to come thither ' (Burnet). It is only fair to Oxford also to say that Cambridge had burned the *Vindiciae* as early as about 1620.

liberal opinions. He cites, for example, the judicious Hooker throughout his second *Treatise* ; and he cites in one passage the royal Solomon, James I. But there is also another book which Locke cites, and with which, indeed, he deals at some length towards the end of the second *Treatise*. It is not the *Vindiciae* ; it is an attempt at a refutation of the *Vindiciae*. It is Barclay's *De regno et regali potestate, adversus Buchananum, Brutum, Boucherium et reliquos monarchomachos*. Barclay was a Scotsman from Aberdeen, who became a Professor of Civil Law at Angers, and published his book in 1600. When he wrote *adversus Brutum*, he was controverting the author of the *Vindiciae*, who was generally styled by his pseudonym. If Locke knew Barclay, as he certainly did, he must also have known the *Vindiciae*, even if he only knew it through Barclay. But a reprint of the English translation appeared, as we have seen, in the year before that in which Locke published his *Two Treatises* ; and he may well have read the translation, if not the original. In any case there is, in more than one respect, a curious parallel between Locke and the author of the *Vindiciae*. Whether Languet or Mornay wrote the *Vindiciae*, it was composed by a person living in Holland (for both of them were there in the year before its publication, and in the year of its publication), and it was composed under the influence of Huguenot feeling. When Locke began his *Two Treatises*, he too was living in Holland; and while he was writing them, the feeling caused by the Revocation of the Edict of Nantes was dominant in his circle. ' It may be said,' writes one of the most recent students of Locke,' that it was in Holland, and in consequence of the intellectual fermentation caused by the Revocation of the Edict of Nantes, that his political doctrines arrived at maturity.'[1]

HERE the wheel has come full circle, and here the argument might fitly conclude. But a word of summary may perhaps be added. The political thought of the

[1] Ch. Bastide, *John Locke*, pp. 96–7. On parallels between Locke and the author of the *Vindiciae*, see Note C at the end of this Essay.

Huguenots, as it is expressed in the *Vindiciae*, found no home and no welcome in France. A chance, indeed, seemed to offer itself during the years of the Fronde (1648–1653) ; but the Fronde was a short-lived movement, which, if it began with the cause of liberty, ended in the cause of class privilege. In 1789, again, it might seem at first sight as if the Huguenot principles had at long last entered into their own ; but it is only a matter of seeming. If the French Revolution adopted the principle of the sovereignty of the people, it made popular sovereignty as powerful and as unitary as ever monarchical sovereignty had been during the last two centuries ; and it left little room for rights of resistance or federal principles. But the principles which were alien to the political unitarianism of France found a more congenial home in Holland, with its mixed system of popular rights and federal institutions ; and while the Huguenots themselves found sympathy and an eventual refuge in the United Provinces, the theory of the *Vindiciae* was developed in that of Althusius—a German, indeed, but a German who lived and worked in Friesland, on the very borders of Holland, and who drew on federal Holland as well as on the federal Germany of his day for the material of his speculation. In England, too, with the rise of the Free Churches, the consolidation of local self-government, and the growth of parliamentarianism, the Huguenot theory found a second congenial home. The federal element of the theory might not appeal to England, but the doctrines of the sovereignty of the people, of the contract, of resistance, of trusteeship, were all readily welcome ; and even the narrow Huguenot conception of the people, under which it was identified with the *officiarii* and the three Estates, found its parallel in the Whig identification of the English people with the magnates and the Commons.

In the English home which it had found at the end of the seventeenth century we may say ' Good-bye ' to the Huguenot theory of politics. Perhaps it had now served its turn and done its work. But it survived, at any rate for a

few, well into the eighteenth century. Robert Molesworth
(afterwards Viscount Molesworth), a supporter of the Orange
cause in Ireland, who went on a mission to the Danish
Court which ended in trouble and a lively *Account of
Denmark*, published in 1694, was a Whig Member of
Parliament, first in Dublin and afterwards at Westminster,
with a taste for letters and political theory. He published,
in 1711, a translation of Hotman's *Franco-Gallia* (welcome
to the Whigs as a vindication of ancient constitutional
liberties, even *in terra aliena*), and he adorned his
translation with a long and lively preface. The memory
of Molesworth's translation survived until the beginning of the Radical movement in 1770, and it was republished for the London Association in 1775.[1] Even
more curious is the story of Thomas Hollis and his passion
for the *Vindiciae*. Hollis (1720–1774) described himself
in one of the many copies of the work which he collected
as *T. H. Anglus, Hospitii Lincolniensis, Regalis et Anti-
quoru msocietatum socialis, libertatis patriae praestantisque
ejus constitutionis anno 1688 recuperatae amator studio-
sissimus*. He was a ' republican ' Whig, who presented
to Sidney Sussex College, Cambridge, its portrait of Oliver
Cromwell (he was a ready giver, and presented books to
Harvard and other Universities), and who wrote at the end
of Molesworth's preface to his translation of the *Franco-
Gallia* the two simple words, ' My Faith.' A wealthy man,
he had a habit of reprinting works of political theory devoted to the cause of liberty, and of adorning his reprints
with emblems of liberty. He republished Locke's *Letters
on Toleration* and his *Two Treatises of Government* ; Sidney
on *Government* : Neville's *Plato Redivivus* ; and other
works. We learn from Blackburne's *Memorials* that the
Vindiciae was ' a favourite book with Mr. Hollis.' ' Many
have been the editions of the *Vindiciae* : Mr. Hollis picked
up as many of them as he could meet with '—among the
rest (as I have already mentioned) the copy used by Walker,
and an edition printed at Paris, in 1631, under the altered

[1] It was reprinted under the title of *The True Principles of the Whigs*.

title of *Vindiciae Religionis*. He acquired an original painting of Languet (whom he firmly believed to be the author, though some of the grounds he alleged were highly dubious) ; and 'intending to procure a new edition of the *Vindiciae*, he caused an elegant engraving of Languet's head to be taken ' (it is figured in the *Memorials*), with a design of prefixing it to the new edition. The edition never appeared. New stars dawned in the firmament ; and when the *Contrat Social* of Rousseau began to shine in 1762, there was no more place, except in the scholar's library, that refuge of extinct stars, for the *Vindiciae contra Tyrannos* of Stephanus Junius Brutus.

NOTE A

The Style of the 'Vindiciae'

One mark of the style of the *Vindiciae* is a sort of epigrammatic *brusquerie*, combined with a perpetual cultivation of antithesis. This gives a forced lucidity and a hard precision to the argument. It suggests to the mind of the reader the habit of the University lecturer, or, again, that of the ' painful preacher.' It suggests, too, the influence of the sharp formulation of Calvinistic theology. To one who has found himself yielding to the temptation of the double or triple antithesis, and has trembled to think that he might be twisting the truth to suit the needs of antithetical necessity, the author of the *Vindiciae*—certainly a fellow-sinner— is at once a comfort and a warning. He even uses the resources of the Latin language to make what may be called punning antitheses. A good instance of his method comes on p. 76 : *Ostendimus antea Deum Reges instituere, Regna Regibus dare, Reges eligere : dicimus jam Populum Reges constituere, Regna tradere, electionem suo suffragio comprobare.*

But the style remains generally trenchant, and sometimes eloquent. ' You talk to me ' (he imagines an objector saying) 'about your patricians and *optimates* and *officiarii regni*. I, on the other hand, can see nothing in them but ghosts and old trappings like those of tragedies. I can see scarcely a single trace anywhere of your antique liberty and authority ' (p. 103).

Such objections stir him to a stinging reply. ' Let not Electors, Palatines, Patricians, and other *optimates* think that they are only created and instituted in order that once, may be, in their lives, at a royal coronation, they may show themselves on view in the trappings of an antique fashion, to play a sort of romantic drama—to take the part, just for the day, of a Roland, an Oliver, a Rinaldo, or some other hero, as if they were on the stage ; to represent, in a sort of a mummery, the Round Table of Arthur ; and then, when the audience has gone home, and the Music has pronounced the epilogue, to think they have admirably played their part. Such things are *not* done in play : they are *not* done perfunctorily : they are *not* the games of boys ' (p. 197). He returns to the theme later, when he imagines *optimatium unus aliquis*, who, instead of facing tyranny like a man, is content simply to admonish the tyrant's aiders and abettors. It is folly as well as cowardice. ' Not only is such admonishment dangerous, and counted as a capital offence, in a state of tyranny ; the man would be acting like one who despised all other assistance, threw his arms away, and quoted the laws and delivered a sermon on justice to a band of brigands in the middle of a wood. That, if you will, is to carry reasonableness to the point of madness. But what is to be done ? Is he to be deaf to the groans of the people, and dumb at the approach of brigands : is he just to gape and fold his arms ? No : if the law assigns the penalties of treason to the soldier who pretends sickness for fear of the enemy, what penalty can be enough for the man who, in malice or cowardice, betrays the people he has undertaken to protect ? ' (p. 206).

I will only add—turning from the style to the scholarship of the author of the *Vindiciae*—that his knowledge of Greek, as I have said in the text of the essay, is more than respectable. He quotes, for example (p. 43), a fragment of a Greek comic writer which proves that he must have read the edition of Stobaeus (who gives the fragment) printed at Venice in 1535. He cites, again, in another passage (p. 171), the so-called Pythagorean writings ; and he quotes, and quotes correctly (probably from Pollux), the oath of the Athenian Ephebi (p. 185).

NOTE B

The Sovereignty of Law in the 'Vindiciae'

Two of the most recent works on Political Theory are Professor M'Iver's *The Modern State* (1926), and Professor Krabbe's *Die Moderne Staatsidee* (1919). It is curious to notice how political theory is still wrestling with the same problems, and wrestling with them almost in the same terms, as it was in 1579, when the *Vindiciae* was published. This is not to say that there is nothing new under the sun. Still less is it to say that the thinkers of to-day are simply the pupils and *glossatores* of the thinkers of an earlier age. It is only to say that the problems remain constant, and that, while each age must wrestle with them in reference to its own conditions, and must keep itself fresh by rethinking solutions afresh in reference to those conditions, there will none the less be repetitions of ancient truths, and sometimes there may even be striking, if undesigned, repetitions of the very forms in which those truths have been couched before.

Professor M'Iver, starting from the theory of ' community ' as the fundamental fact, argues that the State must be regarded as an 'association' which acts as an ' organ of community.' So regarded, it has no inherent power : indeed, in any strict sense, it has no ' power ' at all : it has a ' function ' to discharge, and a ' service ' to render, on behalf of the community, and it is confined to that function and that service. ' It commands only because it serves : it owns only because it owes. It creates rights not as the lordly disperser of gifts, but as the agent of society for the creation of rights. The servant is not greater than his master ' (p. 480). The very language, and the very form of antithesis, have their parallels in the *Vindiciae*. ' Imperare ergo nihil aliud est, quam consulere : Imperii finis unicus populi utilitas . . . Regia vero dignitas non est proprie honos, sed onus ; non immunitas, sed munus ; non vacatio, sed vocatio ; non licentia, sed publica servitus ' (pp. 108–9).[1] Again, ' num regia dignitas possessio est, an potius functio ? Si functio, quid cum proprietate commune habet ? ' (p. 138). And again,

---

[1] The passage is an excellent example of the punning antithesis to which the author of the *Vindiciae* is prone.

'regis nomen non . . . proprietatem, non usufructum, sed functionem et procurationem sonat' (p. 152). Professor M'Iver speaks of 'State,' and the author of the *Vindiciae* speaks of 'Rex'; but the difference does not go deep.

Professor Krabbe contends for the sovereignty of impersonal law as opposed to that of any person or body of persons, 'The modern idea of the State recognizes as sovereign Might the impersonal Power of Right' (p. 2). And again, 'instead of personal Power we have now impersonal Might : instead of *sic volo, sic jubeo*, we have a spiritual sovereignty. In this conception the modern idea of the State reaches its zenith' (p. 37). But the conception of the impersonal sovereignty of law is a very old idea. True, it must be vindicated afresh in each age ; but its vindication began a long time ago. Aristotle said, in a famous passage which affected all subsequent thought, that 'the rule of law is preferable to that of a person, and, on the same ground, even if it be better for persons to govern, they should be made guardians and servants of the law' (*Politics*, iii. 16, §§ 3–4). He also said, in another famous passage (Ibid., iii. 11, §§ 1–2), that 'the generality ought to be sovereign' (ὅτι . . . δεῖ κύριον εἶναι μᾶλλον τὸ πλῆθος), and he grounded his argument on the idea that the meeting of the generality produced as it were a collective person with a collective capacity of judgment. These two sayings were put together in the thought of the Middle Ages, with the result that the people were regarded as the author of law by the power of their collective reason, and the law thus formed was regarded as the final sovereign. Dicta from Roman Law, enshrining the idea of the power of the popular *comitia* to make laws, and the idea that the *princeps* was bound by the laws, added a new corroboration to this way of thinking.

The author of the *Vindiciae* inherits and enforces these ideas. Steeped as he was in law—knowing the civil law, the canon law, the feudal law : the *Sachsenspiegel*, the *Liber Feudorum*, the 'Spanish Code '—he vindicates strenuously, in one of his best passages (pp. 114–116), the sovereignty of law. The 'dooms ' of kings (*arbitria regum*) were found various and contradictory ; laws, 'speaking to all in one and the same voice,' were discovered by the wiser men and the other magistrates ; and kings were assigned the 'function ' of acting as 'guardians, servants, and keepers ' of these laws. From the quasi-historical beginning he rises to a more general argument, in which the basis of law is carried deeper than the invention of 'the wiser men and the other magistrates,' and its sovereignty is more amply and broadly founded. *Sic volo, sic jubeo, sit pro ratione voluntas* is a saying utterly alien from true monarchy and the nature of the normal state. *Ratio*, and not *voluntas*, is the true guide of men. Now *lex est ratio sive mens, ab omni perturbatione vacua* (a translation of Aristotle's ἄνευ ὀρέξεως νοῦς ὁ νόμος ἐστίν);[1] and therefore, as pure reason, it is the true guide. Again, starting from what Aristotle had said about the collective capacity of the generality, and extending his saying to the sphere of the making of law, we may say that *lex est mens, vel potius mentium congregata multitudo*; or we may say more simply, and with more obvious reference to the saying of Aristotle, *lex est multorum prudentum in unum collecta ratio et sapientia*. On this it follows that law is not only reason, but the common reason; and on that it follows that it is sovereign not merely in virtue of being *ratio*, but also in virtue of being the expression of what we may call *communis ratio*. Thus the sovereignty of law is connected with the sovereignty of the community; or rather (for we must not talk of the sovereignty of persons or bodies of persons *as such*), it is connected with the sovereignty of the 'common mind' of the community and its 'common sense' of right and law. This is the conclusion at which Professor Krabbe also arrives. He too connects the 'impersonal might' and 'spiritual sovereignty' of law with the community, and with the presence of representative institutions which permit the community to express a 'common mind.' 'Only where the formation of Law rests exclusively in the hands of a popular representative body can the pure sovereignty of Law appear externally; for a popular representative body derives its significance from what it represents, which is the sense of Law inherent in the nation' (op. cit., p. 36).

NOTE C

The 'Vindiciae' and the Second 'Treatise of Government'

Parallels in detail between the thought of Locke and that of the author of the *Vindiciae*, even if they can be established,

---

[1] *Politics*, III. xvi. 5.

are of no particular value. The real similarity is general, and a matter of the general trend of the argument in the two writers. Locke was not a scholiast or a glossator : he thought out his problems afresh, in the light of contemporary conditions, and with particular reference to his own country. But there are some analogies between the *Vindiciae* and the Second *Treatise* which perhaps deserve notice.

1. In an important passage, the author of the *Vindiciae* inquires into the origin of the State, and of that government of kings which he assumes to be its essential attribute (pp. 107 sqq.). It must, he argues, have been for some great utility that men who were by nature free spontaneously chose *imperium alienum*, and renounced *suae quasi naturae legi ut alienam ferrent*. That utility was twofold. Kings arose to protect individuals from one another by doing justice, and to protect all from external violence by using force to repel force. The Bible and the classical writers of antiquity both illustrate the double function : from both we may see that all kings have been always *judices et duces belli*.

To Locke, too (§ 88), 'the commonwealth comes by a power' vested with two functions—the function of punishing transgressions committed among the members of the society, and the function of punishing injuries done to any of its members by external force. Locke, too, uses the Bible in illustration, more expecially of the second function ; and some of the passages which he cites (e.g. 1 Sam. viii. 20) are the same as those which are cited in the *Vindiciae*.

2. The author of the *Vindiciae* argues that justice is imperfect as long as the decisions given *alia aliis loquuntur* : that it only becomes satisfactory when there are laws *quae cum omnibus una eademque voce loquuntur* (p. 114) ; and that such laws must proceed from ' a congregated multitude of minds ' (p. 116). Locke similarly argues that justice needs ' an established, settled, known law, received and allowed by common consent,' to serve as ' the common measure ' (§ 124), and to remove variety and partiality.

3. The emphasis of Locke is laid upon property. The ' great and chief end ' of commonwealth and governments is the preservation of property (§ 124). To the author of the *Vindiciae* also the purpose of the State is to settle *meum illud et tuum*, and

to pronounce *de rerum dominio* (p. 109). Indeed, he protracts a long legal argument to prove that kings are not the creators or owners or disposers of property, but the agents for securing *ut sua cuique diviti aeque ac pauperi constarent* (p. 134).

4. The author of the *Vindiciae* is full of the language of *curatio*, the *tutor, pupilli*. Government, he is always insisting, is a trusteeship. Locke in the same way harps on the ideas of ' trust,' ' fiduciary power,' action ' against the trust reposed,' action ' contrary to the trust.' To Locke, indeed, the trusteeship is vested in the legislature : to the author of the *Vindiciae* it is vested in the nobility and officials as well as (and apparently even more than) in the Estates General. For both, however, the conception of trusteeship, while it is intended to benefit the people, reduces the people into a sort of tutelage. Just as the *pupillus*, though he is really *dominus*, cannot bring an action without the agency of the tutor, says the author of the *Vindiciae*, so the people cannot act without the agency of the magistrates or representatives to whom it has transferred its authority and power (pp. 210–12). Locke, it is true, is less drastic, and allows the people to act for themselves—even imagining, in one passage, a ' perfect democracy ' in which the people act directly as principals without the intervention of any agents ; but even Locke seems to think that normally the people have appointed a legislature to act as a permanent trustee, so that they have given up their political power to the legislature, and cannot resume it—unless for some breach of trust which is in its nature exceptional.

5. It is in his final chapters, on ' usurpation,' ' tyranny,' and ' dissolution of governments,' that Locke approaches nearest to the particular theme of the *Vindiciae*. It is here that he quotes Barclay's attempt to confute the *Vindiciae*, and seeks to show that Barclay has himself, after all, left a right of *vindicatio contra tyrannos*.

Note.—Since this essay was written, the writer has had occasion to go further into the question of the authorship of the *Vindiciae*. The reader is referred, for his conclusions, to the *Cambridge Historical Journal*, 1930.

IV

PURITANISM [1]

THE name Puritan seems to have taken its origin,
early in the reign of Elizabeth and by the year 1570,
as a nickname given by their enemies to a body
of would-be ' purifiers ' of the ceremonies, the government
and the doctrine of the incipient Church of England. They
were puritans, ' because they think themselves to be *mun-
diores ceteris* ' : they were puritans, because the word might
convey the suggestion and affix the imputation of the
ancient heresy of the Cathars, a term of Greek origin exactly
analogous to the Latin term of Puritan. But what was
hurled by the enemy as an insult was caught up by the
faithful and turned into an honour ; and it was not long
before the Puritans could pride themselves on professing
' the pure or stainless religion.' It is the same alchemy
which transmuted the nickname of Whig into the cherished
appellation of a great party.

In its strict sense the term denotes those members of
the Church of England who, while remaining in the Church,
would have transformed its ceremonies into the plain ritual
of Calvinism, its government into the Presbyterian system,
its doctrine into the Calvinistic doctrine of election and
reprobation. In that sense the Puritans were a Low
Church party, walking to the left of the *via media Anglicana*,
and anxious not only to follow Calvinistic opinion
and practice themselves, but also to make such opinion
and practice the general rule of the Church. But it is
difficult to confine any term to a strict and limited sense ;
and the term Puritan gradually came to receive a double

[1] A Paper contributed to the *Listener* in November 1929.

extension. On the one hand it could be applied to Presbyterians pure and simple, whether they sought to remain inside, or were recognized outside, the Church of England. In such an application the term no longer connoted, as one of its necessary attributes, any membership of that Church. On the other hand, the term could be applied, though this was a far greater extension, to the ' Separatists' who definitely sought to go and to remain outside the Church of England, and to organize themselves in local congregations (such as those of the Congregationalists) or in general sects (like that of the Baptists), on a basis of ' independency.' It has been much debated, particularly by American scholars, whether the term Puritan can properly be applied at all to the Separatists. They did not seek to purify the Church ; they simply stood outside, and how can they be called Puritans ? There is logic in the contention ; but the fact remains that, in England at any rate, the term received a wide extension, and included the Congregationalists and the Baptists as well as the Low Church party and the Presbyterians proper.

NONE the less, it is important to remember that until the year 1662—the year of the revised Prayer Book and the passing of the Caroline Act of Uniformity—the year in which, after a century of struggle in the Church of England, there was a definite parting of the ways—Puritanism was a body of opinion within the Church as well as a body of opinion without. It was not only a matter of the sects who had seceded : it was also a matter of the left wing which had remained. In the century with which we are mainly concerned—the century from the beginning of the reign of Elizabeth to the beginning of that of Charles II —the members of that left wing (and indeed of the whole general body of Puritanism) were never very numerous. During the period of the Civil War—the period which S. R. Gardiner called by the name of the Puritan Revolution—the numbers of the Puritans were swollen partly by the zeal and passion of the times, and partly by the force of fashion which always augments a triumphant party. If, however, we seek to make some enumeration of the body of the Puritans either at the beginning of the seventeenth century, or towards the close, we shall find that their numerical strength was surprisingly small. Scholars have calculated that in the first decade of the century about 3 per cent. of the clergy, and from 2 to 6 per cent. of the laity, were Puritan. When William III attempted a religious census, just after the Revolution of 1688, the statistics showed just over 100,000 male Nonconformists to nearly two and a half millions of male Conformists—that is to say, about 4 per cent. of the one to 96 per cent. of the other.

Puritanism was thus no more than a leaven. Why was it so vital a leaven ? The ultimate cause is the strength of its religious zeal and its moral ardour. But there were contributory causes which deserve notice. It is sometimes said that the Puritan clergy were more learned than the rest. This is perhaps dubious. Professor Usher records the fact that in a list of 281 Puritan clergymen, only 105 had University degrees. But Puritan theology, none the less, had a hold on the Universities in the early part of the seventeenth century, and particularly on the University of Cambridge. The Church of England had no body of theology which could vie with the *Institutes* of Calvin. Puritanism, again, seems to have been strong among the new landed gentry which had arisen in the century of the Reformation, and even in a tolerably large circle of the nobility. It was also strong in the towns, where Puritan ' lecturers ' were paid to preach sermons, often in the afternoon, outside the regular circle of matins and evensong. It is a curious fact that when a Puritan clergyman held a living he had often a salary higher than that of the general run of the clergy. The contributions of the faithful were paid in augmentation ; and when the average salary was £10, or less, a Puritan vicar with a Puritan congregation might receive about £50.

Considerations such as those help to explain the paradox

of Puritanism, the paradox of a strength entirely disproportionate to its numbers. That strength was reflected
in the House of Commons. From the new landed gentry
and the towns there came to Westminster an abundance of
Puritan Members ; and it was commonly said at the time
that three parts of the first House of Commons which met
in the reign of James I (1604) was Puritan. This character of the House accounts in its measures for the rise
of a Parliamentary Opposition, which, beginning on the
grounds of objection to the religious settlement, passed
to the ground of defence of the Constitution, and culminated
in the Civil War.

The geographical distribution of Puritanism was another
source of its strength. It was chiefly concentrated in the
centres of population and wealth—in London and the
Eastern Counties. The Eastern Counties in the seventeenth century were the Lancashire and Yorkshire of their
time. They were the homes of the most intensive agriculture ; they were the homes of the woollen industry.
The Puritanism of the Eastern Counties made them the
core of the Parliamentary cause and the New Model Army.
It also made them largely the source of that movement
of Puritan colonization which helped to populate New
England and to make the American Republic. The place-
names of Massachusetts—Boston and Cambridge, Lynn
and Ipswich—still recall Eastern England.

B UT to understand Puritanism we must turn to its
fundamentals—fundamentals of religious zeal and moral
ardour. Predestination is an iron creed ; and it made, or
tempered, souls of an iron zeal. God is an inscrutable will,
always acting, as it were, by specific decision in every
issue. He is will rather than law—specific decision rather
than general rule. By His will some are chosen to be of
the elect, and called to salvation ; and others, by what
Calvin called an ' irreprehensible but incomprehensible
judgment,' are condemned to reprobation. But it is not
for the elect, in any mood of fatalism, simply to acquiesce

in the operation of inscrutable will and fore-ordinance.
Who shall be certain of his election ?   No man : and therefore it behoves each man, in the solitude of his soul, to
scrutinize himself and to struggle until he attains some
inkling of the Divine purpose.   And even if a man have
conviction of his election, that is no end, and it gives no
acquittal from struggle.   If I am elected and called, I
must remember my election and calling, and do according
thereto.   I am not called into bondage, still less into in-
dolence : I am called into the liberty of the elect and the
strenuous activity of the chosen.   There is an athleticism,
an asceticism, in the Puritan, as of one running for a great
prize which is set before him.   This is the rock of Puritan
faith ; and by its side the formalism of Puritanism—its
objection to the cross in baptism, the ring in marriage, the
surplice—are a very little thing.   Not but what the little
thing sometimes became a large beam in the eye of the
Puritan ; not but what, again, his formalism in objecting to
forms tended to make him a precisian, with a great power
of irritation and even, when he had his way, of destruction.
Stained glass windows and stone sculptures were forms
anathema to his formalism ; and yet that formalism
stiffened itself in its own prim forms of rigid expression.
None the less, when we have made all allowances for the
rigour of its outward case, we must always come back to the
real vitality of the inner spirit of Puritanism.

That spirit was a spirit of struggle.   The symbol of the
Puritan is the figure of Samson Agonistes in the temple of
the Philistines.   There was a struggle to be waged in the
inward man—a struggle for deliverance from the body of
death and for assurance of salvation : there was a struggle
to be waged with the outward world—a struggle against
its cozening forms and all its subtle deceits.   The Puritan
was at war both with himself and the world ; and the
warfare was hard and long.   This conception of warfare
gave a negative quality to Puritanism : the Puritan must
say ' No ' and again ' No,' to himself, to the Church, to
the State, to society at large.   It also gave a certain dualism

8

to the general cast of thought : it made the world a place of unresolved contradictions, and opposed a great and defiant Devil to the merciful God of Grace. But there was a positive behind the negative ; and there was a unity behind the dualism. We must seek the positive core : we must discover the unity of Puritan life.

THE positive core of Puritanism was a deep sense of individual personality, and a resolute practice of individual and personal will. ' Will,' it has been said by Mr. Tawney, ' is the essence of Puritanism.' It may seem a paradox that a creed which emphasized the absolute will and predestined purpose of God should make each of its votaries also the centre of a firm and resolute will of his own. But the Puritan never interpreted God's predestination as his own subjection : he made himself not the slave of divine will, but its image and microcosm. If the will of God ranged the world, and made specific decision on every issue, man's will must act with a similar range. It followed that life confronted the Puritan day by day, and hour by hour, with issues of anxious decision : it followed that his will was kept taut and braced by the exercise of daily and hourly practice. We may call this, if we will, individualism ; and in that sense the Puritan was an individualist. Primarily, indeed, he was the individualist only of the religious life ; but then the religious life was all life, and the religious principle controlled every issue ; and the individualist of the religious life thus became the individualist of the whole of life. In this way solitude—the solitude of a fiery burning soul—became an essential attribute of Puritanism. Now there is a sense in which solitude is one of the greatest of the virtues. It may almost be said that the art of living is the discovery of a balance between the gregarious habit which carries us into society, and the solitary habit which throws us back on ourselves —between the peace of social companionship and social conformity, and the effort of individual life and individual decision. The balance tilts easily towards the gregarious

side ;   and the Puritan who threw all his weight on the other
side did much to redress the balance, not only for himself, but
in the whole general working of our national life ; not only in
the century of his greatness, but also in succeeding centuries.
These are simple and mundane matters in which we may trace
the effects of his influence. He helped to make citizenship an
individual responsibility, a matter in which each must exercise
his thought and practise his will.   He helped to make commerce and industry find their own feet and go their own way,
escaping an old system of paternal protection.   He helped to
make colonization a spontaneous movement ; and when the
colonists had settled in lonely lands beyond the seas, he
helped to give that temper of self-reliance which could
face and conquer solitude.   Yet the solitary habit is only
one part of the balance, and the Puritan was perhaps too
apt to behave as if it were almost the whole.   Any social
system must rest on the virtues of sympathy as well as the
virtues of solitude.   Our English system was long defective
in the virtues of sympathy ; and the solitary quality of the
Puritan life was a contributory cause of that defect.

IF the positive core of Puritanism was insistence on
individual will, and a cultivation of that solitude in
which individual will is tempered and hardened, there
was also a unity in Puritan life ; and there were
ways in which it sought to transcend the tendency towards
dualism which was implicit in its nature.   We have
spoken of Puritan asceticism ; but the asceticism of the
Puritan was never of the sort which renounces the world.
We have spoken of the solitary habit of Puritanism ; but
its solitude was never that of a fugitive and cloistered
virtue.   Puritanism was saved from such consequences
by its doctrine of election, which readily passed into a
doctrine of ' calling ' in the ordinary sense of that term.
Not only had the Puritan been called to grace : he had also
been called to a vocation.   It was his duty to be about
its business : in that way he could show forth fruits, and
by these fruits he could furnish a visible testimony of what

was in him. The world was not a place to be denied : it was a place to be conquered and shaped. The way of conquest and shaping was work—faithful work in an earthly calling or vocation, by which a man might give evidence of the reality of his heavenly calling. Work became a part of the Puritan creed ; and work was the mother of production. The effort and the struggle of the Puritan were thus translated into a shaping of the material world, a conquest of its resources, a victory over its obstacles ; and the unceasing working of God thus found its parallel in the unceasing working of man. This, again, was good stuff for the national fibre ; but this again had the defects of its qualities. Two of these defects have long remained with us. One is a tendency to let work engulf life to the exclusion of thought and reflection. The Puritan cultivated solitude ; but he lost the fruits of solitude when he made his solitude into an office in which he ceaselessly pursued his calling. Another is a readiness to glide into the conviction that the garnered fruits of a secular calling are somehow the evidence of divine election and moral worth, and that property has thus a sort of sanctity. It is only too easy to glide in turn from that conviction into a feeling that an absence of property is an absence of testimony, and an absence of testimony is an absence of worth. And on that basis even a glaring system of social inequality may be condoned, and not only condoned but justified.

WHAT has been said may bring into relief some features of Puritan ethics—the resolute practice of will ; the stoical cultivation of solitude ; the conception of the duty, and even the sanctity, of work duly done in a calling. A system with these features cannot but be informed by a deep moral zeal : but there was an uncomfortableness even in the zeal. The Puritan could not rely on the accumulated moral experience and tradition of his generation. He looked at it and saw that it was evil ; and in any case he was bound, by his faith, to bring the fresh initiative of his will to face each issue. Not only so, but the issues which he had to face were innumerable. Every issue was a moral issue ; and since morality was religion, and to do good was to do the will of God, every fresh step meant an anxious searching of the unsearchable dispose of God. There was a noble anxiety in such a morality ; but it had its dangers. For one thing, it stretched conscience on a constant rack ; and the man who was thus strained might fall into a morbidity of introspection. For another thing, it involved a steady tension of moral effort ; and the man who felt himself keyed to such a pitch might fall into a satisfaction with his own standard which was also a contempt of the standard of the ordinary man. It was a sort of self-complacency which contemporaries criticized in the Puritans. (' Dost thou think, because thou art virtuous, there shall be no more cakes and ale ? Yes, by Saint Anne ; and ginger shall be hot i' the mouth too.') Saddest of all, perhaps, in the Puritan scheme was the absence of any free space of life. If every issue was a moral issue, nothing was in-different, and everything was a matter of moral regimen. If, again, every moral issue was also a religious issue, and every religious issue involved reference to the will of God and to the Bible which revealed His will, it followed that the Bible became the obligatory canon of the whole of life. It was a canon you were bound to follow, and, if you could, to enforce. A Bible despotism was thus a logical outcome of Puritanism ; and in Massachusetts that despotism was for a time realized. The Puritan clergy and the Puritan elect who held the magistracies dispensed with laws on the ground that the Bible was sufficient ; but they made their interpretation of the Bible a rule not only of legal action, but also of moral behaviour. It is another of the paradoxes of Puritanism, but a paradox inherent in its nature, that its philosophy of the resolute practice of individual will could be made to issue in a stringent form of theocracy.

IF we turn from the moral world to the intellectual, we find similar contradictions in the attitude of the Puritan. One of the most fundamental of his theological tenets was that of the inscrutable Divine will acting by specific decision —a tenet parallel to that of the human will acting, in its own small and yet solemn sphere, by a similar rigour of particular will. It was not a tenet favourable to that idea of uniform law on which all growth of human knowledge is ultimately based. John Winthrop of Boston could regard it as a special providence when a spider was discovered in the porridge before it was eaten. It was another remarkable providence when, in a whole library, a mouse confined its ravages to a copy of the Book of Common Prayer. Apart from this way of thinking, theological preoccupation inevitably diverted attention from other and more secular studies. The libraries of New England, till the later half of the eighteenth century, were theological libraries. On the other hand, education, in the whole of its range, from the primary school to the University, owes much to Puritan impulse. The Puritan life, after all, demanded a man who could read and think ; and were it only for the purpose of reading the Bible or training a ministry, schools and colleges were necessary. It was a Puritan Parliament which, in 1649, voted a sum of £20,000 per annum, partly for the two old Universities of England, but mainly for the maintenance of schoolmasters and ministers. Massachusetts had only struggled through some seven years of existence when it founded Harvard College in 1636. But the greatest monument of the Puritan zeal for education is the village school of New England. Wherever a Puritan congregation settled, there was also founded a school. Yet Massachusetts, the home of the village school, was also the home of a strict censorship of the press. Puritanism would teach men to read. But where it had its way, it was resolved to show that it knew—knew only too well—what it was good for them to read.

We may turn from Puritanism in theology, and in the moral and intellectual sphere, to Puritanism in politics. But we must take politics in a wide sense, and interpret

it to include both Church and State and the relations between the two.   Here we must make a distinction between
Puritanism triumphant—the Puritanism of New England—
and Puritanism militant, militant as the creed of a minority,
the Puritanism which was that of old England except for
its brief period of triumph in the years of our Civil War.
In the one we may see Puritanism carried to its logical
outcome and expressed in its logical essence ; in the other
we may see it struggling with circumstances and battling
under adverse conditions.   But a bruised herb may best
express its own inward scent and savour ; and perhaps
we may come to the conclusion that it was struggling
Puritanism which best evolved the genius of its true inner
self.

Among the settlements in New England it was
the Puritan Colony of Massachusetts which most clearly,
and indeed almost solely, showed the qualities and the
defects of triumphant Puritanism.   Rhode Island, under
the influence of Roger Williams, was a home of liberty
and toleration of religious differences : Connecticut, guided
by Thomas Hooker, practised a democracy which demanded
no religious qualification for its franchise.   Massachusetts
was of a more granite quality.   Here the State was a
Church, and the Church was a State ; citizenship was
confined to those who showed churchmanship of the Puritan
type, and churchmanship of that type gave to citizenship
its character, its policy, and its methods.   The system, it
is true, did not permanently last.   By the end of the
seventeenth century it was radically changed.   A democratic movement within brought the members of the community who were not of the elect into some share of control
of the common life.   The more liberal tradition of her
neighbours in Rhode Island and Connecticut penetrated
into Massachusetts.   The influence of the English government, when in the later part of the seventeenth century it
began to recover the reins, was exerted in the cause of
civic liberty and religious toleration.   But while it lasted,
the Puritan policy of Massachusetts was a logical *reductio*

ad extremum of Puritan ideas, and it is instructive to study the main features of that policy.

In the first place there was as rigorous an identification of State and Church, of Citizenship and Churchmanship, as ever Elizabeth or Clarendon attempted. ' No man shall be admitted to the freedom of this body politic, but such as are members of some of the churches within the limits of the same.' As we shall see, the only churches tolerated were those of the Puritan way ; and here was thus a State Church, as much as in contemporary England, to whose members the privileges of citizenship were confined. A law of 1635, parallel to the Elizabethan Act of Uniformity, made attendance at church compulsory under pain of fine and imprisonment. A law of 1638 went further. It enunciated the principle, reminiscent of mediaeval belief and practice, that excommunication from the Church must ultimately entail entire exclusion from civil society and civil existence. It provided that an excommunicated person must seek restoration within six months under pain of ' fine, imprisonment, banishment *or further.*' No wonder that Puritan friends in England warned Massachusetts not ' to fall into that evil abroad which you laboured to avoid at home, to bind all men to the same tenets and practice ' ; no wonder, again, that even the Puritans of England ceased to emigrate to Massachusetts, lest they should lose the liberty they prized. Triumphant Puritanism was at least as rigorous as triumphant Anglicanism.

On this drastic unification of life—the life political and the life religious—there followed other features. One was the absence of democratic principle and practice. We naturally, and justly, associate the English Puritans of the seventeenth century with the rise of English democratic ideas. But the English Puritans advocated these ideas in the winter of their discontent ; and the Puritans of Massachusetts were in a summer and heyday of victory. They believed in the rule of the elect ; and the elect were a small minority. The Puritan village church, though it was based on the democratic idea of a ' church covenant,'

was a dominion of the elect ; and the Puritan Commonwealth of Massachusetts was of the same type. ' Democracy,' said John Winthrop, ' is accounted the meanest and
worst of all forms of government.' In actual practice the
government of Massachusetts was something of an aristocratic theocracy, a combination of the leading Puritan
laymen with the Puritan ministers. Alike in theory and in
practice the idea of the free commonwealth, moved to
common ends by the common will of all its members, was
absent. It could hardly be otherwise so long as the zeal
of righteousness was dominant, and righteousness was conceived as the jewel of the elect. Nor was toleration more
welcome, or more present, than democracy. Indeed, on
strict Puritan principles it would have been a vice rather
than a virtue. No new churches could be organized without
the consent of the magistrates and of a majority of the
elders of existing churches ; and this stereotyped a single
type of church of the Puritan way. When the Quakers
sought entry into Massachusetts, soon after the middle of
the seventeenth century, a law was passed against them
inflicting banishment on pain of death. Four who defied
the law were put to death ; many more were whipped or
imprisoned.

More curious, and perhaps more dangerous, than the
absence of democracy or toleration was the absence, in early
Massachusetts, of any real system of law. We have learned
to believe that law is the guarantee of liberty ; we have
learned to believe that it gives that security, that sense of
acting under known rule in a sure expectation of regular
and fore-known consequences, which is the necessary
condition of an ordered life. But to the early Puritans of
Massachusetts the State was an organ not of the mere
justice of law, but of the abounding righteousness of grace
and election. ' Whatever sentence the magistrate gives,
the judgment is the Lord's.' It was accordingly voted,
in 1639, ' that the word of God shall be the only rule to
be attended to in ordering the affairs of government.' In
practice the Massachusetts assembly passed occasional

laws ; but even the laws were vague.   A law which enacted
that a man spending his time idly or unprofitably should
undergo such penalty as the court thought meet to inflict
was a law which left the magistrate a large latitude.   When
he was instructed by the assembly that, in the absence of
such law, he should determine cases as near the law of God
as he could, the latitude was still larger.   So long as this
system continued, a godly arbitrariness brooded over men's
lives ; and a magistrate uninstructed by law, and acting
in the strength of moral zeal and religious fervour, became
an inscrutable will capable of irreprehensible but incomprehensible judgments.   But this was the inexperience of a
new society ; and it is only fair to add that by 1648 Massachusetts was already beginning to realize the necessity of a
certain and known law.

FROM the triumphant Puritanism of America, which
only enjoyed its triumph for some decades of the
seventeenth century, we may now turn to the militant
Puritanism of England, the Puritanism of a minority
struggling against odds, and necessarily adopting its
tenets to the exigencies of struggle and the conditions
of its environment. The same strength showed itself
on either field ; but it showed itself to more enduring
consequences on the field in which Puritanism was a
minority, engaged in struggle and facing defeat.   It is an
old characteristic of the English, that goes back to *Beowulf*
and the days of the Heptarchy, to love dearly that ' fetter-
ing up of the heart ' (as it is called in an old Anglo-Saxon
poem) and that ' fight against odds ' which the conditions
of the seventeenth century imposed on minorities.   Puritanism, with its insistence on the resolute exercise of a will
trained by spiritual discipline, added a new moral zest
to an old native instinct.   Fighting for faith, against all
powers and principalities, it left a large legacy, even when
it seemed defeated, to the English Commonwealth.   What
were the elements of that legacy ?
French writers have sometimes compared the Puritan

Revolution of the seventeenth century, in its abiding results, to the French Revolution of 1789. There are some respects in which the comparison may be said to hold good : there are others in which, as we shall see, it cannot be justified. One thing we may say of both revolutions : they disengaged clearly the notion of the non-clerical State, which stood on its own account, as a human society, working under a human law on the simple ground of justice and equality. We have seen that this was not in the necessary logic of Puritanism, and that in early Massachusetts a very different notion was followed. But we must allow that it was in its conditional logic ; and we may say that when Puritanism had to face the condition, and accept the limitation, implied in its being the faith of a minority, it adopted freely the principle of the non-clerical State. Clericalism, indeed, never exercised the power in England which it exercised in France. But if it was never *the* enemy, as Gambetta declared it to be for France even at the end of the nineteenth century, there were times when it seemed one of the enemies, and one of the gravest of enemies. Bishops had a control of education, through their power of licensing teachers. Their church courts had a large cognizance even over the life of the laity. Laud attempted to carry the Church still more into the State. The Court of High Commission was not an inquisition, but it assumed large powers ; and the general alliance of monarchy and episcopacy might well seem to menace a clerical régime. Perhaps the lay genius of the English lawyers—always a powerful factor in English life—would of itself have defeated any such tendency. But it was Puritanism which made sure the defeat : it was Puritanism which brought the zeal not of a profession, but of a faith, to curb the enemy. It is true that relics of the old system long lingered. Not till 1871 were the old universities of England fully opened to every citizen, irrespective of religious profession ; and even now their nationalization may be said to be incomplete. None the less, we may say that after 1660 there was no danger of a clerical State in

England. Parliament, indeed, might long require conformity to a particular Church, and long exclude Nonconformists from its own body. But it was the lay parliament of the nation which made the requirement and imposed the exclusion ; and the rigour of such a parliament would alter with the alterations of the public opinion on which it rested.

If Puritanism may thus be said to have contributed to the conception of the non-clerical State, it also contributed to the conception of the limited State. Here the Puritan Revolution differed from the French. The French Revolution installed, early in its course, an unlimited State armed with indefinite power by a community which had banished or suppressed minorities. The Puritan Revolution, even in the period of its brief triumph, adopted, under the influence of its ' Independent ' wing, the notion of ' fundamentals ' which Parliament itself could not touch or vary. A defeated minority after 1660, the Puritans clung all the more intensely to the notion of the limited State ; and they passed to the idea that they were bound to resist if the State overstepped its limits. That idea became embedded in the Whig Party, which, as it included the Puritans in its ranks, included also something of their spirit in its principles. Blackstone was a Conservative Whig, who could speak of unlimited sovereignty ; but even Blackstone embalmed a right of resistance in his *Commentaries*. Nor was it only a matter of a theoretical right. The Nonconformists of the eighteenth century were engaged in actual resistance. They had their children taught as they wished in spite of the law : they stood fast in their faith against the State, and the State, at first *de facto*, in the way of quiet ignoring of things perhaps better left unnoticed, and then *de jure*, in the way of express consent, recognized the ground on which they stood. Gradually the idea of the limited State became almost a fashion. It spread from the world of religion to the world of economics. Was not *laissez faire* best ? Would it not be wiser for the State not only to allow men to think their own thoughts and conduct their own worship, but also to manage their own business and regulate their own trade ? In this way the Puritan tradition passed, as it were, from the chapel to the counting-house : Puritanism, we may say, became allied with political economy ; and the faith of free trade was added to the faith of free religion. It was an alliance which had its dangers. Freedom in the world of religion—essentially a non-competing world, even if churches disagree—is different from freedom in the competitive world of economics. Economic freedom, if it is to mean an economic freedom for all, is a freedom which does not come naturally, but has to be made. It is here that we have to unlearn some elements of the old Puritan tradition. But even as we unlearn them, we may recognize that they had their day, and their justification in their day.

Puritanism was favourable to the principle of the limited State : was it also favourable to the principle, and the practice, of the democratic State ? We have seen that it could reject democracy as a ' mean ' form of government— a breach, as one of its adherents said, of the Fifth Commandment. And yet, wherever it established itself, whether in England or in America, Puritanism carried within itself, whatever might be its opinions of outward and political democracy, the principle of an inner and spiritual democracy. We have to remember that however Calvinistic their theology, the Puritans only rarely practised the full form of Calvinistic organization, with its organized hierarchy of *classes* and synods. Cartwright might attempt such an organization about 1580 : it might be generally attempted, though only for a few years, after the Solemn League and Covenant of 1643 ; but the essential unit of the Puritan scheme was the individual congregation. The members of the congregation were united by a ' church covenant ' ; and though the numbers of those within the covenant were often restricted by a requirement of effective-conversion, and of public profession thereof, the idea of the covenant was essentially democratic. It could easily be transferred to the political sphere ; and it was so transferred by the Pilgrim Fathers of the *Mayflower*, when in 1620 they made the compact whereby they agreed ' solemnly and mutually, in the presence of God and one of another, [to] covenant and combine ourselves together into a civil body politic . . . and by virtue hereof to enact constitute and frame such just and equal laws ordinances acts constitutions and offices, from time to time, as shall be thought most meet and convenient for the general good.' Here is the fundamental democratic idea of the people combining to form a commonwealth and to give it a constitution. Not only in the original framing but also in the actual working of the Puritan congregation democratic ideas were apparent. The congregation chose and ordained its pastors and elders : the mainspring of its life was in itself : authority proceeded from it, and authority was responsible to it. Though Massachusetts might object to democracy, and object logically, Thomas Hooker of Connecticut was also in the logic of Puritanism when he maintained that the people chose its magistrates, and ' they who have the power to appoint officers and magistrates, it is in their power also to set bounds and limitations.'

IN New England as well as in Old England Puritanism was thus a force which helped to lay the foundations of a free Commonwealth, freely based on the common purposes and consent of its members. And it also served, as we have already had occasion to notice, in the laying of the foundations of the British Commonwealth. It was from the Eastern counties of England, in which Puritanism was strong, that the tide of emigration set strongest towards America ; and it was the resolute will and the capacity for solitude inherent in the Puritan temper that made the American settlements successful and permanent. Not that Puritanism was the sole motive for emigration, or that Puritans were the sole emigrants. On the contrary, the land-hunger of the Eastern counties was a potent cause of the English colonization of the second quarter of the seventeenth century, and among the colonists there were a large number who emigrated for the simple purpose of acquiring the free land, owned in freehold, which the New World offered. It has been remarked that even among the 102 passengers on the *Mayflower*, only one-third were certainly Puritans ; and it has been calculated that, of some 65,000 persons who had emigrated to North America and the West Indies by 1640, only 16,000 had settled in the Puritan colonies, and of these 16,000 only about one-quarter were regular church-members of Puritan congregations. But Puritanism was the spear-head of the colonial movement, if it was not also the shaft ; and when we reflect on the great part played by the Puritan colonies of New England in the development of North America, both in the period down to 1776 and in the great period of ' Western movement ' up to and across the Rockies during the nineteenth century, we must conclude that here again the effects of Puritanism were out of all proportion to its numbers. The village church and the village school of the Puritan type have crossed the whole American continent. When we think of Puritanism, we must not think of it only in terms of England, but also in terms of the greater part of the United States of America. We must think not only of Oxford and Cambridge, of English towns, of our English Eastern counties, but also of Harvard and Yale, of American cities, of Ohio and Iowa and the great region of the American Middle West. On our side of the Atlantic, and in our European environment, Puritanism was a factor which stood by the side of, and ultimately had to be mixed with, many other factors — the culture of a neighbouring continent : the German and Swiss evangelical tradition : the Latin and Catholic tradition : and, behind all, an ancient and rooted English conservatism. In North America, even if Puritanism was not entirely isolated (we must not forget the Southern Colonies), it grew in a freer ground and a far less mixed environment. It is in the history and character of North America that its genius accordingly displayed some of its most native and inherent qualities.

THE social and economic aspects of Puritanism have been no less powerful and profound than the political. Critics have sometimes animadverted on the chilling influence which the Puritan spirit exerted on family life. Samuel Butler, dwelling bitterly in *The Way of All Flesh* on the unsatisfactory relations between parents and children at the beginning of the nineteenth century, finds the cause in Puritanism. 'The fathers and sons are for the most part friends in Shakespeare,' he writes, 'nor does the evil appear to have reached its full abomination till a long course of Puritanism had familiarized men's minds with Jewish ideals as those which we should endeavour to reproduce in our everyday life.' Doubtless Puritanism did something to turn the family from a home of loving service to a home of sombre duty. But Puritanism is a familiar cause, which is apt to be alleged in explanation of all sorts of effects, from the rigour of parents to the disrepair of church fabrics. It was not always, or indeed generally, inimical to family life (which it invigorated far more than it corrupted); nor was it, again, always — though perhaps it was more generally — inimical to art and the gracious pleasures of life. If we think, for example, of music, we must confess that there was more music in England in the time of Elizabeth than there was in the time of William III. But we need not blame an intervening Puritanism for the decline. There was music to be heard in good Puritan houses in the seventeenth century; and if there was but little to be heard anywhere in the eighteenth (at any rate, in comparison with Tudor times), the blame is general and national. We may blame Puritanism; but we may blame no less the English Church, which spent itself less than in earlier days

> ' To let the pealing organ blow
> To the full-voiced quire below
> In service high and anthems clear,'

and we may blame the English squires and nobles, who, if they could rebuild their houses and have them decorated by Italian workmen, forgot other and less visible arts.

The economic affinities and the economic consequences
of Puritanism are a theme which has been much discussed
of late, and nowhere more justly or sympathetically than
in Mr. R. H. Tawney's *Religion and the Rise of Capitalism*.
Early Puritanism, as he has remarked, tended towards a
belief that the Bible—the rule of all life—should regulate
all economic dealings and activities. That economics was
in any sense a domain exempt from the operation of that
rule was an idea which Puritanism, in its very genius,
could not but reject ; and the seventeenth-century Puritans,
no less than the Mediaeval Church, were opposed to the
sin of usury and to anything that departed from ' justice '
in the fixing of prices or wages. Such a way of thinking
made for a moral and religious regulation of the sphere
of economic life. But there were elements in Puritanism
which drew it gradually in a different direction. In the
first place there was, as we have seen, an individualism
in the Puritan life which might readily extend itself from
the sphere of religion to that of economics, and might claim
' liberty ' in both. Freedom of worship might lead by
analogy, even if the analogy were mistaken, to the idea of
freedom of trade. In the second place, as we have also
seen, there was an insistence in Puritanism upon ' calling,'
and upon steady work in the pursuit of a calling. This
readily led to an emphasis on production ; and that might
lead to a view of production as something which was moral
as well as economic—something which, because it was moral,
at once possessed moral worth and might justly claim
the autonomy which belongs to the moral sphere. In this
way, once more, *laissez faire*—and a *laissez faire* almost
sanctified by the ground on which it was based—could
be deduced from the Puritan system of thought. In this
sense, too, we may say that the Puritan cause, in its essence
an Antigone protesting against the mere edicts of the State
in the name of the higher and eternal law of God, became
also a business figure protesting against ' State-inter-
ference ' in the name of the sanctity of property. Finally,
and in the last place, we have to remember that the Puritans

9

belonged to the middle classes of our towns. They had the great qualities of a middle class ; and they accentuated those qualities by the stern edge of their self-discipline. They saved and accumulated resources : they gathered capital ; and, denied by the laws of the State any fullness of outlet in political life, they turned to the life economic. Foreign observers have thus been drawn to ascribe to Puritanism the origin of the capitalistic system in England. We cannot deny that it was a contributory cause. It had something to do with the rise of what the Germans call ' Manchesterdom,' and with the growth of the economic habits of Victorianism. It had something to do with the gulf between employer and employed—between those called to production and possession, and those who were called to neither. But if Puritanism, in its later phase, was a contributory cause to such developments, this is not the whole of the matter. Puritanism had an earlier phase in which it enthroned religion as the sovereign of economics. Even in its later phase, it was only one among many forces encouraging the growth of capitalism ; and the capitalism which it encouraged was older, in its origins, than the Puritanism which encouraged it. Above all, it was from the ranks of Puritanism, and from village chapels in which they had learned to think and to speak, that there came many of the leaders of the working-class movement of the nineteenth century. Thus Puritanism helped to supply the antidote to what it had contributed—but only contributed —to produce ; and its ultimate spirit of free individuality expressed itself not only in capitalism, but also in the criticism of capitalism—not only in the idea of freedom of trade, but also in the idea (the idea we are now struggling in England to realize) of freedom of labour.

V

CHRISTIANITY AND NATIONALITY [1]

CHRISTIANITY arose, and grew to power, in a
Mediterranean world—Latin in its western half,
Greek in its eastern, but everywhere penetrated by
ideas of Greek origin—which was generally conceived in
contemporary thought as a single unit or society. That
conception was not primarily or essentially a political
conception, even though, in the days of the growth of
Christianity, a single political structure of Empire embraced
and contained the Mediterranean world. It was rather a
philosophical, or, we may even say, a theological conception.
It had been originally elaborated by the Stoics ; but in the
form in which it was current towards the beginning of
the Christian era, it was the construction of Posidonius
of Apamea, an eclectic philosopher, combining elements
of Platonism with the tenets of the Stoics, whose lectures
in the University of Rhodes were attended by Cicero,
and whose teaching appears in passages of the sixth book
of Vergil's *Aeneid*. On this conception the world was
regarded as a single city of God. God was Reason ; Reason
was a subtle substance, a fiery pervasive aether ; and this
aether, in the form of ' a pure influence flowing from the
glory of the Almighty,' as it is written in the Book of
Wisdom, or, as the Greek philosophers said, in the form of a
material spirit or πνεῦμα, was always ' passing and going
through all things by reason of pureness.' A world so
penetrated by Reason was a world congenial to man, in the
breath of whose being Reason also resided as ' a fragment

[1] The Burge Memorial Lecture for the year 1927.

131

of the Divine ' ; and God was thus knit to man, and man united to God, in a common and intimate city. The ending of human life was the way to a still closer unity. The soul of man sought at death to rejoin the upper aether, which was at once its magnet and its own true nature : angels and ministers might aid it in its ascent ; and even in death man might 'feel at home,' as Dr. Bevan has said, in a universe which was knowable, comfortable, harmonious, and compact.

The philosophical or theological conception of a single city of God, even if it was something distinct from the political order under which it was evolved, neverthless found a natural corollary in that order, which could not but appear to be a reflection, as in a glass, of the ideal laid up in the heavens. Zeno, the founder of Stoicism, who had already taught that mankind should form a single city, had before his eyes the actual pattern of the empire of Alexander. Posidonius lived before the days of the Roman Empire, but he lived in a world whose peoples the Romans already governed by their authority, and on which they had imposed the habit of their peace. The definite foundation of the Empire, and the deification of the Emperors, brought political facts still closer to philosophical and theological conceptions. When the Emperor was worshipped as a manifest god and saviour by all his subjects, the society of the Empire became a quasi-religious society, cemented by a common allegiance which was also a common cult. The city of God penetrated by a subtle Reason was something different from the political society of an empire penetrated by the *numen* of Caesar ; but if there was difference, there was also congruity. The philosopher could count, after all, on an actual political scheme which was one and undivided, like his own ideal scheme of the Universe. The two corroborated one another ; unity answered to unity ; and the harmony which the philosopher sought might seem to be happily established in the correspondence between the πόλις Διός and the *imperium Romanum*.

OUR Lord had spoken, again and again, of a kingdom of Heaven. His teaching, which grew and expanded in the Hellenistic East, among Greek ideas, came readily under the influence of current conceptions of a single and universal society. That influence is already apparent in St. Paul, who held that the Christan Church was a single organic unity—' the fulness of him that filleth all in all '—fitly joined together and compacted by that which every joint supplied, and transcending, in virtue of its unity, all earlier distinctions, whether of Jew and Gentile, or of Greek and barbarian, or of bond and free. But if Christianity could thus make its peace with current philosophic conceptions of the city of God, substituting the penetration of the personal spirit of God for that of an impersonal and material πνεῦμα, it was vastly more difficult for it to come to terms with the actual political order of an empire resting on emperor-worship. As it grew and consolidated its organization, it found itself confronted by the gravest of possible problems. Should the Christian society be purely religious, and should it subtract its members accordingly, in a complete isolation, from a quasi-religious society which cast its incense on the altar of an anti-Christ ? Could a Christian ever appear in the imperial courts, or serve in the imperial army, or acknowledge imperial citizenship in any way or by any act ? Were all these things external, and even diabolical, and was the genius of Christianity a genius of protest, of dissent, of nonconformity ? Or was it possible for the Christian Church, as it had absorbed and transmuted the philosophic conceptions of pagan antiquity, to absorb and transmute its political structure ? Could the Church became a world-society, coextensive with the world-empire ? Could it give the Empire the new aspect of a Christian society and the new cement of a Christian allegiance ; and could it get for itself, in the act of giving, an establishment of its life in the concrete form of an organized and recognized ecclesiastical system ?

The die was cast in favour of the latter choice.

Christianity became both a city of God in conception and an organized universal society in action. The Empire became Christian ; Christianity became imperial. There were deep and cogent reasons for the union between the Church and the Empire. On the one hand, the Church tended strongly to universality ; and the Empire lay ready to hand as a universal scheme in which that tendency might find satisfaction. On the other hand, the Empire, sustained by no common force of public opinion, and resting on no common basis of general will, could only maintain its unity by some common scheme of religious belief ; and as emperor-worship became less of a belief and more of a form, a common Christianity became more and more the one scheme of belief by which unity could be maintained. In this way, and for these reasons, Christianity became, during the fourth and the following centuries of our era, not only Christian, but also Catholic—an organized universal structure, acting from the first through the deliberative organ of its general Councils, and gradually developing for itself the executive organ of a central Papacy. It was a city of God or kingdom of Heaven not merely in idea, or as a conception, like the πόλις Διός of Marcus Aurelius, or the *civitas Dei* of St. Augustine (which was an ideal society of the elect), but as an actual and organized substance. It belonged to the stuff of the visible world of institutions ; and if, as such, it was subject to imperfections and blemishes by which an ideal society cannot be touched, it was yet a living and moving reality, engaged in the process of history and affecting the course of its movement.

The Roman Empire vanished in the West : the Catholic society remained. The one Christian commonwealth of all mankind, conceived indeed partly as an Empire—the surviving image of ancient Rome—but conceived mainly and generally as a Church, is the essential society of that long period of human history which we call by the name of the Middle Ages. It was a fact, and not merely an idea : and yet it was also an idea, and not altogether a fact. Universality was less universal in the world of reality than it was to the vision of thinkers ; and the catholic society, even while it was concrete, faded on its circumference into an ideal haze.   The Byzantine Empire and the Greek Church went their own way ; the tribal societies of Franks and Lombards and Saxons were contained, but hardly incorporated, in the body of Catholic Christianity ; and while, in the earlier centuries of the Middle Ages, the assumed fact of a universal society had no actual fact of some other form of society to challenge its vogue—no nation, and still less any national State— it never squared exactly with the facts of contemporary life.   Neither a pure idea nor an absolute fact, the universal society was a half-way house between the theological idea of a single city of God and the institutional fact of a regular and operative organization of all mankind.   The tribal societies of the Teutons had less of the nature of self-conscious societies : perhaps, indeed, we can hardly say that they had any consciousness whatsoever of their own nature ; but they had their roots in reality, and their kings and assemblies were the potential nuclei of new forms of organization and new conceptions of society.

THE new organization and conception of society which we call by the name of the nation has been gradually built, at different times in different countries, here earlier and there later, during the millennium of human history since the year 1000 A.D.   It germinated within the Christian commonwealth : it sprang from the ashes of the tribal society.   If we examine its origin, we shall find that at some geographical centre, such as London or Paris, a political authority or State arises (the Plantagenets in London, the Capetians in Paris), which gradually gathers a territory around that centre, gives to the inhabitants of that territory a common allegiance, common memories, and a common tradition—a tradition of uniform law and government, uniform speech, a single literature, a common history—and thus establishes the necessary conditions of a national society and national consciousness.   A nation is

not a physical fact or racial group. Racially all nations
are composite and heterogeneous : they are composed of
different stocks and breeds ; and it is not in virtue of any
physical factor of common blood that the unity and identity
of a nation may be vindicated. Nor, again, is a nation
a political structure, or scheme of law and order, as the old
Roman Empire had been. It may be that in part ; but
it must always be something more than that before it can
be dignified by the name of nation. Neither a physical
fact of common blood, nor a political structure of common
law and order, a nation is essentially a spiritual society.
It is what it is in virtue of a common mental substance
resident in the minds of all its members—common memories
of the past, common ideas in the present, common hopes for
the future, and, above all, a common and general will
issuing from the common substance of memories, ideas,
and hopes.

When Christianity meets the nation, and has to make
its peace with national societies and national traditions,
it is meeting something new, and something different in
kind from the Empire with which it had come to terms
a thousand years before. The old political world-society
of antiquity had possessed a universality which answered
to the aspiring and universal genius of the early Church.
Nor was this all. The very defects of the old Empire
had been the opportunities and the satisfaction of the Church.
The Empire, if it had a common law, had no common
language or body of common literature : it had no common
tradition or community of public opinion : it was destitute
of the essential qualities of a spiritual society. It was a
cadre, but it had no *esprit de corps* : it was a channel,
but it needed to be filled with living waters. The Church
could pour its spiritual tradition, its enthusiasm, its passion
for unity and universality, into a mould which lay waiting
for the influx. The nation was made of different stuff. In
its essence it was a negation of universality : it was a
particularist society, confined to a given territory and
peculiar to a given body of persons. In its essence, again,

it was a spiritual society. So far as it was true to itself, and so far as it attained to itself, it was based on the spiritual factors of a common tradition, a public opinion, and a general will, and it drew its inspiration from the spiritual legacy of the past. When Christianity, in the power of its long centuries and the spirit of its great tradition, met the nation, it met something which, if it differed in being particularist in its scope and secular, or mainly secular, in its aims, was none the less, on other and essential grounds, *in eodem genere* with itself.

The problem early arose of the relations between the nascent nation, represented by its monarch or ' State ' (in the original sense of the word in which it is used to denote the person or persons of ' state ' and eminence who are vested with powers of government), and the world-society of the Christian commonwealth, represented by its clergy and above all by its pope. In the early days of the growth of nations it is the monarch who serves as the magnet of national loyalty and the symbol of national feeling ; and nationalism, which in our own days is so closely associated with the cause of democracy that it may almost appear to be the same thing, appeared for many centuries (and not least in the century of the Reformation) under the form and guise of monarchism. National monarchs readily fell into conflict with the clergy of their territory who sought to vindicate independence of royal authority and to plead the overriding claims of their membership and office in the Catholic religious society ; and since the clergy could find comfort and support from the Papacy, such conflicts issued in struggles between kings and popes—struggles such as those which mark the reign of Henry II of England at the end of the twelfth or that of Philippe le Bel of France at the beginning of the fourteenth century. There is a sense in which the Reformation itself, if it be regarded in its political aspect, may be viewed as the last, or, if not the last, at any rate the greatest of those struggles. But Henry VIII, when in the name of nationalism he broke the bonds of Rome and made a national Church, raised deeper issues than had ever been called in question in the previous struggles of kings and popes.

The old struggles between kings and popes had been struggles not so much between rival societies as between rival authorities ; and they had turned on specific questions of jurisdiction, or taxation, or the control of preferments. The deeper question which began to emerge in the age of the Reformation was that of the general relation of Christian society, conceived as a single kingdom of God under the single law of Christ, to the society of the nation; regarded as the realm of a secular yet spiritual tradition covering a particular territory and peculiar to its people. Even before the Reformation the old Catholic society had long been subject to a process of fission. The orthodox Church of the East, so closely associated with the Byzantine State that it might seem one of its aspects, was divided by a gulf from the West ; and within the orthodox Church itself, as it spread among Bulgars and Serbs and Russians, new sub-divisions emerged, which corresponded, in some measure, to societies which contained the germs of a national life. Even in the West it was possible, in the height of the Middle Ages, to speak of an *ecclesia Anglicana* and an *ecclesia Gallicana* ; and as the Middle Ages drew to their close we may find a peculiar position vindicated for the Church in France by the Pragmatic Sanction of Bourges in 1438, or again peculiar rights, such as that of communion in both kinds, accorded to the Bohemian laity by the Compactata of 1433. But the Reformation, as it pursued its course from the Diet of Worms in 1521 to the Treaty of Westphalia in 1648, brought clearly into the light a principle of organization which, whatever its harbingers, marked none the less a new phase in the history of Christianity. Where reformed churches were established—in Scotland, in England, in Geneva, in Holland, in the principalities of North Germany, in Scandinavia—we may see the nation taking for its province the profession of its own form of Christianity, and establishing a national form of religious organization. The spiritual tradition of the new and

secular nation is fused with the spiritual tradition of the old
and Christian society ; and the result at its best is twofold.
On the one hand, the national society may be raised to a
higher power by the consecration of its life through its own
peculiar form of religion. The nation becomes also a
Church ; and it may be something greater in virtue of
being both. On the other hand, the religious society may
be increased in its content and range by the incorporation
of a national tradition and intimacy in the substance
of its own life. The Church becomes also a nation ; and
it, too, may conceivably be something greater in virtue
of being both.

IN no country, perhaps, was the identification of the
Church and the nation more clearly apprehended than it
was in England. The nation and the Church were held to
be one society : membership of the one involved membership of the other : the good citizen was necessarily also
the good churchman. Yet even in England the identification was rather the vision of Hooker and Laud than the
actual and established fact of daily life. The ideal of the
national Church has been challenged among us during
the last three centuries from two different sides. In the
first place—in order of time, and perhaps also in order of
importance—there was the challenge of Nonconformity.
To the Nonconformist the radical principle of the Reformation was not a national Church, which would only be a new
body of death in place of the old, but liberty of conscience.
Liberty of conscience meant the right of all men to associate
freely in voluntary societies according to the inclinations
of their belief ; and the voluntary religious society, as wide
or as narrow as the number of its free adherents might
determine, was accordingly vindicated as the proper
organization of Christian life. In the second place, there
was the challenge offered to the national Church by the old
universalism and the Catholic tradition—a challenge which
sprang to new life in the Oxford Movement, and lives
to-day among those who are still inspired by its principles.

To the convinced Catholic, if we may use that word in a broad and general sense, the Reformation left intact the continuity and the universality of the Catholic tradition ; and to him the proper organization of Christian life is the historic and universal Church of Christ, transcending the nation, as it transcends the sect or confession, and uniting the whole round world in a single society.

Fundamentally as the two challenges differ, and widely as Catholicism diverges from Nonconformity, they are yet allied in their attitude to the principle of nationality and the conception of a national Church. The one would assert the principle of the free Church within the free nation : the other would vindicate the august and sovereign nature of a single Church which lies outside, and yet embraces, the nations ; but both would refuse to accept the identification of religious and national society. Both, too, may be said to have shown in the past, and to show in the present, an international trend. The Nonconformist bodies of one country maintain their connexions with cognate bodies in others ; and the Nonconformist influence in our national politics has been generally directed towards the support of liberal ideas of foreign policy—the encouragement of struggling national causes ; the advocacy of the free course of trade across national barriers ; opposition to wars of aggression ; sympathy with the restriction of armaments and the general cause of peace. Driven into opposition to a national State which sought to enforce religious conformity, Nonconformists have also been led to support international policies which similarly sought to curb its aggressive tendencies. The international activities of Catholicism have been less conspicuous, but the adherents of the Catholic tradition have also sought to maintain contact, and even to achieve reunion, with cognate religious bodies in other countries ; and the genius of universalism which informs their creed has made them alive to the general movement of European opinion and tender towards the general cause of European comity. The members of a national Church may have narrower sympathies. Wrapped in the intimate life of their own country, they may be inclined to support all its public policies : they may corroborate national pride and encourage national isolation. Christianity, it may be said, should be a brake upon the nation.   It should check by its universality the self-centred particularism into which a nation may readily fall : it should meet with its own gospel of peace the combative passions which are so easily roused by national sentiments. Balance is a law of life ; and it may be urged that a balance is better obtained if Church and nation are organizations of a different order, rather complementary to than identical with one another.

THE question of the relation of Christianity to nationality is, however, even more fundamental than the questions which are raised by the existence of national Churches. What we have to ask ourselves, in the last resort, is whether the nation itself—the principle of nationality and the passion of nationalism—can really be fitted into the Christian conception of the order of the world and the purpose of history.   A devout Christian may well say to himself, in the secret of his soul, that the essence of Christianity is peace, the inclusion of all mankind in a single faith, and the union of all humanity in a single body under Christ its Head.   Why, he may ask himself, should national differences persist, and why should the world be divided among different national traditions, with all their inevitable divergencies and antipathies ?   Can such an order of the world be divine, and can a process of history which has achieved such a result be justified ?   These are questions that have to be faced.   In any attempt to reach an answer we may begin by reflecting that the unity of human society is indeed a precious thing, but that no unity has any real virtue unless it has some content, some substance of common feeling, some depth of spiritual tradition.   A society is only a real society in virtue of such content, such substance, such tradition.   Now the essence of the nation is the substance of its tradition.   It is a real society of the mind,

with a common mental content resident in the minds of all
its members—a content which has been built by the generations, and is at once a large inheritance from the past and a
generous bequest to the future.   When we think of such a
society, we cannot call it merely secular, or altogether
earthly.   We are rather driven to the generous faith of
Mazzini, to whom the nation was a divine society.   Man, he
believed, was united to God by a communion which issued
in duty to Him ; but he was also, and in consequence,
united to his fellow-men (because they also were united
in communion with God) by associations, especially the
associations of the family and the nation, which were units
divinely appointed for the discharge of man's duty to
God.   The association of the nation was thus consecrated :
its essence was mission : its purpose was the discharge of
the duty divinely laid upon it both by the riches of its
own internal development and by the aid which it gave to
other nations in the development of their life.   No nation,
Mazzini held, could live for itself alone : each owed a duty
to others, to the general system of Europe, and to humanity
at large.

Nations, like men, must be judged by their fruits ; and
it is not possible to applaud all the fruits of national activity,
either in Mazzini's own country or elsewhere.   But it is
equally impossible to regard nations and nationality as an
aberration of the process of history.   It has always been
one of the tenets of Christianity—a tenet which it inherited
from Hebraism ; a tenet by which it was, from the first,
distinguished from contemporary Greek philosophy with
its doctrine of the repetition of cycles—that God has a
purpose ; that each event in history is unique ; but that
all are links in the progressive chain of the unfolding of
that purpose.   The units and associations through which
the divine purpose has operated in history are various.
There have been city-states ; there have been would-be
world-empires ; there have been tribal societies, large and
small ; there have been, and there still are, nations.   Of
all these forms it can hardly be denied that the nation has

the greatest power for good, whatever the harm it has also done or may yet do. If we look at its origin, we shall recognize how deeply religious elements were implicit in its very beginnings. The nation is a product of Western Europe : it sprang to life among the tribal societies which had entered the western half of the Roman Empire after it had become Christian ; and it was cradled in Christianity. It is a just remark of Dean Church that if Christianity came to the peoples of the Mediterranean when they were already formed, it came to the peoples of Western and North-Western Europe when they were still in the process of being made. The religious factor was from the first a great element in the spiritual tradition of the Western nations, and the influence of the Church played a large part both in securing their unity (the unity of Anglo-Saxon England, for example, was in no small measure the work of the Church) and in determining their moral ideas and the very substance of their law. We may not follow Mazzini in regarding the nation as a divinely appointed society, but we have none the less to confess that religion has entered into its making and become part of the substance of its inherited tradition. Even the secular nation which repudiates any recognition of Christianity is penetrated by a past which is itself penetrated by Christian tradition.

Nor are the fruits of the nation, in its modern operation, alien from the habit of the Christian temper or the spirit of Christian principle. If there is one doctrine which is firmly rooted and embedded in Christianity, it is that of the infinite value of human personality, which makes men capable of sonship of God and inheritance of the kingdom of Heaven. If there is any test of human progress along a line of purpose through the course of history, it is the test of progressive recognition, in human societies, of what we may call the worth of persons. Now the work of the nations has enriched and dignified human personality. From the days of the French Revolution the nations have more and more organized themselves as

States, and national States have more and more arranged
their lives on the basis of democratic government. Nationality and democracy have gone hand in hand, not merely
as parallel or simultaneous causes, but in virtue of an inner
connexion, by which a system of self-government naturally
arises as soon as States become coextensive with the national
societies in terms of which men readily think and feel, and
in the area of which they readily form the public opinion
and general will that are the basis of self-government.
National States issuing in systems of democratic self-
government have enhanced the worth of persons by the
gift of the suffrage, and by eliciting and enlisting, for the
purposes of national discussion, the interest and the opinion
of all their adult members. Where a national system of
education has been added, and the nation has determined
to awaken the intelligence and to form the character of
its children, another and very great force has been brought
into play for the enrichment of personality and the increase
of worth of persons. Perhaps we are apt to judge the value
of nationality too much by the nature of international
relations, and too little by the quality of the internal national
life which it inspires. Yet men may be fairly judged
no less by what they are at home than by what they are in
society ; and nations too may be weighed as much by what
they do to improve the life and the worth of their own
members as by what they do externally in their relations
to one another.

All in all, we may say of the nation that it is a creation
of the human spirit—feeling its way to an ideal of righteousness, here in one manner, and there in another—which has
helped to liberate men by its methods of free self-government and to educate them by its system of free education ;
which has incorporated in the substance of its tradition
religious elements, and has given expression in its literature
to ideals and aspirations made musical and intimate by
the appeal of a national language. None of these are small
things ; and national literature in particular—at once the
expression of national life, and an impression upon it ; at

once the gift of a nation to itself, and a national contribution to common human culture—may be counted heavily to the credit of the nation from which it proceeds. In all these things there is at least a potential nobility which deserves recognition. And if we believe, as a convinced Christian will readily believe, that there is a plan and the unfolding of a purpose in the movement of human history, we shall say that a development so long in its continuance, and so comprehensive in its range, as the development of nations has been, must be recognized and even, if possible, enhanced by Christian countenance and comfort. If the nation can be regarded as part of the purpose and plan of the world, it is for Christian faith to wrap itself round the nation, and for Christian doctrine to enfold the nation in its scope.

CHRISTIANITY did not begin as a Church. Our Lord was a teacher of men. Transcending all other teachers, He was yet like all great teachers in this, that He sought to produce a ' conversion of the soul ' which would result in a new ' way of life ' among His disciples. Teaching and discipleship were the words which He used ; but as more and more souls were converted by His teaching, and the new way of life was trodden by more and more disciples, the Christian school became little by little a great Christian Church. Yet the essence of all teaching remains the teaching itself ; and whatever the organization in which it has issued, the essence of Christianity is still the teaching and spirit of its Founder. Organization is a human mould ; but the human mould does not make the divine spirit which runs into its form any the less divine ; and different moulds may contain the same spirit at different periods of time. The original mould of Christianity was the mould of the universal society, which the philosophers and the statesmen of antiquity had combined to proclaim or to establish. But it was the mould of a particular time and a particular season in human affairs ; and the fertility of that process of human history,

10

which is no mere series of chance events or of cyclical repetitions, was not exhausted by the production of that mould.   The nation is the new mould of our modern times —a mould originally produced, by particular influences of the historical process, in Western Europe, but a mould which is establishing itself, by the contagion of example and the force of suggestion, in the East as well as the West and the New World as well as the Old.   The spirit of Christianity has in each age to make its terms and arrange its accommodation with the developments of the historical process.   It did so in the last centuries of ancient history, and formed a universal organization of its life to match the universal society of those centuries.   It may do so equally in the later centuries of modern history, forming national organizations to match new national societies.   We may readily admit that it is easier for a new Church, seeking a form and a shape of order, to run into some existing mould, than it is for an ancient Church, which has found its form and shape, to change them to suit some change in the contemporary moulds of human life.   Christianity has centuries behind it ;   and it carries the weight and the casing of the centuries.   But whether it assumes a national form, or remains super-national, or runs on non-national lines of voluntary organization, it is everywhere confronted by the great and looming figures of national societies, and it has to adjust its teaching and its activities to their existence and their aspirations.

I have already said that the nation is a deeper and richer society, in virtue of its spiritual tradition, than were its precursors ;   and I have already suggested that churches and nations are both the gainers by mutual contact and co-operation.   A Church which draws into itself the spirit of a national tradition may increase its appeal to its members ;   and the common fund of Christianity may be all the richer, and all the more living, for a larger variety of settings and interpretations.   In the same way the nation which draws into itself continuously, and not merely in its first beginnings, the inspiration of a religious faith and a religious purpose will increase its own vitality. A nation is most active, and most truly national, when it is possessed by a religious conviction—not, I hasten to add, the conviction of those moments of aberration in which a nation regards itself as God's own chosen instrument for working out His intentions, but the conviction of a resolute and permanent faith which makes a nation firm in the pursuit of a cause, such as (to take but one example) the cause of the abolition of the slave trade and slavery as things contrary to Christian principle. Our own nation has suffered from its moments of aberration, in which it has dreamed sad·dreams of an English God and God's Englishman ; but in its more sober and permanent disposition it has been inspired by a not ignoble notion of national duty to aid the oppressed—the persecuted Vaudois, the suffering slave, the oppressed nationality—and it has been most characteristically national when it has most felt such inspiration. And indeed it follows, if a nation be in its nature a spiritual society, that it will be most itself when it is most stirred by spiritual motives and purposes.

I am far from believing in the pure divinity of the nation, or from subscribing to any doctrine of the divine right of nationality to an absolute self-determination. Nations are human societies, created in time, with the imperfections of the temporal ; and they are subject to the eternal religious principles which exist not in to-day or yesterday, but for ever. They live and move in the ambit of the Christian spirit, and the actions which their leaders take in their name must be judged by the degree of their conformity with that spirit. But if they are human societies, it does not follow that nations are also secular—at least in that sense of the word in which it is used as the antithesis and the negation of the religious. We offend against the essence of the nation if we emphasize its secularity, or regard it as merely an earthly unit for earthly purposes. Its tradition began its life at the breast of Christianity ; and its development in time, through the centuries of our millennium, has not been a development utterly away from its nursing mother.   There is something of a plan in its growth : there is something of progress in its achievements. We are prone to make distinctions in our thinking, and to harden them by the terms which we use for their designation.   But life and the heaving movement of history are sometimes less distinct than our thought, and much less distinct than our terms ; and the distinction between the secular and the religious—the nation and the Church— is perhaps less profound than we are apt to think.   France, it is true, has tended to follow, since the Revolution of 1789, the lines of a secularist nationalism ; but in England our national tradition has been opposed to the idea of a merely secular society for secular purposes standing over against a separate religious society for religious purposes.   Our practice has been in the main that of the single society, which if it is national is also religious, making public profession of Christianity in its solemn acts, and recognizing religious instruction as part of its scheme of education. It is a practice which has its sanctions.   Our national Church was perhaps something of an accident in its beginnings, but it is neither fortuitous nor erroneous in its continuance. The form of Christianity which seeks to penetrate and to elevate the nation, making itself coextensive with the national society, and seeking to infuse its own essence into the national tradition, is a form which may carry furthest, and infuse deepest, the teaching which is the essence of Christianity.

I MAY seem to have dwelt long on nationalism in an address which in its nature should be devoted to internationalism.   I can only plead that, if we are to have a healthy and effective internationalism, those who are labouring to promote the union of nations must first of all understand the nature of the units to be united, and understand them no less—and indeed even more—in their strength than in their weakness.   There is a form of facile internationalism which lays such stress on the first part of the word that it tends to forget the second.

A League of Nations means nations as well as a League, and if there were not nations the League would be a bond uniting a number of zeros. Nationality is not in its nature an enemy of internationalism—though it may be in its excesses. We may even say that the more nationality there is—the more each nation has developed and deepened and enriched its tradition—the more there is likely to be a League of Nations. A developed and deep and rich national tradition makes a nation less discontented, because it can rejoice more in its own abundance ; and it may make it more ready to give, because it has more to give. It is here, perhaps, that the work of Christianity lies, in the development and deepening and enrichment of the national traditions of the different nations. A national Church has its way made easy for such work ; but any form of organization based upon Christian faith can operate, in its measure, on the nation within which it is active. The great international function of Christianity lies in the deeper spiritualizing, within each nation, of that national tradition which is already, in itself, a spiritual thing. Links of junction and leagues of union matter, and matter profoundly ; but the intimate concern of Christianity lies perhaps even more in the penetration by its spirit of the bodies to be linked and the nations to be leagued than in emphasis on the machinery of junction or union. The kingdom of Heaven is within you ; and it is within each nation that the foundations of the ideal world of fair dealing and justice and goodwill and peace have to be laid. And this is the accommodation or adjustment which Christianity can everywhere make to the supreme fact in the social structure of our modern world—the existence and aspirations of nations.

It has been the gist of this lecture that Christianity and nationality are not enemies, and indeed are so far from being enemies that the union of their two traditions, whether in the form of a national Church or in some other way of interaction and interpenetration, may be conceived as a natural stage of the historical process of human life.

The more that Christianity acts upon each nation in its own internal life, the more it elevates all nations to a height at which they can dwell together as equal spiritual societies —the more, again, it unites them by giving a common content to their various traditions. A nation is no ignoble thing. If men can be led by its appeal, as we know that they can be, to lift themselves out of themselves into a concern for its general well-being, they can escape by their devotion to it from the narrow and individual selfishness which so readily besets us all ; and if in turn the whole nation can ' lift itself out of itself,' with the aid of the Churches, into a conception of national mission—an ideal of national ' station ' in the general society of mankind, and of the national duties appurtenant to that station—it can also escape, through that conception and that ideal, from the broader and corporate selfishness which is the defect of nationalism. It is the mission of the Churches within a nation to co-operate for common action upon its life towards that end ; and it is equally the mission of the associated Churches within each nation to aid the associated Churches of other nations, wherever and whenever they can, in promoting the cause which is common to all—the deeper steeping of all the nations in the spirit of a common Christian teaching and tradition. The work of Christianity, in its relation to nationality, is that Christianity should penetrate more and more the spirit of each nation, and that, upon that basis, a common Christian effort should play its part in ensuring that common understanding among the nations which is at once the root and the fruit of any abiding friendship.

VI

THE DISCREDITED STATE [1]

IT is perhaps not an untrue saying, that the State has generally been discredited in England. Indeed, foreign lawyers have been known to say that the State has never existed in England. Notions of *imperium* and *majestas* have not flourished in these islands, except in the Byzantine days of Henry VIII. Austin, who, one is told, was not particularly skilled in English law, and could blunder shockingly in Roman law, may have theorized about *majestas* ; but his own difficulties in fitting his theory of sovereignty into the framework of English politics seem to show that it is fairly remote from the *genius loci.* A sovereign and majestic State, a single and undivided *imperium*, lifted above the conflicts of society, neutral, mediatory, impartial, such as Hegel conceived and such as German theorists still postulate—this we have not known. Our State is on its executive side a bundle of officials, individually responsible for their acts, and only united by a mysterious Crown which is responsible for nothing and serves chiefly as a bracket to unite an indefinite series of integers. Our State on its legislative side, as Hegel told us a hundred years ago, is no pure State, emancipated from society : it is trammelled in the bonds of *bürgerliche*

[1] A Paper delivered before a Philosophical Society in the University of Oxford in May 1914. I should express myself differently in some respects to-day. The experience of the last sixteen years has altered any theory I may have had when I wrote the paper. But I have reprinted it here as it was originally delivered, partly because I thought it might have some historical interest, and partly because the last two paragraphs indicate that I was aware, when I wrote, of the ' relativity ' of the views which I was then expressing.

Gesellschaft; and our legislature, composed of members of this society, ' sacrifices objective freedom or rational right to mere formal freedom and particular private interests ' (*Philosophie des Geistes*, § 544).

With a bracket-enclosed bundle of officials, and a socially trammelled legislature, we cannot have a State, a German will say ; or if we have a State, it can only be discredited. History cannot elucidate, but it may at any rate illustrate, this discredit. Let us take three illustrations. The feudal baronage of the days of Magna Carta were good syndicalists —and indeed the best syndicalists throughout history have been the upper classes. For organized labour like theirs they felt that the State had no message. They asserted a right of striking against the State : they claimed a class-privilege of legalized rebellion whenever the class-privileges which they had defined in Magna Carta suffered infringement. Their syndicalism had a good mediaeval philosophy at its back. They could appeal to contract and natural law. The king ruled on contractual terms ; if he transgressed the terms which he had promised in his coronation oath to observe, they were quit of their *fides* and might betake themselves to *diffidatio*. Moreover, natural law rules the world, including States and kings ; and if class-privileges are included under that elastic head, class-privilege rules, or overrules, the world of States and kings. In other words, the feudal barons were not unacquainted with the eminent dominion of natural rights.

A second illustration follows logically, if not chronologically : 1688 is no far cry from 1215. Locke speaks of property instead of class-privilege ; and since we all *may* have property, he seems more universally kind. Be that as it may, he inaugurated a long period of our history. The right of property, not only in things but in persons— not only for use, but also for power—has raised its head against the State for these last two centuries. Once more contract, always inimical to the State, has served as a philosophy ; and in the name of freedom of contract a great organ of freedom has had its long winter of discredit.

But two may play with the same doctrine. The natural rights of labour may be urged as well as the natural rights of property. They are being urged to-day. This revenge of labour on property has its ironies. The worst of the natural right of property was its want of logic. While it claimed immunity from the State, it could only exist by the protection of the State. Its motto was, You must keep your hands off me ; but you must stand in front of me. Labour has learned its lesson from property ; and with an almost equal want of logic, perhaps the more pardonable because it has good precedent, it claims immunity from the State for its trade unions in the same breath that it demands recognition by the State of their rights.

A third illustration touches different ground. Men may claim not a mere natural right to privilege, or property, or labour, but a right divine to worship free. Robert Browne, of Corpus Christi College, Cambridge, had little use for the Elizabethan State. Henry Barrow, of Clare, was of the same way of thinking. Congregationalism, which ranks these two Cambridge men among its founders, simply turned its back on the State. Calvinism, in one sense more drastic, in another sense more complacent, recognized the State, but made it the organ of a spiritual consistory, and enlisted its secular arm for enforcing the final judgments of an ecclesiastical tribunal. It is Congregationalism, however, and not Calvinism, which has influenced English political thought most deeply. The first and most striking agent of that influence was Sir Harry Vane, Milton's contemporary. Vane, taught by his experience of religious intolerance in America, had early come by the principle of ' soul-liberty,' which Roger Williams, father of toleration, had made the basis of his community at Providence in 1636. Soul-liberty, Vane urged, was exempt from and higher than the State. ' Magistracy,' he wrote, ' is not to intrude itself into the office and proper concerns of Christ's inward government and rule in the conscience ; but it is to content itself with the outward man, and to intermeddle with the concerns thereof in reference to the converse which man ought to have with man.' The doctrine may seem to us trite and conservative; it was new-minted and radical to an age which thought in terms of the one society, the church-state, whose membership was compulsory, and whose rules, alike the ecclesiastic and the politic, were equally binding on all its members. Milton celebrates Vane as a new Cortez who has seen a new Pacific:

> 'To know
> Both spiritual power and civil, what each means,
> What severs each, thou hast learned, which few have done.'

Believing that the individual can never forfeit to the State his soul-liberty, Vane equally believed that the community can never alienate its own inherent if limited sovereignty. The responsibility of each individual for the saving alive of his own soul, the responsibility of each community for the determining of its own life, these are the two divine burdens of humanity. No wonder that Vane's philosophy had a deep influence on T. H. Green, who had a notable sympathy for English Nonconformists. Vane said on the scaffold, 'The people of England have long been asleep. I doubt they will be hungry when they awake.' 'If the people of England should yet awake and be hungry,' Green writes, 'they will find their food in the ideas which, with much blindness and weakness, he vainly offered them, cleared and ripened by a philosophy of which he did not dream.'

English Nonconformity has been the main influence in the discrediting of the English State, just because it has been the noblest. Antigone has confronted Creon these 250 years with the declaration that his mortal decrees were not so strong as to outspeed the unwritten and unfailing law of God. The pity is that our English Antigone has had Midas for her ally. For the Nonconformist defiance of the State has been confirmed and corroborated by the defiance of the economic man, with his appeal to the unwritten and unfailing law of free contract and free competition. Our two distinctively English products in the sphere of the mind—and we may take these to be Nonconformity and political economy—have been shrewd enemies of the State. It is curious to notice that he who wrote *The Man versus the State* was reared in Nonconformist circles and nourished on political economy. It was for a paper called the *Nonconformist* that Herbert Spencer wrote his first essay on politics—*The proper sphere of Government* : it was in the agitation against the Corn Laws that he first took any active part in politics. And the whole assumption of the validity of natural rights which Spencer so largely drew from these two influences is an assumption that still lies at the back of ordinary English thought and prejudice. Few Englishmen might know what you meant if you spoke to them of natural rights ; but most Englishmen believe in natural rights. Professor Halévy, a close observer of things English, noted, in a recent letter to the writer, that ' the old eighteenth-century idea, exploded as it is, of the abstract rights of the individual is quietly gaining ground in the world of actual English politics.'

THE measure of the ground gained is the number of the new ' isms ' that are current. Their number sometimes surprises, and men feel that they live in new and unstable days. The quiet Victorian peace of the last half of the nineteenth century has perhaps lulled us into forgetfulness. But there were many ' isms ' abroad in the tumultuous years between 1789 and 1848 ; and there were ideas spreading even in the years of Victorian peace which are now sown broadcast. Two of these—Tractarianism and Marxianism —suggest some reflections. They have in some sense taken the place of the old Nonconformity and the old economics in resistance to the State. Curiously enough Nonconformity is now if anything conformist. It is Elizabethan : it will accept a State definition of religion for the purposes of teaching in elementary schools. The real Nonconformist of these days is the high Anglican. Ever since 1833 he has felt the claim and urged the rights of the Church of his conception against the State and its menace. He has felt that his

Church is a substantive body independent of the State, with its own origin in divine foundation, its own continuity in virtue of apostolical descent, its own rights in virtue of its origin and continuity. Newman wrote to his fellow-clergy in the first Tract for the Times : ' A notion has gone abroad that [the people] can take away your power. They think they have given and can take it away. . . . Enlighten them in this matter. Exalt our holy fathers the bishops, as the representatives of the Apostles . . . and magnify your office as being ordained by them to take part in their ministry.' Here the protest is not the protest of Roger Williams for individual soul-liberty : it is a protest for group-liberty. And Marxianism, a philosophy which probably owes much to English inspiration, and certainly owes something to the inspiration of Thomas Hodgskin, indicates a similar change. The economic defiance of the State is no longer the individualist claim of the economic man for *laissez faire* : it is the cry of class consciousness, the collective voice of Labour. Interpreted and expanded by Sorel, Marxianism urges the need for the liberty of the proletariate consciousness and culture from the contamination of the bourgeois State, just as Catholicism demands the freedom of religious consciousness and the religious idea of life from the coercion of the secular State. Nonconformist soul-liberty and economic individualism have both surrendered the defiance of the State to new challengers. The challengers are now groups, challenging in the name of groups ; but the challenge is still there.

The English State is thus accustomed to discredit. And to tell the truth it has never sought to take great credit to itself. It has not magnified its own office, or exalted its own dignity. It has left its officers to be responsible for their official doings to the ordinary courts and by the ordinary rules of the common law. Habeas Corpus enables the judges to review any act of the executive which has resulted in the imprisonment of a subject. No official can swell with pride as the embodiment of the State, or boast that the clothes he wears distinguish him from his civic brethren. Our forefathers at the end of the seventeenth century would not even allow the State, in the shape of the Crown, to contract our National Debt. The National Debt is owed, and the interest on the National Debt is paid, by ' the Publick.' While law has not been tender to the State, it has been tender enough, intentionally or no, to all manner of groups. Here we touch on that peculiarly English thing, the Trust. The State replied to Nonconformist defiance, at any rate in the eighteenth century, by turning the other cheek. For one thing it passed annual Acts of Indemnity to secure those Nonconformists who had violated its laws by taking office without the due subscription ; for another, it permitted the conception of trust to shelter Nonconformity in possession of its chapels and funds. The trust, as Professor Maitland has shown, preserved religious liberty. And the trust has also served trades unions. It has permitted them to accumulate and to hold the funds without which their activities would have been impossible. It may indeed be urged that the trust has sheltered group-life more fully than any legal recognition of the ' real personality ' of groups could have done. Hidden behind their trustees, groups have thriven and grown unnoticed. The recognition of their real personality would have meant their coming more fully under the public eye ; and the public eye might have refused to wink at the doings of bodies which it could see, while it never even blinked at the activities of groups which were hidden by the screen of trust.

Nor have groups merely flourished in our country under the shelter of trusts. They have flourished anyhow and anywhere. England is a place where they seem always to have been budding and maturing. In this clubable country groups and associations are always arising freely and acting as freely. We have thrown off in an easy and light-hearted way groups like the East India Company, which, as we may read in our statute book, can have financial transactions with the English ' Publick ' as an independent entity, so that in 1786 the Public stands indebted to the

Company in a sum of more than four millions. In the same easy way this English State has thrown off groups like colonies, which manage to combine independence with allegiance ; and within her own borders she has thrown up those associations called parties, which are well within the State, and yet so far from being altogether under the State, that they have a habit of taking the State in tow and ' running ' it after their own devices. Nonconformist bodies, trade unions, great semi-sovereign companies, self-governing colonies, political parties—they have all budded freely, matured easily, and gone very much their own way.

IT is curious that, while English thought and practice have never been particularly favourable to the claims of the State, two Englishmen, Hobbes and Austin, should have been preachers of a doctrine of *majestas* which recognizes and, one may almost say, consecrates those claims. The doctrine has a long history, and its history proves that it is not of English origin. As stated by Austin it runs as follows : ' Every positive law, or every law simply and strictly so called, is set by a sovereign person, or a sovereign body of persons, to a member or members of the independent political society wherein that person or body is sovereign or supreme.' In other words, all laws are the fiat of a sovereign ; all sovereigns are persons or bodies of persons of a determinate character ; each independent political society has one and only one such person or body of persons ; and every such person or body of persons has indeterminate or unlimited power. This is a theory of an admirable simplicity ; but it is not the theory of Bentham, who recognizes the possibility of a limited sovereignty [1] ; it

___

[1] Cf. the *Fragment on Government*, chapter iv. §§ 34–6. ' What difficulty there should be in conceiving a state of things to subsist in which the supreme authority is thus limited [by an instrument of convention, setting assignable bounds to its power], what greater difficulty in conceiving it with this limitation, than without any, I cannot see.' Bentham, writing in 1776, thus anticipated, more than ten years in advance, the principle of the United States Constitution. (I owe this reference to the kindness of Sir F. Pollock.)

fails to square with the facts of English political life and structure ; and it is, one may suspect, French in its immediate and perhaps papal in its ultimate origin. In the eighth chapter of his first book, the French legist, Bodin, defines *majestas* as *summa in cives ac subditos legibusque soluta potestas*. This majesty is the *differentia* of a State : ' a state transcends a corporation by the fact that it embraces a multitude of citizens and towns within the protection of the majesty of its power.' For support of the transcendence and omnipotence of this majesty Bodin appeals, and very naturally appeals, to the supremest of all sovereigns, the papal chair. Innocent IV, he writes, ' who understood best of all men the rights of sovereignty, and who had put under his feet the authority of almost all emperors and Christian princes, said that supreme power belongs to him who can take away from ordinary law.' It is indeed the high papal view of the *plenitudo potestatis* which really inspires Bodin, as Bodin inspires Austin. As the Papacy is the *fons et origo* of the government of the august commonwealth of Christian men, so the sovereign is the ἀρχή—the ἀρχή in both senses of the word—of the public conduct of the members of each independent political society.

A modern clerical writer—inspired by the teaching of Acton, who fought papal infallibility, and stimulated by the writings of Gierke, who champions the real personality of those corporations relegated by Innocent IV to the category of *fictae personae*—has set his lance against this high and dry doctrine of sovereignty. Dr. Figgis, representing those tendencies of advanced Anglicanism which have been mentioned before, has written more than one philippic against the Innocentine and Austinian notions of sovereignty. If one looks at the ecclesiastical community in itself, he contends, the Innocentine notion is fatal to the true federal character of the Catholic Church ; if one looks at the ecclesiastical community as engaged in the life of a State, he argues, the Austinian notion is destructive of the rights of that community, because it is fatal to the true federal character of the State, and because it is only on the basis of the recognition of its federal character that the rights of its component communities can be preserved. Advocating a federalistic view alike of the Catholic Church and of the State, Dr. Figgis ingeminates the phrase 'inherent rights of associations.' He returns, in a word, to the old idea of natural rights, but he resuscitates that ghost by giving it blood to drink—the red blood of real corporate personality. It is in the name of real group-persons that Dr. Figgis can renounce the doctrine of an 'omnicompetent State' confronting and controlling a 'sum of atomistic individuals'; it is in this sign that he will victoriously instal the doctrine of a partially competent State of a federal character, embracing in a kind of co-partnership—and not, as Bodin says, in the transcendent majesty of power—real groups which have also their competence in their sphere.

II

THE problem of resistance is in actual life always a problem of groups. Theorists may set limits to the State in the name of the individual; practical resistance is always a matter of group-consciousness. What is a group? Has it a personality beyond the persons of its members, and a will beyond their wills? Maitland, following and interpreting Gierke, has answered that 'the fellowship is a real person, with . . . a will of its own.' Professor Geldart, in an inaugural lecture on legal personality, cautiously writes that 'there seems to be at least a *prima facie* case for holding that our legal theory ought to admit the reality of a personality in permanent associated bodies, or at least of something so like personality that we may provisionally call it by that name for want of a better.' The problem is perhaps the simplest and most terrible of all problems. It is the problem of universals : the problem of identity and difference. It is as easy for a mind without the philosophic compass to drift into the *res praeter res*, and to see all as identity, as it is to run up against the *nomen de rebus*, and to see all as difference. Perhaps neither fits the facts ; perhaps the Identical, in this matter of groups, is neither a real person nor a nominalist fiction. Let us call it an idea, and see into what dim port we drift with that pilot. William of Wykeham had an idea, somewhere about 1378 ; to-day there is a group, or fellowship, of St. Mary College of Winchester in Oxford, and this Paper has been written in a room that belongs to this idea, and its writer is somehow, being Fellow of Wykeham's college, related to this same idea. What has happened is that this idea has entered into a continuous succession of persons. They have retained their personality, but they have coloured their personality with the idea : a new personality has not arisen, but a new organizing idea has served as a scheme of composition for existing personalities. We have it on Aristotelian authority that the State is the same as long as its scheme of composition is the same. Its identity resides not in any single transcendent personality but in a single organizing idea permeating simultaneously and permanently a number of personalities. As for the State, so for all fellowships ; there may be oneness without any transcendent one. We may alter our organizing idea ; we may turn a tragic chorus into a comic chorus. We do not kill a personality that existed before, or create a personality that did not exist before : we alter our organizing idea.

Law has to bring these permanent and organizing ideas, which unite persons together in lasting schemes, under some rubric or title—trust, contract, *persona ficta* or real person. The rubrics of law are not reality ; they are cases in which to put reality ; but the cases may fit reality well or badly, and since reality has a way of growing, they may help or hinder its growth. Apparently the cases called trust, contract, and *persona ficta* all hinder growth, and cramp the living texture of reality within the limits of a rigid trust-deed, or a hard bond of contract, or a limiting charter of incorporation such as must go to the creation of a *persona ficta*. Much may be said for the rubric of real personality as a rubric of the lawyers and for the lawyers ; and much might be said in this connexion on a fascinating problem—how far legal categories are created by the demands of social growth, and how far legal categories create or rather determine social growth itself. But to the plain man the simple necessity is the necessity of preserving the organizing idea fresh and growing, freshly apprehended as a motive by each mind in the organization, and freely growing with the growth of mind, as a wider outlook discovers fresh implications and fresh relations of the idea. Ideas have their pathology ; and they suffer from two main diseases. They may become mere bundles of blue paper swathed in red tape : we may have trust-deeds in lieu of ideas ; and the religious idea itself, which is the true and only unity of any Church, may pass from an idea to a creed, and from a creed to an empty formulary. Again, they may become office chairs and organizing secretaries. This is the tragedy that is always enacted when an institution becomes mere officialdom, or a Church mere sacerdotalism. Great is the magic of office chairs, and the hard-driven word organization too often covers an ample paucity of ideas. But we need not escape blue paper and office chairs by flying to real personalities which are perhaps, in any other sense than that of legal categories, the ghosts of imagination. Ideas are, and are not fictions : they have hands and feet ; but they are not persons, any more than they are fictions.

We may eliminate personality and will—transcendent personality and transcendent will—from associations ; we may be content to speak of associations as schemes in which real and individual persons and wills are related to one another by means of a common and organizing idea. We may conceive the State as such a scheme based on the political idea of law and order ; we may conceive it as containing, or at any rate co-existing with, a rich variety of schemes based on a rich variety of ideas. We are all members of the one scheme and partakers of the one idea ; most of us are also members of many other schemes, and partakers of many other ideas. The ideas are in relation to one another ; perhaps they are in competition with one another. If it is so, it is a competition of ideas, not of real collective personalities. To apprehend this point of view is already a certain gain. We are rid of the idea of an internecine struggle between the real personality of the State and the real personality of other groups. We cease to feel murder in the air. Real ideas cannot be killed : they can only die by the suicide of their own excess, or the slow internal decay of their own life. Again, when we talk of real persons, we attach to them an intrinsic value as such, because we feel that all personality has value. At that rate we should see value in the Mafia [1] or Camorra.. If one talks rather of ideas, one can keep something more of critical poise. One can argue with ideas : one can show that they are partial or erroneous ; one can deflate a bubble idea with a prick of logic.

BUT the problem remains to be faced—if not to be solved, for it is perhaps theoretically insoluble—whether there is any graded hierarchy of associating ideas, and whether we can ascribe sovereignty to one associating idea. A passion for the *reductio ad unum*, such as inspired the *De Monarchia* of Dante, may urge us to seek a dominant One ; and finding that One in the associating idea of the political community, we may speak of the sovereignty of public opinion. We may urge that there must be a single source of adjustment to determine the relations of associating ideas one with another, to criticize each scheme of association on its merits, to abolish associating ideas that are dead, to reinvigorate associating ideas that are dormant. Whether empirically or theoretically considered, the matter is by no means easy. Empirically we may see that other associating ideas than that of the political community have claimed,

[1] It is curious to note that the word Mafia is applied both to the organizing (or disorganizing) idea, and to the society which it unites. Dr. Murray defines Mafia as ' the spirit of hostility to the law and its ministers prevailing among a large portion of the population (of Sicily) . . . also the body of those who share in this anti-legal spirit.' It would seem that the Sicilians are good enough philosophers to give the name of the organizing idea to the society which it constitutes.

and—what is more important—have received a final and
absolute allegiance.   This is most conspicuously true of the
religious idea, which political theory has a way of neglecting.
The final allegiance of the thorough Romanist lies with
Rome, and not with Westminster.   The allegiance of Sir
Harry Vane, 'in the office and proper concerns of Christ's
inward government and rule in the conscience,' lay not
with the magistracy, nor even with the sacerdocy, but with
the indwelling Christ.   The mediaeval world knew no
unitary political sovereignty.   Mediaeval thinkers might
indeed conceive of a final and ultimate law of nature,
whether as an 'indicative law' and the dictate of reason
as to what is right, or as an imperative rule and the will of
God ; but just because they ascribed sovereignty to this
law of nature, insomuch that all laws and all executive acts
contrary thereto were *ipso facto* null and void, they could
not and did not ascribe any sovereignty to a political
superior.   It was possible for the associating idea of the
feudal privilege of a class to erect itself into an ultimate
value, and to claim and exercise the right of legal rebellion
against the authority of the State.   The conception of an
ultimate State Sovereignty entered England with the
Reformation.   Its zenith is the year 1539, when Parliament
ascribed to Henry VIII's proclamations the force of law,
and by the Act of the Six Articles took the very ark of the
religious idea itself into the sphere of its regulation.   But
State Sovereignty was shattered by Nonconformity and
shot-ridden by the Great Rebellion.   And if to-day some
may see a new Henry VIII in the guise of a sovereign public
opinion, the syndicalist will none the less claim exemption
from the bourgeois State for his idea of class, the nationalist
will claim immunity from the denationalized State for his
idea of the nation, and the right hand of the churchman
will lose its cunning if he forgets Jerusalem.   Even a quiet
and cautious scholar like the President of Harvard will tell
us in his last book that public opinion, which is in effect
the opinion of the majority, is only dominant within the
sphere of those things in which the minority will voluntarily

consent to the decision of the majority, and that outside this sphere there lies an area of issues which a prudent State will never raise, because it is impotent to decide.

Public opinion, the associating idea of the political community, would be uniquely sovereign if it were absolutely homogeneous. That it never is ; and that, some of us may hope, it never will be. Any community is a field of competing ideas ; and with the growth of mind we can only expect a richer competition. It may be urged that heterogeneity of opinion is a symptom of an imperfect community, which has never thought itself together. It may also be urged that the opposite is true. The pullulation of new organizing and associating ideas is not a sign of poverty of the mind. The formation of new idea-centres, and the organization of men round those centres, is not likely to cease. One may rejoice as well as grieve to see Ulstermen and Irishmen, labour-men and churchmen, swarming after new guiding ideas to new hives. The apiarist is troubled : he wants all his bees in his own private orchard. But there is something to be said for the bees Their guiding idea may be imperfect. It may contain a narrow and imperfect synthesis of data ; and the nationalist idea, for instance, may on occasion lead men to seek a life that is narrow and poor in comparison with the wider and richer life of a great culture-state. But ideas have also to be measured by their effects on persons — in a word, if a very loose word, by their subjective value. An idea may be one-sided, but it may enlist the whole personality in its defence as nothing else could. If it does, it has after all its value as a vital and energizing factor for the individual. One defends democracy not as a form of government but as a mode of spiritual expression—an eliciting and enlisting force, which draws from us energies of thought and of will which we should never otherwise expend. The same defence may also cover this sphere. And there is another thing to be said. Admitting for the moment that the State idea is the broader and wider synthesis, it may, just because of its breadth, be an imperfect synthesis, which only achieves success by neglecting factors for which it should find room. It may be a forced and bare universal, purchased at the cost of many of its individuals. The very attempt of factors which conceive themselves neglected to push themselves forward as absolute wholes on their own account may serve as an incentive to a truer synthesis. If bare unitary sovereignty is, as it seems to be, such a forced and bare universal, we should only rejoice in its practical criticism by the logic of fact.

III

ON what lines men may achieve, if ever they can achieve, a single associating universal, it is difficult to see. Churches, at any rate, seem likely always to be recalcitrant elements. As things now are, the high Hegelian unification seems at least premature. When Hegel tells me that ' the being of the State (on its objective side) is the in-and-for-itself universal,' and that yet ' the State, as self-knowing and self-acting, is pure subjectivity and *one* individual ' ; when I hear that I, ' seeking to be a centre for myself, am brought by the State back into the life of the universal substance ' —I throw up my hands. When I take things as I find them, I cannot see that universality, sovereignty, call it what you will, is the unique property of any one association. Other times, other fashions ; and again *tot sententiae, quot societates*. At different times different societies may claim a final allegiance ; and at one and the same time two or more societies may tug at the same heart-strings with equally imperative demands. No associating idea seems to engulf the whole man ; and any man may have to face that solemn conflict of duties, which his membership of two different societies, his divided allegiance to two divergent ideas, may at any moment awake. There is no set solution of the dilemma. One is thrown back on the ' leaden canon ' of Lesbian builders—' for the canon of the indeterminate is itself also indeterminate.' Either way one seems bound to lose. Whether one unsheathes the sword for the idea of

the political society—the idea which requires as its bare
minimum the observance of law and order—or for the idea
of the other and rival society of religion, or nation, or class,
the thumb is turned down against the gladiator. Either
the pains and penalties that attend outraged law and order,
or the ostracism or excommunication which attends desertion
of the other group.

The prospect seems desolating. And most of us are not
Childe Rolands, nor do we come to the dark tower. From
anxiety and suspense, from the condition of unstable
equilibrium, we deliver ourselves into the obvious and
primrose path towards the greener valleys of law and order.
Quod principi placuit legis habet vigorem. No associating
idea, we may comfort ourselves, can have absolute validity
or inherent right save one. Men who live together in a
community must have an ultimate source of adjustment of
their relations. That ultimate adjusting force, itself unad-
justed, gives all rights except its own ; and all rights are
therefore derivative, none are inherent. You may talk—
and here you hit most shrewdly—of the inherent rights of
Churches ; but what of Mormonism ? You may talk of
the inherent rights of proletariate consciousness ; do you
also admit the inherent rights of capitalistic consciousness ?
You may talk of the inherent rights of nationality : what
of Albania ? After all, the Idea of the State is the idea
par excellence—all-embracing, all-subsuming, all-adjusting.
Other ideas are partial ; other ideas need criticism and
adjustment. One may praise famous associations such as
did bear rule in their kingdoms ; but the tyranny of the
association over its own members may be greater than any
coercion exercised by the State over associations ; and the
State may and will be an organ of the freedom of persons,
which is the only freedom, if it curtails the freedom of
associations, which is only a paper freedom.

Yet some may still set a lance against the State, however
daunted. The State is the organ of freedom : it is also a
vehicle of force. Its sphere is automatism ; it does external
acts to produce external results. Other associations need

consent the more as they use force the less ; they must act more in the spiritual sphere, and seek to supply motive ideas in order to produce spiritual reactions. Again, the State may be broader ; but is it many-sided, or one-sided ? It rests fundamentally on the idea of law and order in the external converse of man with man ; and the cultural ideas which it has superadded, turning itself from a plain grocer's shop into a Whiteley's emporium, have not altered its foundations. And therefore it is perhaps after all no final source of adjustment. It may be that there is no other source of adjustment among the associating ideas of a many-sided community except omniscience, which we admittedly do not possess. It may be that the State-idea is but *primus inter pares*—as ultimate as, but hardly more ultimate in the last resort than, other ideas which can quicken the pulse and fire the heart. Our universal may thus turn out to be a federal sort of thing. The State may be an educator of citizens : the Church may also be an educator of church-men, with a ' right of entry ' as such. The State may have its Westminster Parliament : the nation may also have its Dublin Parliament. The State may be an area of political action : the trade union may also be a field of political action. It hardly meets the point to urge that the Church will not have its right of entry, or Dublin its parliament, or trade unions a political levy, until the State has issued its permissive law. The State is not prior to law ; and Gierke will tell us that ' law is the result not of a common will that a thing shall be, but of a common conviction that it is.' Browning can write

> Justinian's Pandects only make precise
> What simply sparkled in men's eyes before,
> Twitched in their brow or quivered on their lip,
> Waited the speech they called but would not come.'

In a word, law, as has already been said, makes cases to hold reality, though it may affect reality very vitally by the kind of case it makes.

The Austinian notion of sovereignty is such a case.

The reality it seeks to contain is the associating and organizing idea of law and order. The difficulty is that reality is wider than the case, for there are other ideas, in practice equally ultimate with this idea ; and reality is therefore cramped by its case. In foreign affairs, it is true, there is a point in emphasizing the independence or ultimacy of a determinate political authority : only upon such terms can it negotiate with any finality. Indeed, changing the venue of our metaphor, we may say that sovereignty is a lotion for external application. But it ought to be labelled ' Poison—not to be taken internally.' Internally, it leads to a false view of law, which it degrades into the mere will of the sovereign. ' The human mind,' Professor Wallace wrote in one of his lectures, ' must be disabused of the delusion that it makes laws.' Sovereignty fosters the delusion. Internally, again, it leads to a false unification and simplification of the rich complexity of the fact. It substitutes unitarianism for federalism, a corner in lieu of competition.

This may seem anarchism. Really it is polyarchism. And as for the problem of polyarchism—the problem of unstable equilibrium—why, after all, *solvitur ambulando*, it is likely to be settled by the needs of mere ordered life. This is the ultimate necessity ; but it is not an absolute or invariable necessity. It varies with times and seasons. The sixteenth century was a time and season for *salus populi lex suprema.* Within, there was need of taming fully a still half-tamed nobility, of laying securely the red spectre of social unrest : without, nations were assuming ' the state and posture of gladiators ' in their dealings one with another. Machiavelli could preach the State ultimate, the State undivided : he could warn his new prince that he would ' often be forced, in order to maintain his state, to go to work against faith, against charity, against humanity, against religion.' Years of ordered life have permitted the germination of other ideas than the indispensable minimum idea of law and order ; they have brought us polyarchism for monarchism. If the indispensable basis of law and order has been well and truly laid in sound hard concrete, it is all for the good. If that basis is not secure, if the building of our common life shows cracks and signs of subsidences, if the enemy without should see a gaping opportunity for his battering-ram, the cry of ' Back to law and order ' will be great, and will prevail. Perhaps the hour is not yet. But if it should strike, there is no fear for the State, or for the idea of law and order. There is rather fear for other societies, other ideas. The idea of law and order, when it is roused, is one of the cruellest things in history. Think of the suppression of the Parisian Commune in 1871.

THE discredit of the State is a sign that it has done its work well, and is doing its work well. When the judge gets white gloves at assize after assize, we can afford to think of putting up the shutters of the jails. The State will come into credit again, with a rush, at the double, as soon as it is seen to be doing its work badly. In the use of my private income I like to support charity and all manner of good causes. If it comes to a pinch, I have to say to myself, as somebody said to Talleyrand, ' It is necessary to live.' In our social life we are swarming hither and thither after associating ideas not only of law and order, but of religion, nation, class. If it comes to a pinch, we shall forget that we are anything but citizens. Through our mouths the State, which is nothing but ourselves organized in an ordered life, will then say to itself, ' It is necessary to live.' And there is no Talleyrand to say to the State, ' I do not see the necessity for it.'

VII

THE ' RULE OF LAW '[1]

I

THE passing away of the ' rule of law ' may seem to many honest observers to be the mark of the hour. A number of antinomian philosophies appear to be current ; and a social philosophy which turns the ordered state into the passive area of a truceless war between labour and capital has penetrated even beyond the schools. Here, however, we shall be concerned not with the schools or their philosophies, but with the actual facts of justice and administration in a state which we shall assume to be an ordered whole of life within the domain of law. We have to ask what is actually happening to the·law and to the administration of the law in the English community of to-day. Can we trace any leakage or escape from the rule of law ? By such leakage or escape, it must be premised, we are not to understand failure of the Courts to act where it is generally understood that they may and legally possible that they should act. Such failure, whether owing to resistance or to fear of resistance, may be lamentable, but it does not defeat the principle of the rule of law. We are rather to understand the definite exclusion of the Courts from action, and the legal impossibility of their action, within the sphere of such exclusion. Now it does appear, and it is beginning to be said, that the executive department

[1] A Paper contributed to the *Political Quarterly* of May 1914. I have omitted some passages which were merely addressed to questions of the hour. On the other hand, I have not sought to bring the paper up to date, because it seemed to me that there might be some value in keeping a record of an approach made, even before the war, to a question which is more than ever engaging attention to-day.

of the State has succeeded in subtracting a large area of action from the cognizance of the Courts ; and what we have to consider is how far the executive has actually escaped, or is actually escaping, from the rule of law, and how far such escape can be defended.

It will be noticed that the terms 'rule of law' and 'cognizance of the Courts' have been used convertibly. This use of terms is permissible, and indeed obligatory, in England, where there is no separate administrative law, separately administered, and where all the law that there is is administered by the ordinary Courts as they stand.[1] In England the rule of law is coterminous with the cognizance of the ordinary courts : it is the rule of the judicature. This is an inheritance from Henry II. He made all men, including his own royal officials (witness his Inquest of the Sheriffs), justiciable by his ordinary judges ; and that tradition has been unbroken for seven centuries. It has become the general tradition of the Anglo-Saxon stock, in all places in the King's dominions, and even outside his dominions ; it has become, and it still is, the differentia of the Anglo-Saxon form of State from the continental form. Not our Parliament, or our parties, or our Cabinet, but the rule of our judicature constitutes our form of State a different species. Our judges can pass upon any legal issue which can be framed as a point of law for their decision. We have no distinction between private law and public law ; because our ordinary judges administer all the law that there is, that law is one body. There is not one law for acts of public authority, and another law for acts of private citizens : the same law embraces both, and the same judicial rules of procedure—the same tests of the admissibility of evidence and the same methods of testing evidence —cover both.

---

[1] Martial law, in the sense of the law under which the soldier lives by virtue of the annual Army Act, does at first sight appear to be a separate administrative law ; but it does not, as is well known, subtract the soldier from the cognizance of the ordinary Courts for any acts for which a civilian would be cognizable there.

This is the principle of the rule of law ; and this principle has affected the whole of our legal conception and treatment of State action. The result is a highly individualistic conception and treatment of such action. One may almost say that there is no such thing as an action of the State in England ;[1] one may almost say, indeed, that legally there is no such thing as the State. There is a bundle of individual officials, each exercising a measure of authority under the cognizance of the Courts, but none of them, not even the Prime Minister, wielding the authority of the State. These individual officers are, it is true, united by an abstraction termed the Crown, whose servants they are conceived to be.[2] But the Crown is an abstraction, and not a living agency. We are still left with the fact that the State as such does not act in England : a multitude of individual officials each separately and severally act. What is more, these officials are all equally servants of the Crown. The postman is the servant of the Crown as much as the Postmaster-General. He is not the servant of the Postmaster-General : his contract is with the Crown. If he does wrong in the discharge of his service, the onus cannot fall on the Postmaster-General (unless, indeed, he has given specific *ad hoc* instructions) ; the onus will fall on the Crown, or rather, it would fall on the Crown if the Crown could do wrong, which by the hypothesis of our law it cannot do. And indeed, apart from legal hypothesis, it is difficult to see how the Crown can do wrong. It is not a person, but at best a personification. It is not a living agency ; it has no real personality, though the law may attach to it such a measure of personality as belongs to a ' corporation sole.' Since it is not a personality, there is no question of its responsibility. Responsibility is the shadow cast by personality ; but we cannot have the

[1] True, there are ' acts of State ' ; but these are acts done out of England, for instance in time of war.

[2] Not all officers of the State are necessarily officers of the Crown. There are officers who derive their powers from Statutes, and who are thus, if one looks at their origin, officers of their Statute (or Statutes) rather than of the Crown.

shadow when there is no person to cast the shadow. Just because it is a mere personification, the Crown is sacrosanct : it has no duties, and no responsibility for the fulfilment of duties.

And so it comes about that the State, which surely exists, at any rate as much as a railway company exists, is nevertheless irresponsible, as a railway company is not. Here is escape or leakage from the reign of law, which is not new, but at any rate five centuries old. ' The King can do no wrong.' It is true that the Crown can be sued for breach of contract : if the Admiralty breaks a contract with Vickers & Maxim, there is a legal remedy. But even here the remedy is peculiar : it takes the form of a petition of right, and is regarded as a matter of grace. In the more important sphere of torts the Crown is immune. For the tortious acts of its officials it has no manner of liability. A mail-van driver may run over me. He is the servant of the Crown, but the Crown is not concerned ; and the Postmaster-General, his joint servant in the eye of the law, is equally unconcerned, unless he has given him specific instructions to drive furiously, and made him his agent for the time being, which is a thing unlikely and anyhow difficult to prove. I have, of course, my action against the mail-van driver : he has committed a tort. But he is a man of little substance, and my satisfaction is likely to be equally little. Still, that is the rule of law, as it was laid down in the case of *Bainbridge* v. *The Postmaster-General*, in 1906. The Postmaster-General is not liable for the negligent acts of subordinate officers, unless there is direct proof that he has ordered or directed these acts ; and, of course, the Crown is not liable.

Let us alter the case. Let us suppose that the driver who runs me down is in the employ of the Great Western Railway Company, and is driving one of their vans. The position is in one respect still the same. I cannot sue the directors of the railway company in this case, any more than I could sue the Postmaster-General in the other. The van-driver and the directors are joint servants ; **and** the directors are only liable if they have ordered or directed the specific acts of the van-driver. But in another respect the position is very different. I can sue the Great Western Railway Company as well as the van-driver of the company ; I cannot sue the Crown as well as the van-driver of the Crown. If there is G.R. on the van I have only one action, which lies against its driver ; if there is G.W.R. on the van I have two actions, one of which lies against the driver, the other against the company. And the point is that the company is a person of substance, and my satisfaction is likely to be substantial.

Why should I not get satisfaction also from that great company the State ? There is no reason at all why I should not—except legal form. How then can legal form be altered ? There are two legal ways. The one is to make the Post Office into a company, or rather a corporation, able to sue and to be sued for all purposes. The other is to make the State itself into a company or rather a corporation, equally able to sue and be sued. Which is better ? It seems the simpler way, at first sight, to make the department concerned—Post Office, Admiralty, or what not—departmentally liable. But there are difficulties. As a matter of fact the Post Office is already, for certain purposes, a corporation ; but that did not help Miss Bainbridge. It was partly incorporated in 1840, and further incorporated in 1878 ; but it has been incorporated so far as to derive the benefits, but not so far as to incur the liabilities, of incorporation. The same seems to be true of other bodies and departments which have also been partially incorporated ; and so far as it goes at present, incorporation of departments does not seem to provide a solution. It is true that the incorporation might be made a full and complete incorporation ; but even then difficulties might arise. Each department would try to avoid liability ; each department would try to shift liability to another department. There would be tedious and expensive litigation. And after all, the department is not the real person. The real person in whose service the tortious official is

employed is the State.   And the real cure is to recognize
the State as a juristic person, with its responsibility and
its liabilities.

OVER two hundred years ago the State, under the name
of ' the Public,' entered into a great liability.   It became responsible for the National Debt.   The National Debt
was not contracted by the Crown (events of the reign of
Charles II made men suspicious of the Crown), but by ' the
Public ' of England.   All we have to do nowadays is to
extend the liability of the Public.   If it could owe and pay
my forebears the interest on their share of the National
Debt over two hundred years ago, why should it not owe
and pay me to-day the damages for my broken leg if its
driver runs me down ?   We must cease to hide the true
juristic personality of the Public under the bushel of the
Crown ; we must cease to degrade the Public (as we have
continued to do, except in this old matter of the National
Debt) into a mere set of individuals—minors, as it were—
for whom the Crown acts as trustee.   Let us abandon the
false conception of the Crown as trustee — irresponsible
trustee—for a sort of unincorporated club : let us boldly
bring into daylight the Public itself as a corporate person,
a real agent, responsible for its actions.

It would be a great gain merely from the legal point of
view to make this change.   The whole confused conception of the Crown — corporation sole in itself, and yet
trustee for the Public, which nevertheless, though a sort
of minor, has to contract for itself the public debt—breeds
darkness and lets tort escape its due punishment.   To
substitute the Public for the Crown is not to substitute
a Republic for Monarchy ; but it is to substitute light for
darkness, truth for sham, a reality for a personification,
responsibility for irresponsibility.   Such a change would
not only be a gain in the legal sphere : it might possibly
involve a consequential gain in the constitutional sphere.
The whole, or almost the whole, of the ' conventions '
which constitute so large a part of our constitution flow

from the conception of the Crown. They are conventions
or understandings which regulate the prerogative of the
Crown. Now it has been said that the prerogatives of the
Crown are the privileges of the Public. But the world, as
recently as 1911, was by no means clear on this point ; and
the uncertainty about the ownership of these prerogatives
may even yet produce grave consequences. It is easy to
confuse the Crown with the King ; and if a party preached
this confusion, and the King himself became a party to
this confusion, there would be rocks ahead. Just as we
need a clear conception of the juristic personality of the
Public for ordinary legal purposes, so we also need a clear
conception of the relation of the King and the Public in
matters constitutional. We ought to be sure that the
King, in any action he takes, is acting on behalf of the
Public, and therefore on the basis of public opinion, and
therefore by the advice of the ministers who have come
from, and in their day of reckoning go back to, that opinion.
In ordinary law and in constitutional law the final authority
and the final responsibility of the Public should be our
sheet-anchor.

But this is another story, and we must return from high
matters of the constitution to ordinary law. What we
have here to urge is simple. What is needed is, in the first
place, the conception of the State or the Public as a legally
responsible person ; and, in the second place, the application to this person of the idea of agency in such sort that it
shall admit responsibility for the acts of its servants done
in its service. As we have already seen, this admission
of responsibility by the State would not divest its agents
of their responsibility. What we should have would be
double responsibility of both, instead of the sole responsibility of the agent. In this way an objection that might be
raised against the policy of fixing responsibility on the
State disappears. It might be urged that if we make the
State responsible, we protect the official, and that the protected official, with the State at his back, will use his powers
more loosely. Each policeman and tax-collector will feel

12

himself an incarnation of the idea of the State. But this
does not follow. Each policeman and tax-collector will
still be responsible before the Courts for his acts. Mr.
Crane, whose manner of repairing a footpath in which
telegraph wires had been laid was alleged to be responsible
for Miss Bainbridge's injuries, will still (if the allegation is
true) be liable for what he has done ; but Miss Bainbridge
will now be able to bring an action not only against Mr.
Crane, but also, and at one and the same time, against the
Public, whose servant he is.

II

HITHERTO we have considered the State as a party
in litigation ; we have urged the responsibility of the
State for the acts of its executive officials. We now turn
to consider the State as judge ; or rather, we turn to consider the executive officials of the State as judges. It is
easy to make a simple division, and to say that the executive
administers and the judicature judges—that the executive
does all administration, and the judicature does all justice.
But the division cannot be made. The judges, especially
on the Chancery side, do a great deal, or have in the past
done a great deal, of administrative work. They have had
to administer trusts and to make schemes for charitable
foundations. On the other hand, the executive is, as a
matter of fact, finding more and more that it has to assume
judicial functions in the course of its administrative work,
especially in the departments of education and of social
reform. In this sense one may say that there has been
a great development of administrative justice in the last
few years. But this fact does not stand alone. There
has been a still greater development of administrative
legislation. Statutory Orders and Provisional Orders form
the great bulk of our modern legislation ; but they are laws
enacted by administrative departments, subject, of course,
as the departments are in general subject, to parliamentary
control. In a word, our administrative departments not only

administer ; they also legislate ; and they are tending more and more to exercise judicial functions. It is this exercise of judicial functions by the executive departments, removing as it does a large field of legal issues from the cognizance of the Courts, which seems to many to involve an escape from the rule of law, and to be therefore in its essence wrong.

It is urged that the exercise of judicial functions by executive officials means bad justice. Persons possibly unskilled and certainly prejudiced are set to do the grave work of the law. Without any strict judicial procedure, they decide legal issues for the proper testing and settle-ment of which a strict judicial procedure has been estab-lished by centuries of growth. Under the sway of their party chiefs, they decide issues in which party feeling is involved, and they cannot escape if they would from wresting their judgements to support the interests of the dominant party. Here, the adversary urges, there is being instituted ' in the name of democracy a Star Chamber more repugnant to the manners and traditions of English-men than the hated Star Chamber which was swept away in 1641. . . . But it will not be tolerated. The right of appeal to the Courts and the right to have the Courts of Justice open to the world . . . are heritages for which Englishmen have fought and died, and it is inconceivable that we have reached a day when these will be relinquished at the bidding of Mr. Lloyd George.' [1]

These are brave words. And no one will deny that there is a danger that the leaders of democracy may seek to force the pace towards the millennium by quasi-judicial Commissions. ' In Indiana a commission, consisting of three surgeons, is empowered to select for treatment [sterilization], from reformatories or other State institu-tions of a similar nature, persons " deemed by them to be unimprovable mentally and physically, and unfit for procreation." ' This haste to realize eugenic ideals ' is in effect a punishment imposed by a Board which differs from a Court of justice both in its constitution and in the

[1] *Land Union Journal*, November 1913, p. 11.

fact that the prisoner is not heard in his own defence or represented by counsel.' [1] But though such dangers may loom ahead, the exercise of some amount of judicial authority by the ordinary executive departments is to-day inevitable. Be the machinery of our courts never so admirable, it works slowly, and it works expensively. Moreover, its whole structure is adjusted to the defence of property and the repulsion of attacks upon or injuries to property. We do not blame the law—we only state its limitations—when we say that it tends to the conservation of vested rights. Now issues may arise which cannot properly be brought under the notion of property—issues in which persons, and the life and health of persons, are the vital concern. Can an unhealthy tenement be demolished ? The law can only answer the question in terms of property : the Local Government Board can and must entertain considerations of persons and of general social policy for the betterment of persons. Efficient administration of Housing Acts demands judicial condemnation of improper houses by those who administer such Acts. They may not desire such judicial powers : one hears from their own lips that their instinct is to shrink from such a new responsibility. But the powers are inevitable ; the responsibility is unavoidable. On the one hand there is absolute need for the expert. Questions of housing, knotty points of insurance, problems of educational policy arise, on which the judges have not the knowledge or the point of view which will enable them to give a real solution. Here the accumulated experience of the executive official is a necessary and indispensable guide. On the other hand, there is an equally absolute need for a process which is expeditious and inexpensive. Here we have to face the fact that the ordinary process of the Courts is neither. We have also to recognize that there is a demand for a sort of social justice administered by officials responsible to the general will of the country and alive to the new developments of social conscience

[1] Schuster, *Eugenics*, pp. 244, 247.

and the new needs of social policy.   The social problems
of the sixteenth century demanded the Star Chamber of the
sixteenth century, whatever its tyrannies and whatever its
unpopularity may have been in the seventeenth century ;
and it may be urged that the social problems of the twentieth
century have also to find their Court of solution.

BEFORE we can come to any decision on the issue we
must look at the facts themselves.   A number of departments have during this century been vested with a power of
giving judicial decisions without any appeal to the ordinary
Courts.   The Board of Education is a striking instance.   The
most obvious example of its judicial powers is that which was
conferred by the Education Act of 1902.   Under Section 7
of that Act the Board of Education has authority to decide
contentions between the local education authority and the
managers of non-provided schools, in so far as they concern
the maintenance and the efficiency of those schools.   Under
this section arose the Swansea case.   The local education
authority of the borough of Swansea had increased the
wages of the teachers of provided schools, but of provided
schools only.   The managers of a non-provided school
complained to the Board of Education that the local education authority had thereby failed to maintain non-provided schools in the state of efficiency contemplated and
commanded by the Act.   The Board of Education sent
down a barrister (Mr. J. A. Hamilton [1]) to hold a local inquiry.   He found that the non-provided school had earned
its grant, and was *pro tanto* efficient, but only because
its managers had supplemented the salaries of its teachers
from their own pockets.   The local education authority
had therefore failed to comply with the Act.   The Board
of Education, however, decided, in spite of his finding,
that there had been no such failure, on the grounds (1) that
there was no statutory right of the managers of any particular school to receive for their teachers any particular
scale of salaries, and (2) that it had not been shown that

[1] Afterwards created Viscount Sumner.

the moneys provided by the local education authority were inadequate to maintain the school in a state of efficiency. The issue was carried to the Courts, and the Courts took cognizance of the issue, in spite of the fact that the Board had a final power of decision, on the ground that it had acted *ultra vires* and beyond the limits of the Act. The issue was decided against the Board : it was held (1) that the decision of the Board was based on disregard of the duties imposed on the local education authority by Act of Parliament, and was therefore without jurisdiction ; and (2) that the Board, in deciding that it had not been shown that teachers could not be obtained at a lower rate of salary, had not decided the real issue. Moreover, it was held that the findings of fact on which the decision of the Board was based were not judicially made ; in other words, that the Board had decided a judicial issue without judicial process. The whole case seems to afford the strongest argument against the use of judicial powers by executive departments. It suggests, in the first place, that such departments may be liable to the animus of party—for the Board of Education apparently obeyed the animus of a party against denominational schools—and, in the second place, that the officials of these departments are apt to decide judicial issues without proper judicial procedure. Here, if anywhere, we see the danger of setting persons who may possibly be prejudiced, and possibly unskilled, to do the grave work of the law.

But there are still other dangers. There is no record of the decision of the Board of Education, and there is no stability about its decision. The decision is promulgated as an *ipse dixit* of the Board, without any statement of grounds ; if the grounds were stated in the Swansea case, it was only because the Board had been brought into Court. Nor can there be any stability. The Board which under the influence of one party chief decides one way may under the influence of another party chief decide another way *in pari materia*. If the President of the Board desires a stable decision which will outlast his own administration

he has to go to the Courts.   There are cases which might
have been settled by the Board under Section 7 of the Act
of 1902, and which have nevertheless been carried to the
Courts ; and the reason would seem to be a desire for
greater stability than the Board can give.   The same
instability may arise in another way.   Any decision of an
executive department, though *ex hypothesi* final, will be
challenged and taken to the Courts by an aggrieved and
litigious person (and in this country we may always count
on an abundance of such persons) if he, or rather his counsel,
can possibly detect a loop-hole.   Counsel may find such
detection possible ; and the Courts, to which the issue is
thus carried, will have a natural bias in favour of entertaining the issue, because they are at once inclined to
magnify their office and likely to feel a professional jealousy
of any claim of the executive departments to a jurisdiction
which ousts their own.   Departmental decisions are thus
auf Kündigung ; they are liable, as it were, to a month's
notice.

There are other judicial activities of the Board of Education.   It has taken over from Chancery and the Charity
Commissioners powers of interpreting and making new
schemes for educational trusts.   Again, it has to decide
disputes which arise under its own regulations.   For
instance, a school may not refuse a pupil except on reason-
able cause.   A head mistress dismisses a girl because she
insists on wearing a ring, and because the rules of the school
forbid the wearing of jewellery.   The girl, however, is
engaged, and wishes to wear her engagement ring.   Here is
an issue which the Board of Education has to decide.
Indeed, the tendency of teachers is to erect the Board into
a universal judge, and to make it, for instance, a court of
appeal in cases of dismissal ; but the policy of the Board
is always to refuse to take cognizance.

It would take us too far afield if we attempted to sketch
the judicial activity of the Ministry of Health, for instance
in matters of housing, or that of the Board of Trade, for
example in matters of shipping.   But there are some

features in the system of National Insurance, in the form in which it was originally introduced, which deserve our attention. If what has been said of the judicial activities of the Board of Education may dispose us to be critical of the justice done by executive departments, the system of National Insurance may perhaps bring into relief another side of the matter.

The National Insurance Commissioners, under the Insurance Act of 1911, are vested with large judicial powers. We must here distinguish between health insurance and unemployment insurance. Under the former head the Commissioners themselves (1) act as a Court of first instance, in deciding (a) whether any employment is such as to constitute an employed contributor, and (b) what the rate of contribution shall be ; and (2) act as a Court of appeal in deciding (a) disputes raised by or with approved societies, and (b) disputes raised by or with insurance committees. There is only an appeal to the law Courts under (1)(a). In any question, that is to say, turning on the definition of an employed contributor—or, in other words, in any question of liability to the *onus* of insurance —there is an appeal to the County Court, with further appeal to a judge of High Court appointed by the Lord Chancellor ; and it is further possible for the Commissioners to take such a question themselves to the High Court in the first instance, without giving any decision of their own. The Commissioners, therefore, have the grave power of deciding whether I shall or shall not come under the operation of the Insurance Act, and whether I shall or shall not pay contributions accordingly ; but I have an appeal to the ordinary Courts of the land, which, however, if I am a poor man, as *ex hypothesi* I am—for otherwise there can be no question of contribution—will not be very valuable.

Referees may be used in questions of health insurance, to act as a Court of appeal, in lieu of the Commissioners, in questions of disputes raised by or with approved societies or insurance committees. In questions of unemployment insurance, referees, and not only referees but an umpire, are regularly used. Claims for benefit are settled by an administrative officer ; but a dissatisfied claimant may require the officer to report the claim to a Court of referees. The officer must give effect to the recommendations of this Court ; but he may, if he disagrees, appeal for a final and conclusive decision to the umpire. This procedure holds good not only for claims for benefit, but for the determination of questions connected with such claims. The Court of referees, it should be explained, consists of an equal number of employers and workmen, chosen from panels constituted by the Board of Trade, with a chairman appointed by the Board of Trade : the umpire is appointed by the Crown. The system of referees and umpire is exceedingly interesting ; it is a model likely to be imitated in other spheres. The local referees, who are paid for their services by the Board of Trade, bring a wealth of amateur local experience to their judicial work : the umpire, who is the final judge, is a permanent expert whose time is entirely devoted to these judicial issues. One is reminded of some features of Prussian *Verwaltungsrecht*, where, in the lower ranges, local and elected citizens give the decision, and where, in the higher ranges, there are permanent judges appointed and assigned for the decision of administrative issues. Under the system of unemployment insurance, as under the Prussian system of *Verwaltungsrecht*, the decision of administrative issues depends, in the lower ranges, on a body of ordinary citizens, and in the higher ranges on judicial officers (not indeed judges proper, but none the less judicial officers) specialized and detailed for the purpose of administrative justice. The umpire is not an executive official, nor a nominee of executive officials. He is a quasi-judge, appointed, like a judge, by the Crown. We shall probably be right in detecting in the umpire the model which might be followed in dealing with judicial questions arising in the course of administrative policy. The ordinary judges, we have seen, will hardly serve our purpose : there are objections, we have also seen, to the allocation of judicial functions to the ordinary departments of administration. This quasi-judge, who stands between both —who has the independence of the judge, and the close contact with actual problems of the administrator—is perhaps the solution of our difficulty.

THESE are the facts ; what is their bearing ? They seem to look both ways. On the one hand, we may condemn the justice administered by executive departments or commissions. We may charge them with three grave faults—a lack of proper judicial procedure ; a lack of impartiality and of due detachment from the prejudice of party ; a lack of any conservative or stable tradition. They may find verdicts without due hearing of evidence according to proper rules ; they may administer not the dispassionate law of the impartial State, but the biased policy of a prejudiced party ; and whatever they do, the works of their hands may not be established, partly because a new administration with a fresh prejudice may inaugurate a new set of decisions, partly because a litigious citizen may succeed in invoking the ordinary Courts to upset old decisions on a nice point of law. On the other hand, we may feel compelled to endorse the new development of ' administrative law ' as something inevitable. We may charge the ordinary Courts with faults, or rather with limitations. They start from a postulate of property, and they arrive at a defence of vested interests : they will deal with a covenant between landlord and tenant when it has been broken—they cannot vary it when it has become impossible. This is a limitation inherent in law, and not an aberration of law. But law has its aberrations. It is slow ; it is expensive ; it is painfully public. Judges as well as officials may be unskilled ; and indeed, in many matters where officials have necessarily much knowledge, the judges have probably little. Courts may be as much prejudiced as departments. There are juries as well as judges ; and even if the judge is free from prejudice in favour of economic doctrines current in his youth (and not all judges are), the jury is very likely to be obsessed by the *idola fori*—by the limitations of a ' business ' outlook on life. Nor is the case in favour of ' settling the matter out of Court ' altogether negative. The executive policy of a government, when it runs into the particularities of insurance or housing, raises judicial issues which can only be settled in the light of that executive policy, and by those who are familiar with the whole set of facts to which it is addressed. If the government is to be forced to go to the Courts whenever such a judicial issue is raised, it is really being forced to abdicate. Policy is being confused with law, and matter of administration is being made matter of jurisdiction.

On the whole, our motto may well be *Spartam nactus es, hanc exorna*. We have here a new and necessary development : we must adorn this development by such safeguards and methods of improvement as we can devise. There are several methods of adornment. In the first place, there is needed a clearer distinction between matter of law and matter of policy. The new development has grown in a haphazard way to meet the needs of the hour, and it has not grown very logically. We may have judges deciding a matter of policy for the Board of Trade ; we may have the Board of Trade deciding a matter of law for the judges. These anomalies, the natural results of an unforeseen and uncontrolled development, have to be removed. In the second place, the institution of the referee, and still more that of the umpire, deserve consideration and probably extension. If there is something to be said against the assumption of judicial functions by the executive officials of departments, there is little if anything to be said against the discharge of such functions by quasi-judicial officials to whose decision the executive officials can refer contentious matters which they prefer not to decide themselves, which it is better that they should not decide themselves, but which cannot be properly decided in the specifically legal atmosphere of the ordinary Courts. We may perhaps look forward to a day when the Local Govern-

ment Board will have its umpire ; when the Board of
Education will have its umpire ; when, in fine, each executive department concerned in social policy will have its
administrative judge or judges.

Such an institution would meet, and meet fully, the
charge of want of skill which may be levelled against ' lay '
justice. What will meet the other charges of want of
stability and want of impartiality ? Both charges might
perhaps be met to some extent, if the practice were introduced of giving the grounds of decision, and if a formal
and considered judgment were pronounced, at any rate
on important points.   Prejudice might be banished by such
publicity ; stability might be secured, if such judgments
could be cited as precedents *in pari materia*.   But there
are grave objections to such a course. It is a safe departmental maxim that you should never state your grounds.
If you come out into the open you are only inviting trouble.
Again, precedents are of little value, and may be a great
disadvantage, in matters of administration. One wants
elasticity and adaptability ; one needs to escape from,
rather than to come under, the binding obligation of precedent.   All the arguments for extra-judicial justice would
disappear if we made it purely judicial.   There is a further
and still more vital consideration. The administration
must always be subject to parliamentary responsibility.
That is a fixed and final principle of our constitution.   But
an independent system of administrative jurisprudence
proceeding on the basis of precedent would tend to escape
from parliamentary control. The series of *res judicatae*
would become its own standard ; and the control of Parliament would be defeated by the appeal to the custom of the
administration.

But if the parliamentary responsibility of executive
departments makes it difficult for them, in the course of
their judicial activities and decisions, to deposit a uniform
and binding body of administrative case-law, it does not
in any way militate against the idea of some judicial review
of those activities by a body other than Parliament, or of

some appeal against those decisions to a court of a judicial character acting on judicial considerations. On the contrary, the parliamentary responsibility of executive departments is the very reason why there should exist some such system of review and appeal. The judges of the ordinary law are independent of Parliament and its parties and its currents. They judge without fear or favour, whatever the complexion or the tone of the House of Commons. Any form of judicature which is responsible to Parliament is amenable to parliamentary pressure. The Board of Education would have decided otherwise in the Swansea case if there had been a different party majority in the House of Commons. We cannot, therefore, comfort ourselves by thinking that responsibility to Parliament is a sufficient guarantee against any abuse of extra-judicial jurisdiction. On the contrary, we have to confess that an appeal from an administrative department which may possibly be deflected by party considerations to a Parliament which is certainly organized on party lines is an appeal from prejudice to prejudice— we may almost say, from a less to a greater prejudice. Yet we cannot but feel that there should be some method of effective appeal. The decisions of administrative officials, or of their referees and umpires, ought not to be always final. An appeal to the ordinary Courts is *ex hypothesi* impossible as a general rule ; for if the limitations of those Courts make some other procedure necessary in the first instance, the same limitations equally preclude an appeal from that other procedure to those Courts. But is it foolish to suggest a sort of *Oberverwaltungsgericht* for England ? Should we lose, and might we not gain, if it were the rule that wherever referees or umpires stated a case the case might be carried to a final Court of State ? In the seventeenth century Chancery seemed likely to develop into such a Court : Bacon argued in favour of such a development ; and ' the fact that it was a Court of Equity would have enabled it to make exactly that judicious mixture of law and discretion by which an administrative **Court can in certain cases reconcile justice to individuals**

with the public necessity.' [1] The common law was too
strong for Lord Bacon ; and the development of Chancery
in the eighteenth century has made it impossible for it
to play such a part to-day. But we can conceive that
the Judicial Committee of the Privy Council might serve
such a purpose ; and the suggestion that this Committee,
or some similar committee, should become a final Court
of State is perhaps worthy of consideration. A Committee of Privy Council which contained judges and expert
officials might do real service in this direction. It would
be free from any particular departmental bias, and it would
correct such a bias. As a permanent Court, lifted above
the play of parties, it might correct the ardour of prejudice.
Above all, it might bring stability into the system of administrative decisions. At any rate, as a final court of
interpretation, it might help to prevent the variation of
decisions from one administration to another.

Whatever its effect, the intention of this argument is
directed not against, but towards, the rule of law. Any
such system as is here advocated does not exclude the
ordinary Courts. It does not exclude, in the first place,
concurrent jurisdiction of the ordinary Courts and of
administrative judges in any issue which raises at once
matter of policy and matter of private right, as many issues
may ; it does not exclude, in the second place, appeal
from the administrative judge to the ordinary Courts in
any issue in which, as in the Swansea case, matter of general
law arises out of a matter of policy. Not only so, but the
system here advocated would in one sense extend the sphere
of the rule of law. It would tend to make such administrative law as we have no longer, as it has hitherto been, a
matter of routine, and of unstable routine, administered
haphazard and with no little shadow of turning, but a
matter of stable law, administered in a legal way by men
of a legal character, and subject to the review of a higher
Court which would make for the stability and permanence
of the whole system. And after all, the transmutation of

[1] Harrison Moore, *Act of State in English Law*, p. 31.

administrative routine into administrative law is surely an extension of the rule of law.

TWO considerations suggest themselves in conclusion. The first is this. *Sans le savoir* (he will not add *sans le vouloir*), the writer finds, at the end of his discourse, that he has been advocating something like the Prussian system of administrative law. Professor Dicey set the fashion against administrative law ; but he was concerned with the French rather than the Prussian system, and his interpretation even of the French system altered as he observed what he called its growing 'judicialization.' [1] At any rate two things may be said on behalf of administrative law as it exists in Prussia. In the first place, it is not administered by executive officials, but by administrative judges. In the second place, it does not exclude, but it coexists with, the system and rules of the ordinary Courts ; and the bias, so far as there is any bias, is in favour of these Courts. The State, under the name of the Fisc, can be sued in the ordinary Courts. The administrative Courts and the ordinary Courts may have concurrent jurisdiction in the same issue from their different points of view. The administrative Courts often use the ordinary civil law ; and the supreme civil Court (*Reichsgericht*), which has the interpretation of civil law, has known how to maintain its sphere and assert its scope. If we in England should recognize the liability of the State ; if we should extend the system of administrative judges already adumbrated in our referees and umpires ; if we should institute a final Court of State—we should not be sailing an unexplored or uncharted sea.

One final consideration. We have spoken of the State as a person when we were discussing its liabilities as a party to litigation. The same conception may be of service

---

[1] A year after this article was originally published there appeared the eighth edition of Dicey's *Law of the Constitution*, with a new Introduction. I would refer the reader particularly to Section B of the Introduction (on the Rule of Law), and more especially to pp. xliii–xlviii.

when we think of the State as a judge. The idea of the
State is one which is little grasped in England. We think
of a bundle of officials when we use the term ; at most
we rise to the conception of the ' Government,' and even
by that we only understand a partisan body of leaders.
It is the penalty we pay for our individualism and our party
government. At our best we may concede, like the Duke
of Wellington, that the King's government must go on ;
but even here we do not get to the State, but to a personification of the State. If we could only realize the State
as a person, and look at our officials as the agents of that
person (a conception, for obvious reasons, very much easier
for a German than for an Englishman), we might fare
better. The National Insurance Commissioners are not,
after all, a set of party whipper-snappers, to be abominated
by all good men of the opposite party : they are not even,
in any real sense, servants of a mysterious Crown. They
are the agents of this commonwealth of England. ' His
Majesty's Judges ' are also agents of this commonwealth,
this ' Public,' this State—call it what you will. Even
without the prefix Re, and whether or no we desire that
it should be added, the Public of England is the Sovereign
of England. The Government is its agent ; departments, referees, umpires, as well as judges, are its agents.
Our loyalty to the Public demands our recognition of its
agents. The Government is the accredited representative of a great power ; why spend one's days in examining
and disputing its credentials ? Departments, referees,
umpires are representatives, just as the judges are representatives. And who shall say Nay to those whom the
Public has duly, and by process of law, accredited as
its representatives ?

VIII

THE STUDY OF POLITICAL SCIENCE [1]

I

A PRELIMINARY modesty becomes a new professor; and a deprecatory preface to his inaugural discourse is not only a decency, but also a debt, when the new professor is sitting uneasily in a new chair to expound a subject which, he well knows, many of his hearers will regard as certainly nebulous, probably dubious, and possibly disputatious. Happy is the Cambridge man, with history bred in his very bones, who returns to Cambridge, after years of devotion and service, to declare the ascertained mysteries of the muse Clio; [2] but unhappy, thrice unhappy, is the Oxford man, who comes to Cambridge for the first time, dripping from seven years of immersion in the bewildering complications of the University of London, to profess an uncertain subject about which he has already forgotten more than he ever knew. To come to Cambridge—the home of exact knowledge, where men walk on the razor's edge of acute analysis—and to come, with such an equipment, for the exposition of such a subject, is a bold and desperate thing. I can only promise, as I do with a genuine sincerity, to attempt to ascertain the nature of my subject : to seek to discover the facts, if such there be, which form its basis ; and to try to analyse, as best I can, their significance and implications. And I may perhaps be allowed to

[1] An Inaugural Lecture delivered in the University of Cambridge in 1928.
[2] Professor G. M. Trevelyan, who had only the term before delivered his Inaugural Lecture as Regius Professor of Modern History.

13

take some measure of comfort from the reflection that such experience of affairs as I have had in London during the last seven years may give to my lectures that tang of reality which my subject especially needs. No philosophy of human life can live by books alone ; and political philosophy, no less than other forms, must study the busy hum of affairs in the cave before it can move into the upper light of contemplation.

You will not expect me, after what I have said in my preface, to begin the body of my discourse by any precise definition of my subject. It is a subject which has come to be known in this place by the name of Political Science. I am not altogether happy about the term ' Science.' It has been vindicated so largely, and almost exclusively, for the exact and experimental study of natural phenomena, that its application to politics may convey suggestions, and excite anticipations, which cannot be justified. If I am to use the designation of Political Science, I shall use it, as Aristotle used πολιτικὴ ἐπιστήμη, to signify a method, or form of inquiry, concerned with the moral phenomena of human behaviour in political societies. I should prefer to call such a method or form of inquiry by the name of Political Theory, because I should hope, by the use of that name, to avoid the appearance of any excessive claim to exactitude, and I should be indicating more precisely the nature of the inquiry, as simply a ' speculation ' (θεωρία) about a group of facts in the field of political action, a speculation intended to result in a general scheme which connects the facts systematically with one another and thus gives an explanation of their significance. If that name be adopted, a respectable and honourable antiquity may readily be vindicated for the subject I have to profess. It was studied by Aristotle : it was expounded by St Thomas Aquinas : it was discussed by the venerable Paley, a light of this University, in his *Principles of Moral and Political Philosophy* ; and it has been treated continuously, during the last seventy years, by a succession of distinguished men in both of the older Universities.

IN the cultivation of political theory as a subject of University study Oxford has perhaps been more systematic, if less many-sided, than Cambridge. The Oxford school of Literae Humaniores, the glory of my old University, has produced what itself may almost be called a school of thinkers (for Oxford naturally runs to ' schools ' and ' movements ' of thought) in T. H. Green and F. H. Bradley and Bernard Bosanquet. Nurtured on a double inspiration, the ancient oracles of Greek philosophy and the modern mysteries of German idealism—blending Plato with Hegel, and Aristotle with Kant—these Oxford thinkers have advanced to the creation of original philosophies on the principles of political obligation, the duties of social station, and the general theory of the State. Their influence on generations of Oxford men has been profound ; some who have sat at the feet of their political wisdom have in after days been called to handle the political destinies of their country ; and they have shown that they had not forgotten the lessons which they once learned.

Cambridge, always more individualistic, has never produced a single dominant mode or prevalent body of opinion in the field of political theory. But Cambridge has none the less been the nursing-mother of a rich and various speculation. Now it has fostered a philosopher, and now an historian—now a lawyer, and now a churchman—who has turned to the study of politics and made, from his own particular angle, some new and vigorous contribution to its development. There is the honoured name of Henry Sidgwick, a philosopher who took both politics and economics for his province, and who, steeped in the teaching of John Stuart Mill, expounded with a rigorous integrity, and a scrupulous analysis, the purely English tradition which makes the utility of individuals the canon of all institutions and the criterion of every policy. There is Sir John Seeley, Regius Professor of Modern History, one of the earliest discoverers of the existence of the British Empire, a scholar of masculine vigour and a robust realism, who regarded political science as the fruit on the branches of history, and, drawing his principles of politics from a study of the modern working of the English constitution, turned the attention of Cambridge scholars towards that study of political institutions which has continued to be endemic.   There is Lord Acton, Seeley's successor, *clarum et venerabile nomen*, a profound and pregnant thinker on all European affairs ' as well civil as ecclesiastical,' who cherished a delicate and fastidious love of liberty, believing that the independence of the Church in the State had been, and should continue to be, its bulwark, and dreading those nationalist enthusiasms which seek to make a national State into a destructive tyrant ' crushing all natural rights and all established liberties for the purpose of vindicating itself.'   No influence has been more profound in this place than that of Acton ; and I would commemorate among those who felt and propagated that influence the name of Neville Figgis, whom I was proud to call a friend ; who adorned with incisive wit and industrious scholarship all the themes of political theory which he touched ; who loved and prophesied the cause of liberty, both political and religious (I shall never forget his taking me round the garden of the house of the community in which he lived at Mirfield, and suddenly exclaiming, ' Barker, I really believe I'm a syndicalist ') ; and who, if he had lived, would have been an occupant as proud as he would have been worthy of the chair to which, in his stead, I am called.   I cannot but glow as I think of his memory.   Admiration and affection were his due ; and he had his due from many.   And there is another name which comes last, but is very far from being the least—a name which also kindles a glow in the minds of those who have heard his voice and fed on his thought—the name of one who was worthy, in his field, to be counted by the side of Acton, and who, along with Acton, filled the mind and determined the thought of Figgis —the name of Maitland. I can cite no greater name.   I can only record the measure of the debt which I owe to the man who wrote, in his own inimitable style, the opening chapters of the *History of English Law*, the introduction to *Political Theories of the*

Middle Age, and the essays which deal with or touch on the problems of politics in the three volumes of his *Collected Papers*. How massive was the monument which he erected ; how stately and delicate was the style of its architecture ; and how far-reaching has been the influence which his teaching, and in particular his teaching about the character of associations and the nature of their personality, has exerted.

I cannot but reflect, as I think of the writings of these Cambridge scholars, how many of them were vowed to the cause of liberty. If Oxford, with its strong corporate sense, about the origin of which I have often wondered, has professed the cause of the body politic, Cambridge, once the apostle of Protestantism and always the apostle of freedom, has followed the banner of individual autonomy. It is the banner which claims my allegiance ; and I am proud and comforted to think of the great men who formed the tradition which I shall follow. The chair of Political Science is a new chair ; but behind it stretches a line of solemn and majestic shadows. There is Sidgwick, with his scrupulous regard for the canon of individual liberty : there is Acton, for whom history was above all the history of freedom : there is Maitland, whose dissertation for his fellowship at Trinity was ' a historical sketch of liberty and equality as ideals of English political philosophy,' and whose theory of associations has nerved both defenders of the liberties of Trade Unions and champions of the rights of churches in the modern State. Thinking of these things, and seeing behind me these great figures, I may say of my efforts, as with infinitely less reason Ranke said of his in his inaugural lecture, *Non attingunt metam, sed meta posita est.*

II

AMONG the precursors whose names I have mentioned there were at least four—Seeley and Acton, Figgis and Maitland—who had devoted themselves to the study of history ; and Sidgwick himself, philosopher as he was, had

198 CHURCH, STATE, AND STUDY

studied the development of European polity. There is an obvious affinity between history and political theory ; and it may well be a way to the better understanding of the nature of political theory if I turn to consider how far it proceeds on the ground of history, and how far it takes wing and transcends the bounds of historical study. Herodotus, the most garrulous and lovable of story-tellers, could not tell the story of the Persian wars without passing into political reflections ; and in his third book he makes a number of Persian grandees, after compassing the death of the false Smerdis, proceed straight from assassination to a calm discussion of the inherent merits, and the inevitable defects, of monarchy, aristocracy, and democracy. The austere Thucydides mingles a pithy and astringent phil- osophy with his severe narrative of the Peloponnesian war ; and alike in the Melian Dialogue, the funeral speech of Pericles, and the passage on sedition in his third book, he gravely attempts *rerum cognoscere causas*. As the historians of Greece became philosophers, so the philosophers became, if not historians, at any rate students of history. Plato himself, idealist as he was, and however cavalier he might generally be in his treatment of history, attempts a review of the lessons of the past, in the third book of the *Laws*, before he proceeds to build an ideal State. The *Politics* of Aristotle is built on the solid foundations of Greek experi- ence ; and its political theory was compacted and cor- roborated from a study of 158 constitutions, of which we possess an example in the treatise on the Constitution of Athens. The practice of the Greeks may seem to confirm the theory which Seeley expressed in a well-known jingle, ' History without Political Science has no fruit : Political Science without History has no root.' And if this be so, history will be but philosophy—political philosophy— teaching by examples ; and political philosophy in turn will be simply history precipitated in a patterned shape of generalities.

But I take leave to doubt whether Professor Trevelyan should be termed a root, and, still more, whether I deserve the appellation of fruit.   History and political theory march together for all the length of their frontiers ; but they are separate and independent studies.   Let us assume, for the purpose of argument, the truth of Croce's proposition that ' every true history is contemporary history '—that it is a history of the present regarded as containing the past, or, if you will, of the past regarded as constituting the present. Let us further assume the truth of another saying of Croce, that ' dead history revives, and past history again becomes present, as the development of life demands them,' or, in other words, that in a given present some element of a distant past, acquiring a new vitality from a new congruity ·with the life of that present, may become once more a creative force, as the Greek past did at the Renaissance. On these assumptions we may proceed to admit that there is much political theory which has been bred partly from the stimulus of present experience, but partly also from the study and stimulus of some congruous past which has become alive and present from its congruity with present experience.   The political theory of Rousseau, for example, was born of Rousseau's experience of the Republic of Geneva and of his study of the parallel city-states of the Greek past in the biographies of Plutarch and the dialogues of Plato.   The political theory of the Whigs in the seventeenth century sprang equally from a mixture of contemporary political experience and the study of precedents and analogies in a congruous past—particularly, perhaps, the reign of Richard II, which was affected by the Whigs for its records of constitutional opposition and its example of a king's deposition.   But while we may readily admit the debt of such political theory to the study of history, we must equally admit the possibility of a great and influential theory of politics which has no definite basis in history.   It may be the method of a political thinker to assume as his axiom certain views about the nature of the human mind and the end of human life, and to deduce a systematic theory from those views.   This was the method of Spinoza ; it was the method of Plato when he wrote the

Republic ; and it is fundamentally the method of Aristotle, who—however historical, and even empirical, he may appear—was none the less purely philosophical in his explanation of the existence, his conception of the purposes, and his derivation of the institutions, of the true or normal State.   In this way, and in this sense, history and political theory may be independent, if conterminous, powers.   You may have a political theory which is a good theory without being rooted in historical study, just as you may have history which is fine history without issuing in any fruit of political science.   For to relate what actually occurred, *wie es eigentlich gewesen ist*, is a task worthy of the greatest historian ; and he who tells some noble and stirring story in noble and stirring prose may mix true art with genuine history and carry every vote.

NOT only is political theory a study which is, or may be, independent of the study of history.   We may go further, and say that it is a study which loses its true nature, and puts its neck unnecessarily under the yoke of happening and the routine of historic sequence, if it occupies itself largely with problems of history.   It is concerned with questions of being rather than with those of becoming : it has to discuss what the State is *semper et ubique*, rather than what it was at this time or in that place, or how it developed from one form into another.   It is true that John Stuart Mill once wrote that the fundamental problem of all social speculation was ' to find the laws according to which any state of society produces the state which succeeds it.'   He was following Comte and the Positivist theory of successive stages in a superseding process of development, by which, for example, the industrial regime ejects the military as ' positive ' thought ousts ' metaphysical.'   But to anatomize the history of society and thought into separate sections divided by deep abysses—as if it were a desert of Arizona traversed and split by great cañons—is to forget the continuous eternities both of society and of thought. There are questions of political theory which are the same yesterday, to-day, and for ever. Why does the State exist ? What are the purposes for which it exists ? What are the best and most congruous means for their realization ? These are its fundamental problems ; and it is thus concerned less with historic processes (however generally and even abstractly they may be conceived) than with the fundamental realities—essence, purpose, and value—which transcend the category of time. We must admit, indeed, that the state exists in time, and may vary in form, if not in substance, from age to age. We must equally admit that political speculation has often dressed itself in historical language, and that the theory of the Social Contract, for instance, has sometimes been expressed in terms which suggest an historical account of the actual genesis of the State. But even the theory of the Social Contract is, at bottom, a philosophical theory rather than an historical narrative. It is an attempt to explain, not the chronological antecedents, but the logical presuppositions, of the State—to show, not how it came to be, but on what assumptions we can explain its being. Hobbes himself, after an account of the state of nature which imposes the necessity of a social contract, remarks ' It may peradventure be thought that there never was such a time . . . and I believe it was never generally so . . . howsoever it may be perceived what manner of life *there would be,* where there were no common power to fear.' In a word, the whole theory is a matter of an hypothesis, or assumption, on which the existence of the State and its government can be explained ; and it does not profess or claim historical validity. There is a profound remark of Hobbes which may serve as the conclusion of the whole matter. Philosophy ' excludes history as well natural as political, though most useful—nay necessary—to philosophy ; because such knowledge is but experience, and not ratiocination.'

' Most useful—nay, necessary.' Nurtured as I have been in history, I should be the last to decry its utility, and, indeed, its necessity, for the purposes of my subject. Any true philosophy must be one which has been immersed in experience—and yet has escaped the peril of submersion in its wide and brimming flood. A philosophy of politics must especially be immersed in a double experience—that of the past and that of the present. It must be based, in the first place, on a knowledge of what Sidgwick called ' the development of European polity '—a knowledge of Greek democracy, of Roman imperialism, of mediaeval institutions both feudal and ecclesiastical, and of the mingled parliamentarianism and nationalism of modern Europe. It must be founded, in the second place, on a real acquaintance, deeper than can be derived from the study of books alone, with the forms—and not only the forms, but also the spirit and working—of contemporary institutions. The parallel chair in the sister University bears a double designation : it is a chair of political theory and institutions. In this University too the study of political institutions has been cultivated, for many years past, by a number of lecturers ; and one of the papers set in the first part of the Historical Tripos is primarily concerned with ' a comparative survey of Political Institutions and their development, with some reference to the history of Political Theory.' Such study, and such survey, has a natural and obvious fascination. Who is there who cannot read with delight the memorable works of Bryce on *The American Commonwealth* and *Modern Democracies*, or President Lowell's lucid treatises on *Governments and Parties in Continental Europe* and *The Government of England* ? From this point of view I can well understand why the University, even if it has not specifically used the word institutions in the designation of the new chair, has included in the Professor's terms of appointment a generous clause which permits his absence, during one term in every three, in order that he may study abroad the actual working of institutions or the actual development of theory. I have thought how I could best take advantage of this permission, and while I may take some liberty to myself, I am inclined to think that I shall not fly away much, or for long, from the cage in which I am more than content to sit and sing. There are some far flights (I can think of three) which I desire to undertake during my tenure of the chair ; but I believe that I may occasionally desire to spend the academic year in the company of my colleagues. For one thing, my own bias leans towards the side of theory, and it is probably best for me to run with the bias. Other professors will contribute, in time to come, what I have failed to give ; and the subject of the chair is vast enough to permit some measure of selection and specialization. Meanwhile I am happy to think that a number of University lecturers in the field of history are lecturing, and will continue to lecture, on political institutions. I will help whenever I can, and wherever I have fresh knowledge to contribute ; and though it may not be given to me to survey mankind in China and Peru, I will remember that Capetown and Delhi and Washington are not inaccessible, that vacations are sometimes long, and that continental journeys are often short. For the rest, I will cultivate my garden in Cambridge, and I will comfort myself with the austere reflection that though absence might endear me more, presence may make for greater continuity of study and instruction. The uninterrupted movement of a University's life, as I have had some occasion to observe, does not pause for the absence of any Professor ; nor does the business of any other body or society in which he may be interested. And I feel it the duty of a Professor of Political Science to interest himself, as far as he may, in the life and affairs of the community in which he lives. It is difficult, I confess, for a professor to practise what he professes ; but χαλεπὰ τὰ καλά—all good things are difficult.

I SEEM to have diverged from history into an auto-biography of the future ; and I must return from green fields into the dusty road. I have spoken of history and political theory as separate things : let me put them together and treat of the history of political theory—or, as it is often called, the history of political ideas. It is a fascinating subject, just as the history of philosophy is a fascinating

subject. And just as, I imagine, you must know something
of the history of philosophy to be a good philosopher, so
you must certainly know a good deal of the history of
political ideas to be a tolerable political theorist. In
thought, as well as in action, the roots of the present lie
deep in the past ; and Hegel had his foundations in Plato,
as Bosanquet, in his turn, had his foundations in both.
The more the development of political ideas is studied, the
richer will be the development of political theory—provided, I hasten to add, that it is studied as a means and
not as an end, and provided again that it is studied in its
breadth as well as its depth. Let me explain these two
provisos. The first is simple. To study and to understand
previous theories about a subject does not absolve a teacher
from the duty of himself understanding the subject itself.
It is possible, but not perhaps very useful, to know all
political theories without attaining a theory ; and there
may be more wisdom in less knowledge, if it is brought to
a point and used as a tool of original thought. The danger
of some subjects of speculation—I would cite in evidence
literary criticism as well as political theory—is that they
may be choked, as it were, by the history of their own past.
The second proviso which I have made raises larger considerations. When I speak of considering breadth as well
as depth, I mean that besides political theory there is what
I would call political thought, which is as broad and wide
as the general community from which it proceeds, and
which, in any study of political ideas, must be considered
no less than political theory, however deeply such theory
may delve. Political theory is the speculation of individual
minds, self-conscious and analytic ; political thought is the
thought of a whole society, often but dimly conscious of
itself, and yet pervading and shaping political life and
growth. The complex of political ideas which we may call
by the name of political thought is implicit in, and has to
be gathered from, its own actual and historical results—
the development of Athenian democracy, the growth of
the English constitution, the general unfolding of national

ideas and aspirations in modern Europe.   It is embedded
in institutions, from which it must be disengaged ; and it
may even be, as it were, interred in the political vocabulary
of a language, from which it may have to be exhumed, as
Professor Myres has shown in a recent work on *The Political
Ideas of the Greeks*, by a patient study of etymologies and
the nuances of meaning attached to political terms.   Whatever the sources from which it may be discovered, it is a
matter of profound moment ; and no history of political
ideas can be complete which does not reckon with *Staats-
gedanke* as well as with *Staatslehre*.

I HAVE spoken long of history in its relation to political
theory.   If I speak but briefly of a study cognate to history—the study of law—my brevity must be regarded less as
the measure of my respect than as the index of my ignorance.   But I hasten to say how readily I admit that political
theory can never afford to neglect the study of legal ideas,
and how gratefully I recognize the debt which my subject
owes to a succession of great legal thinkers.   Legal ideas
have formed, or contributed to form, the institutions of the
state ; and they are still the bony substance, or supporting
vertebrae, of its subtly compacted organs.   The family is a
legal rather than a natural institution—an institution which
was thought into existence by the primitive lawyers who
made its rules, rather than brought to birth by innate
instincts [1] :   property, too, is a conception of the lawyers ;
and the State itself, in one of its aspects, is a legal framework which lawyers have largely built and whose anatomy
they have discussed in treatises on *Staatsrecht*.   In England,
indeed, with its unwritten constitution and its conception
of the general sovereignty of a single law, there has never
been any separate *Staatsrecht* ; and the study of constitutional law has been part and parcel of the general study
of common law.   But perhaps for that reason, and because
there has been no separate compartment of study, but only
a disengaging of broad constitutional principles from the

---

[1] Eduard Meyer, *Geschichte des Altertums*, I. i. (3rd edition), p. 17.

body of our law, the thought of the lawyers has exercised all the more influence on political ideas and speculation. Blackstone is justly famous ; the name of one of his successors in the Vinerian Chair—that of Dicey—deserves to be had in lasting remembrance ; and I have already celebrated the name of a great occupant of the Downing Chair of the Laws of England in this University, Maitland, who not only showed that the history of English Law was an essential part of the history of English politics and political ideas, but made his exposition, by his style and his genius, a part of English literature. In the more general field of Jurisprudence Cambridge produced Maine, if Maine adorned Oxford ; and Maine, pursuing an historical method of inquiry, made the general history of law at once illustrate and check political theories, whether of the patriarchal origin of society or of the formation of the State by a Social Contract. Nor, outside England, and not to mention other English names, such as that of Austin, can I forget the work on my subject done by the lawyers of the Continent— Bodin, Grotius and Montesquieu, Gierke and Jellinek, Duguit and Esmein. The debt is profound ; and I cannot, even at the risk of egotism, forbear to mention what I owe to the teachers of law in my own old University with whom I have had discussions, or, I had perhaps better say, from whom I have had expositions. I will only add that I hope to be allowed to renew the indebtedness here. Political theory and its teachers must consort not only with history and historians, but also with law and the lawyers.

III

BEFORE I turn from history and the cognate study of law to consider philosophy, I desire to say some few words about psychology, which is, as it were, a half-way house on the road I am travelling. If in the days of Seeley, and in the general tradition of Cambridge, the study of politics has been mainly connected with the study of history ; if again in the days of T. H. Green and his successors,

and in the general tradition of Oxford, it has been connected
with the study of philosophy—in the world outside it has
come more and more to connect itself with the growing study
of psychology.   Political theory would sometimes seem to
be turning itself before our eyes into social psychology.
Theorists of an older type are censured for basing their
theory on a very imperfect observation of the human mind
and the tendencies of human conduct, and the new science
of mental and moral behaviour is promising to supply the
defect.   There is some justice in the censure, and some
actual delivery accompanies the promise ; nor can I be
blind, even if in this matter my eyes are a little held, to
the new substance and new inspiration brought into social
studies by writers such as Tarde, MacDougall, and Graham
Wallas.   But I cannot but say to myself—it may be from
hardness of heart and an obstinate clinging to the gospel
I once received—that psychology is a fashion (I have seen,
in my lifetime, more than one fashion of thought) : that
fashions change ; and that the quiet hodden grey of
philosophy endures.

In its modern form psychology runs into the mould of
natural science.   Like physics, it decomposes its subject-
matter into atoms and electrons which it calls by the name
of instincts.   Like biology, it works from the primitive to
the present ; it explains the present in terms of evolution
from the past ; and it may be led to refer the behaviour
of civilized man to the instincts developed in man's rude
beginnings.   Decomposing the mind into instincts, it may
miss the unity secured to the mind by a pervading and
freely moving reason which ' passeth and goeth through all
things by reason of her pureness,' and makes the mind move
freely as a whole towards its chosen purposes.   Referring
the present to the past, and explaining social behaviour
to-day by primary and primitive instincts, it may forget
any standard of value, and blend the high with the low in
a common continuous substance.   The dignity of man may
suffer, and he may become not a little lower than the angels,
if the study of his mind is treated as the study of so much

mechanism. On the other hand there can be no doubt that the study of psychology in its various forms—and there are very various and divergent forms of the study—has added new substance to political theory. If the study of political institutions and legal principles brings us face to face with what Hegel would call Mind Objective—mind concrete and deposited in a solid and stable fabric—the study of psychology presents us with mind subjective, the subtle spinning of mental processes which forms the living stuff of Society and the State, the play of emotions, sentiments, instincts, and habits, which lies behind and peeps through political and legal systems. Nor does social psychology only add to knowledge : it may also claim to be a practical and applied science. I have been told that its aim is entirely practical ; that it might be described as a sort of social therapeutics ; that just as the doctor studies physical processes with a view to stimulating or inhibiting or modifying those processes, so the social psychologist studies psychical processes with a view to similar control. In a word, he wishes to know how normal man behaves in the presence of a given stimulus in order that he may discover how far you can change his behaviour by changing the stimulus. Perhaps there may be a remedy for the evils of states if psychologists are kings, or kings have the spirit and power of psychology ; and a statesman who has studied psychology may be the better aware both of the difficulties which he has to face in men's instincts and modes of behaviour, and of the methods by which he may overcome those difficulties. But there is a certain danger in that form of applied psychology, not unknown to statesmen, which leads to spell-binding and *réclame* ; and there is also a tendency even in pure students of the subject to let their view of human nature suffer from their observations of the working of the human mind. The political theorists who used psychology even before it existed—and one may perhaps speak in such terms of Machiavelli and Hobbes and Bentham—were apt to think that mankind was a little breed. Greater knowledge has bred greater respect ; but even now the observation of mass-behaviour may lead the psychological student of ' human nature in politics ' to feel —half in sadness, and more than half in kindness—how little real wisdom goes to the government of the world.

THE affinities of psychology, when it is regarded or studied as a branch of natural science, are affinities with biology.   If it be true that psychology has added new content to political theory—and of that, whatever else may be said, there cannot be any doubt—it is also true that biology has laid it under a debt.   It is not only a matter of the theory of evolution, which has influenced all thought in every field, and has turned political theory to the study of social development ;   nor is it a matter merely of the idea of adaptation to environment, which has led some political thinkers to regard a people's political ideas and institutions as a way of life adjusted to suit regional features and needs.   The service which biology can render to political theory goes farther than these things.   What has happened in the past is that biologists have elaborated their own theories in their own field, and that students in other fields have borrowed these theories and applied them to their subject without adequate consideration of their relevance or validity in the study of that subject.   Ideas of struggle for life and survival of the fittest, which have their value in the domain for which they were elaborated, have thus been, as it were, lifted and transported to the alien domain of human society.   It is the natural fate of new and seminal theories that, by being applied too generally —as if they were panaceas or universal ' open sesames '— they should again and again be misapplied ;   but neither Darwin nor Einstein can be blamed for the indiscriminate zeal of those votaries of novelty who find the secret of the universe in each new discovery.   I need not, however, linger over what has happened in the past.   What has now begun to happen in the field of biology, and what is likely to go farther, holds far more promise.   Instead of sustaining a sort of theft, biologists are beginning to lend.   They have

14

turned their attention to 'the biological foundations of society,' if I may quote the title of a work by an old colleague of mine, the late Professor Dendy : they have taken into their province (to quote again, and this time from the title of a lecture by a great Cambridge biologist, Dr. Bateson) the study of the relation between ' biological fact and the structure of society.' The growth of Eugenics—a subject of profound importance for political theory—is an example of the contribution which biology may make when it turns to the study of biological fact in its connexion with social structure ; and that is perhaps only one example of what we may justly expect. Biology has perhaps greater contributions to make to the study of human welfare than any other science. And in this place, celebrated by the names of great biologists, it is fitting for a Professor of Political Science to acknowledge existing debt, to anticipate further obligation, and to promise neither to neglect biological fact in his own inquiries nor to be slow in grasping any chance of co-operation with students of biology in the general field of social investigation.

IV

I COME in conclusion, and I come with a genuine feeling of modest stillness and humility, to the great subject of which I conceive the subject of this chair to be a province, a border-province, if you will, but none the less a province. That subject is philosophy, and especially moral philosophy. As I see it, political theory is primarily concerned with the purpose, or purposes, which man proposes to himself as a moral being, living in association with other moral beings, who at once desires and is forced to pursue his purpose or purposes in the medium of a common life. It is a study of ends, and of the modes of realization of those ends ; and since ends have supreme value, and determine the value of other things which serve as their means, it is a study of value or values. Here it may be said to touch the sister science or theory which is called economics. Economics is also concerned with values ; and if originally it concerned

itself only with money value, it has been led inevitably to
the study of social value and the measurement of the difference between the one and the other. ' This consideration,'
Marshall has remarked, ' will be found to underlie nearly
all the most serious modern economic studies.' Economics
and politics thus run up together into philosophy ; and
moral philosophy (or moral science) is the basis, or apex,
common to both. For such philosophy is a study of ultimate value ; and that is a necessary criterion for those who
pursue the study of social value, whether in the field of
political life and institutions, or in that of economic life and
production.

It is here, and in this conception of political theory as
moral philosophy applied to the life of the whole community, that Plato and Aristotle still remain masters.
Plato combined ethics and politics in a single dialogue
which he entitled, ' polity, or concerning righteousness '—
the dialogue which we call the *Republic.* Aristotle wrote
separate treatises on *Ethics* and *Politics* ; but the one is
related to the other, and both are concerned with the study
of the human good, which is ' the same for the individual
and the state,' though it ' appears a greater and more
perfect thing to have and to hold ' when it is exhibited in
the life of a good community. In the *Elements of Politics*
and the *Principles of Political Obligation* the method of
Henry Sidgwick and T. H. Green is fundamentally similar.
Whatever the difference of their views, both of these thinkers
postulated a conception of the human good, and both of
them attempted to determine, on the basis and by the
criterion of that conception, the system of relations which
ought to be established in a political community. In its
essentials the problem of political theory is a constant. It
has to determine the end, or ultimate value, which governs
and determines the life of political society : it has to discover the appropriate and congruous means by which that
end may be realized, that ultimate value actually enjoyed.
But in one age one aspect of the final good may be emphasized, and in another another ; and the means of realization

also vary, not only with variations in the aspect of the final good selected for emphasis, but also with the variations of the medium—by which I mean the congeries of contemporary institutions, customs, conditions, and problems—in which realization has to be achieved. That is why political theory is always new as well as always old, and why it is constantly changing even while it remains the same.

IS there any aspect of social well-being which particularly needs emphasis to-day, and is there any means for its attainment which offers particular promise and demands particular study ?   If I can answer these questions, I shall have given some clue to the prepossessions with which I start and the lines which I hope to follow.   I will say at once that there is one aspect of social well-being which lies heavily on my mind at the present time.   I assume that the general end of society is the development in each member of a full personality, which on the one hand issues in the individual doing or enjoying of things worth doing or enjoying, and on the other hand flows in the channels of harmonious co-operation with other and like personalities. The human good, in the form in which it is pursued in the state, is the energy of individual moral wills acting for their own appropriate objects in a regular system of organized co-operation.   On the one hand individual energy, on the other social co-operation ; on the one hand free initiative, on the other organization.   The pendulum swings slowly from this side to that in the development of humanity ; and now it may seem to pause here, and now there.   Yet freedom remains a precious thing ; and an individual moral will, even when it has to act in harmony with other and similar wills, must essentially be free if it is to be moral— for free action only is moral.   The cause of liberty was proclaimed by Mill, as it was proclaimed by Milton : it seemed a cause which was accepted : it is a cause which is being threatened.   Its enemies wear no ignoble faces. There is the puritanism of administrative zeal, concerned for the setting in order of a thickly populated and sadly complicated society, full of contacts and conflicts of interest which seem to cry for adjustment. There will always be men who would fain leave the world a tidier place than they found it ; and we cannot readily blame them for a misguided zeal. There is, again, the passion of social enthusiasm, aflame for a creed and consumed by desire for grasping quickly the sorry scheme of things and remoulding it instantly new. Such passion will not readily stay to gain consent, and it may move to its end like a rushing impatient wind, taking ultimate acceptance for granted, and ready to impose a dictatorship until it comes. Liberty is thus threatened alike from the right and the left—at once by the sober administrator and by the ardent reformer. And meanwhile the methods by which men once thought that liberty could be made secure have themselves fallen into discredit. It is not so long ago since democracy was a word of power, and men were ready to suffer for the cause of free parliaments and a free suffrage. To-day the word and the cause are under suspicion ; and there is a feeling abroad that the people, too vast to be moved except in moments of passion, when movement may become a tyrannical frenzy, are a managed multitude which the controllers of the machine can manipulate at their will. We have to face a reaction against the old faith in liberty and popular government ; we have to admit that the political hopes in which men once dressed themselves were sanguine. But the faith and the hopes abide. There is no better way for the management of men than the way of self-management ; and in the long run it is the only possible way. It is true that the burden of self-government is heavy. It makes great demands on the intelligence and the interest of every citizen. But the demands which it makes are its justification. A form of government which elicits and enlists the mental and moral energy of a whole civic body for its working is a good form of government. Yet the justification will only be theoretical unless the energy is really present. And it will only be really present if electorates can develop an instructed and interested public opinion, which is neither tyrannical in its occasional pressure nor apathetic in its general laxity. The formation of such a public opinion is the crux of our politics.

IF liberty is the aspect of social well-being which needs emphasis to-day, and if liberty demands a living body of public opinion for its realization, is there any means for attaining such a body of opinion which offers particular promise and demands particular study ? There is an answer which is painfully obvious, but which, in the hope that the obvious may also be true, I shall none the less venture to give. That answer is ' education.' It is an old saying that we must educate our masters. It is an older saying, repeated again and again in the *Politics* of Aristotle, that the citizen must be educated in the spirit of the constitution under which he lives. That saying, with a new application, and, it may be, with a new depth of interpretation, is one which may well be repeated to-day. The theory of education is essentially a part of political theory. It is not so much a matter of psychology, with which it has been generally connected in the Universities and Training Colleges where it is taught (though I admit that the study of psychology has a value for the theory of education, as it has for political theory in general) : it is rather a matter of social theory—of grasping and comprehending the purposes, the character, and the needs of Society and the State, and of discovering the methods by which the young can best be trained to achieve these purposes, to maintain and even improve that character, and to satisfy those needs. To Plato the State was essentially an educational society, and its activity was first and foremost a training of its members to understand, and understanding to fulfil, the duties of their station in the community. I believe that we shall come to take the same view. A national system of education is a comparatively new thing with us ; and we only see in part the services it can render, and the significance it may assume, in the scheme of our national life. That it may give us the instructed and interested public opinion

which we need for the safety of democracy is only one of
the expectations we may perhaps legitimately form.   It
may also help to form, and even to strengthen, civic character, banishing some of those shadows—the shadow of a
restless instability ; the shadow of a gregarious and imitative
habit—which have been cast upon it by the urbanization
of our life.   It may train men not only to do their work in
the world, but also to use the time of their leisure—that
time which is the growing-time of the spirit ; that time in
which the spirit of man, casting aside its shackles, can
expand and exult in the free play of its faculties, released,
and at the same time realized, in the delight of music and
literature, the joy of thought and discussion.   For to bring
the matter to a clear and simple point, I cannot but believe
that it may well be part of the function of the state, and a
part which ought to be emphasized in political theory, that
it should promote from its own funds, and encourage by
its own institutions, not only education in the narrower
sense in which we habitually use the word, but also (if I
may use a word soiled by some dubious use) that broader
and more general culture which includes, among many other
things, the hearing of good music and the seeing of good
plays.

BUT this is too exciting a theme for the end of a lecture ;
and I must fall into a quiet final cadence.   I know
enthusiasts who would call the theory of education the core
and centre of social theory ; and I am almost persuaded to
be such an enthusiast myself.   I do not wish, in devoting
myself to political theory, to relinquish the interest which
I have more and more come to feel in the matter of education.   I believe, on the contrary, that in virtue of that
very devotion I am likely, and indeed bound, to feel an
even greater interest.   Any scheme, therefore, that may
be launched in this University, either for its fuller participation in the training of teachers, or for its sharing, in
other ways, in the preparation of social workers (and are
we not all such ?) in other fields—any plan intended to

secure, in the noble words of the Bidding Prayer, ' that there may never be wanting a succession of persons duly qualified for the service of God in Church and in State '— must necessarily command the fullest measure of my attention.   Not that I come with any scheme which I wish to press.   μὴ γένοιτο.   I only come with a desire to learn and a wish to help.

IX

HISTORY AND PHILOSOPHY [1]

PLATO spoke of an ancient difference between philosophy and poetry. We may perhaps speak of a certain modern difference between philosophy and history—or at any rate between teachers of history and teachers of philosophy. Every teacher is apt to magnify his own subject, and naturally prone to magnify it most at the expense of the nearest and most closely related of other subjects. When teachers of different subjects are brought closely together—as they are in Oxford common rooms and Cambridge combination rooms—they are driven to take stock of one another ; and the philosopher may rally the historian with a nimble dialectic, while the historian, who has more of the *esprit positif*, will pursue his Parthian foe in the heavy armour of ' facts.' ' You philosophers,' he will say, ' love to theorize about provinces, such as the State, into which you have not travelled and of which you have made no survey. The real stuff is not in you. You are detached from affairs : you say you are spectators of all time and existence, but when it comes to the point, you retire from the dust and heat under the shelter of a wall. It is we historians—students of things that have actually been done or are actually being done— who have an instinct for affairs and a sense of reality : it is we who can bring the lessons of the past to guide the making of the future.' The philosopher, with his ironic modesty, may admit the impeachment ; but he will shoot some rankling arrow. ' Yes,' he will say, ' you historians

[1] Based on an Address delivered before the Historical Association in London, January 1922.

are great travellers and surveyors. You accumulate much
knowledge (or rather memory—for knowledge is a deep
thing) of events and institutions ; but I wonder whether
you ever attempt to think together all this memory, or to
find its significance and plan. It may be that you do ; in
fact, I believe that I have noticed an occasional attempt
here and there. But I doubt if these attempts have carried
you very far. For you assume, whenever you make these
attempts, that historical process is the explanation of
existence, and that the sequence of events preceding any
given thing is the explanation of that thing. Does that
assumption really help you to think things together, or to
find any significance or plan ? '

If I may make a personal confession, I would admit
that these sayings of the philosopher long left me with
an uncomfortable feeling. I remembered (as a teacher of
history I hope I may be forgiven for ' remembering ' rather
than thinking) the dictum of Hobbes, that philosophy ' excludes history as well natural as political, though most
useful (nay, necessary) to philosophy : because such
knowledge is but experience, and not ratiocination.' I
said to myself that any knowledge I had was ' but experience ' ; I admitted to myself that history only dealt with
' How ' and not with ' Why '—that it only explained how
things came to be, and did not and could not explain why
they were or should be. I realized (or thought that I did)
that to know how private property came to exist is not to
know why it should exist, any more than to know that
common property once existed in the dawn of time—if
indeed it did—is to know that it ought to exist in these
latter days. History does not explain values, on which
alone a *raison d'être* can be grounded ; and this is because
values are not due to the growth (or, as I would rather say,
remembering that history is the record of human will and
action, to the *making*) which constitutes the historical
process. Nothing possesses value because it has grown, or
was made long ago, or has been made by a long process :
everything possesses such value as it possesses, in that

field of institutions with which history deals, because it
serves, and to the extent to which it serves, a moral purpose. We are always cheating ourselves into the conviction that continuity of duration or antiquity of origin
is itself a value ; but we must always criticize continuities
and antiquities by a criterion which is beyond time. In a
word, the historian, with all his historical values, must come
before the bar of philosophy. And there—to take one
instance—all the many nationalisms which feed on the
historic method, with their memories of Cuchulain and
Stephen Dushan and other heroes and glories, will be asked
to change their language ; and the question will be, not
' What have you been ? ' but ' What can you do for the
moral betterment of humanity ? '

While I was in this frame of mind, I came across, and
I read, a work by Benedetto Croce on history.[1] The thesis
of this work, if I understand it rightly, is that there is really
no difference between history and philosophy. History *is*
philosophy, and philosophy *is* history. If we are to adopt
such a thesis, and to make such an identification, it would
seem that we must change the connotation of one or both of
the terms which are thus identified. It may be that we
must assign a new sense to the term ' philosophy ' ; but at
any rate it appears necessary that we should give a new
meaning to the term ' history.' If the terms are identical,
an investigation of either should lead to an understanding
of the other. A philosopher would naturally start with
philosophy. Those who have been trained in history may
be forgiven for starting with history.

WHAT then, is history, and with what does it deal ? It
is natural to answer that it is a method of inquiry
which deals with what has happened, exactly as it happened,
or, as Ranke said, ' *wie es eigentlich gewesen ist.*' In other
words, which appear to be words of an obvious truth, it deals
with the past. But does it really deal with the past ?
That is exactly the question.

[1] *The Theory and History of Historiography.* Eng. Trans., Harrap, 1921.

We have to remember, first of all, that much of the past is irretrievably gone and forgotten, and has left no memorial, as though it had never been. This is partly the result of accident ; but it also springs from the wise economy of the human mind, which has forgotten the unessential. And this may remind us that in our modern civilization, with all its apparatus, we are debarred from forgetting. We have paper, the printing press, libraries, archives : we preserve everything : the wise economy of the mind cannot operate ; and trouble is prepared for our descendants. But of the past that is past we can at any rate say that what survives is a part—the part which accident and economy have conspired to leave—and not the whole.

In the next place we have to notice that when we deal with such of the past as still remains, and still is present with us, we select. We select not only in the obvious sense of choosing this particular period, or this particular country, or this particular aspect (economic, or constitutional, or biographical), but also in the further sense of picking this or that part of the record of our period, or country, or aspect, as the substance of our thought and the staple of our exposition. An historian is like an artist—like the painter of a portrait or a landscape : he selects what has significance and interest. Such significance and interest are present in two cases and under two conditions. They are present, in the first place, when the element selected is a root of the present, which survives in the present and is thus contemporary with it. The institutions of our Teutonic ancestors—their villages and their assemblies—are elements of the past which are roots of our present ; and they have a significance and an interest for us accordingly. But significance and interest may also be present when the element selected is an analogue of the present ; when it is spiritually akin to the present ; when it is an inspiration, and, as it were, a spiritual root of the life of the present. The past of republican Rome was such an analogue to the men of the French Revolution : it was something spiritually akin, from which they drew inspiration ; it was a motive force for the time in which they lived—a force surviving and contemporary. And age by age we may similarly see some period of the past flashing into contemporaneity with the present, as the wheel of time revolves, and becoming, in a spiritual sense, which is none the less deep because it is spiritual, a living part of the real present.

It follows that history is, after all, concerned with the past which is present—present either as a root or an inspiration of the present—and that 'past history, if it really is history, that is to say, if it means something and is not an empty echo, is also contemporary.' This view, that all history is contemporary history, depends ultimately upon a conception of philosophy. According to that conception time is the area of the operation of mind or spirit. In each age the spirit is struggling for self-consciousness. In order to attain self-consciousness it must comprehend those elements in its present life which have come from the past. It is the function of history to aid the attainment of self-consciousness by giving a description and by showing the derivation of those elements. If we think of his work of description, we can only say that the historian is describing the 'present' and writing 'contemporary' history. If we think of the elements described, we may say that they existed in the past, or that they are derived from the past; but we must also say that they are still present, because they are forces still operative in the operation of the spirit.

A T this point we may pause to make an observation. The spirit has its phases, which vary from age to age. Its constitution and operation were one thing in the age of the Renaissance; another in the age of Enlightenment, of which Voltaire was the prophet; and still another in the age of Romanticism which followed the French Revolution. On this it follows that the past which was present to the spirit, and was a part of its constitution and operation, in each of these phases, was a past that varied with each phase. The mediaeval past, for example, viewed as a past which was still present, was one thing to the men of the

Renaissance, to whom it was a dark and inimical age of obscurantism, to be overcomè at all hazards : it was another thing to the men of the Enlightenment, who pitied its ' Gothic ' absurdity : it was still another thing to the men of the Romantic movement—an enchanting Age of Faith, with its church-bells still ringing through the centuries to call humanity to its devotions. The past thus varies according to the phase of the spirit in which it is present : it is not a fixed datum, but a Protean thing which can change from shape to shape. This is not to say that its facts, events, happenings, institutions ever alter. It would be a pure absurdity to say anything of the kind. It is only to say that the significance and interest of the past alter from age to age. There is a past which is constant ; and there is also a past which changes. Of the two it is the past which changes—which undergoes re-interpretation—which matters most ; for it is this past which is part of the fibre of the present. And here we touch another paradox. Not only does the past change : it also lives and dies. A past age may sometimes be alive, because it is present and part of the life of the present ; and it may at other times be dead, because it has no significance or interest, and is no part of the constitution of the spirit in its present phase. The Greek past, for instance, lived in the age of the Renaissance ; but it was dead—or very nearly dead—in the early Middle Ages. To-day it is alive and vigorous again. ' If the twentieth century searched through the past for its nearest spiritual kin,' writes a Greek scholar, ' it is in the fifth and following centuries before Christ that they would be found. We are to-day in a position, as no other age has been, to understand Ancient Greece, to learn the lessons it teaches, and, in studying the ideals and fortunes of men with whom we have so much in common, to gain a fuller power of understanding and estimating our own.' These words may lead us to a final paradox. What is nearest to us in thought—what must particularly and primarily be comprehended if we would comprehend ourselves and our own age—may be what is very far from us in time. We are naturally apt to believe that, if we would understand the twentieth century, we must first study the nineteenth ; and we push our pupils—or they push us—into the study of what seems emphatically ' modern ' history. But this is perhaps a short-sighted view. It is Pericles, and not Bismarck, who is really modern, because it is he who is our nearest spiritual kin. It is Greece of the fifth century before Christ, and not Prussia in the nineteenth century of the Christian era, which is present in the spirit of this age as its analogue and inspiration. If we would study contemporary history, we must study the history of classical Greece.

BUT it is time to recur to the argument. That argument, at the point at which we paused, and turned as it were down a side lane, had reached the conclusion that the historian describes the ' present,' and writes ' contemporary ' history. We have now to carry this conclusion further. If history describes the present as containing—and indeed as being— all the past that is still present as a root or an inspiration of contemporary life and thought, then we may say that after all history does give an understanding and an explanation of what we are and where we stand. History which is just the record of a past which is past, and an account of the process of that past couched in the form of a sequence of events, is not an explanation, but only a serial or a journal which has no significance or plan. History which is a description of the present as containing in itself the past— history which is an account of the past as still alive in the present—this may be an explanation, and a mother of understanding. On the former conception of history it would follow that it is a temporal sequence, as of a chain with many links, which produces and makes the present. But this is not the fact. It may only be one link of the chain, and that a link which (in time) is far removed and very early, which produces and constitutes the present. The Greek conception and practice of democracy, for instance, may be the link that is present and helps to make the present ; and the other links of the chain of time may be dropped and ignored by the spirit in its present phase, as things which possess no significance or interest for its operation.

But if history be an explanation, and a mother of understanding : if, as the theory of Croce would suggest, 'its ultimate—which is also its present—import is an account of what we now are and where we now stand ' : if ' its message comes into such an account, distils and sublimates into such a quintessential judgment on the present '—then we may bring the argument to its final conclusion, and we may say that history is philosophy. History makes us spectators of this present time and this contemporary existence, with all the past that they contain : history is the achieved self-consciousness of the spirit in its present phase, viewing itself in all its fulness as containing the past which is part of its present. It was said of old that history is philosophy teaching by examples. If it were that, it would not be philosophy, but a mass of empirical precepts. It is philosophy in the higher sense of a deep and rich understanding of the present—the present seen in all its connexion and contact with its roots and its inspirations in the long far-reaching past. ' When history has been raised to the knowledge of the eternal present,' Croce concludes, ' it reveals itself as one with philosophy, which for its part is never anything else but the thought of the eternal present.'

MANY may demur to this conclusion. There is a history, they will say, which is not philosophy. There is a history which is a story of the past, exactly as it happened ; and the human mind, with its boundless and divine curiosity, will always crave to know the story of what has happened just because it happened, and exactly as it happened. There is a touch of nature which makes us all kin : we think nothing human alien from ourselves : the Incas of Peru or the Aztecs of Mexico—they *were* ; and just because they were, and because they were men, we shall always desire to know their story, and we shall always turn to history for their story. The wardrobe of a mediaeval king :

the panoply of a mediaeval knight : the structure of the *Great Harry* : the rig of a frigate—these, too, were all in the world once upon a time ; and we desire to know what they were.

Yes, we desire to know ; but we have to avoid the *progressus ad infinitum.* There is no end of the things that were ; and there is no end of the stories which might be told about them. But are such stories history ? And is it not wise to have some definite conception of history—what it is and what purpose it serves ? The danger before historians is that they should become story-tellers of the infinite. ' All things are defined—and limited—by the function they discharge and the potentiality they possess.' It may be wise for the historian to acknowledge that his function is to aid each age to the attainment of self-consciousness, and that his potentiality rests in his ability to describe all the roots and the inspirations of the past which go to constitute the living present. He may be well-advised to become the ally of the philosopher ; and in the issue he may be rewarded—and astonished—by finding that he has become a philosopher himself.

We may make two observations which show the need for an alliance between the historian and the philosopher. In the first place, every history that is a genuine history implies some view of the world. If we call Herodotus the father of history (he is rather the eternal child of history), we shall find in the first book of the father of history, in the story of the fortunes of Croesus, a philosophy concerning the ways of the gods towards men—a philosophy which runs through the whole of his ἱστορίης ἀπόδεξις. And if there is much history nowadays which has no view of the world, and is rather a compilation of facts (which men sometimes call by the name of research), perhaps it is not history. In the second place, every philosophy that is a genuine philosophy implies some knowledge of the present world, and of the factors which have gone to constitute that world ; and the name for that knowledge is history. For the object of the study of the philosopher is spirit, or mind.

15

And mind is not a timeless or abstract thing : it sits at the roaring loom, and weaves its living web. Plunged in time, concrete in history, it is ceaselessly thinking and making and being in successive presents. In each present it must attain self-consciousness ; in each present it must find its philosophy. There is no final philosophy, just as there is not, and never will be, any final history of any age or movement—be it the Periclean age or the decline of the Roman Empire or the Great Rebellion ; and the reason is in either case the same. And just because there is no final philosophy, every philosopher should be so far an historian as to recognize that his philosophy is a philosophy of his own present, and to ensue accordingly—what he can only attain if he studies history—a knowledge of that present in all the fulness of its manifestation.

THIS is the end of the argument, if I have understood Croce aright, concerning history and philosophy. It remains to point some morals. One of these concerns the curricula of the various schools of history which are now established in most of our universities. If the historian must also be a philosopher, the historical student must be trained in philosophy as well as in history. What, then, are we to say of the curricula in these schools of history ? We can only say that they are almost exclusively concerned with outlines or surveys of history, partly English, partly European—outlines or surveys in which the field of ' ancient ' history (in many ways the history which is most contemporary) is left uncultivated, and any reference to the living present is absent ; while, if there be any philosophy, it has generally two defects—it is treated in isolation, in a compartment by itself ; and it is only that one part of philosophy which goes by the name of political science. Yet moral philosophy is of the first order in a study which is concerned with the will and actions of men ; and even the metaphysics of an age may be of primary importance for the understanding of its life. Who can say that he knows much of the Middle Ages if Realism and

Nominalism remain to him unfathomed terms of art ?   The study of the history of an age should go hand in hand with the study of its philosophy.   There is much to be said for those Oxford schools which combine the study of the history of the ancient world with that of its philosophy, or, again, the study of modern philosophy with that of the history of the modern world which started with the Industrial Revolution, the Revolution in America and the French Revolution.

There is another moral, which concerns research ; and this must be mentioned with bated breath.   There is a great vogue of historical research in these days.   But it is possible to wonder whether some of this research is not a mistaken imitation of the sort of research that is necessary and valuable in natural science.   Natural science is a great process of discovery of the elements and the facts of the natural world.   In that multitudinous world research is imperative.   To control the natural world, we must know it ; to know it, we must have at our service a vast mass of induction based on a vast observation.   The world of human action is a different world.   Its facts are not new pieces of matter, or new resolutions of matter into ever tinier and tinier elements.   They are, as it were, fragments of mind—creations of the spirit, and indeed parts of the spirit—which we have to make alive again by thinking them back into life.   Discovery of the fact is important here, as it is in the natural world ; but interpretation and vivification of the fact matter most.   To concentrate simply on the discovery of the fact is to forget the half which is greater than all the rest.   Through such forgetfulness historical research may run to waste.   Whatever may be the needs of natural science, thinking is the thing which we need in the world of human action.   I wish I knew more facts :   I wish I had discovered *any* facts ;   but I wish most of all that I might understand better the facts which I know—and yet do not know, because I do not understand them thoroughly.   We ought all to dig for new facts ;   but if we stop at that, the gain is not very apparent.

All that has happened is much as if we had dug sherds out of a hole in the ground, and piled them in a heap by the side of the hole. It is not clear, if we stop at that point, that the sherds collected in a heap are better than the sherds in the ground. One can only hope that they will be useful to those who come after and can use the material.

I would conclude by saying once more (I only repeat Croce) that the natural world is one thing, and the human world another ; and natural science is one thing, and human history another. Natural science deals with matter, reduced to the nicest and finest subdivisions—all the matter it can find, and all the sub-divisions—an infinity, as it were, of infinitesimals. It employs a busy host of co-operative workers, eagerly watching one another's work : the results attained by an Austrian botanist to-day may affect the conclusions of an English professor of genetics in a few weeks' time. No research need here be wasted : every discovery may tell. It is otherwise with history. History deals with mind and the operation of mind ; and the supreme necessity is that the historian should bring a living mind to the understanding of the operation of man's mind. Co-operation will help ; but the great efforts of the historian have to be made in the loneliness of thought. Thucydides went deeper than perhaps any other historian into the minds of the men whose actions he described. He had researched abundantly for his facts ; but it is his supreme merit, which makes him still the greatest of his-torians, that he thought his facts through, and thought them down to their foundations in the minds of his con-temporaries. And this he did himself, and by himself. And unless this be done, we may say that the writing of history is

> ' Work that obscures . . .
> Making our not-returning time of breath
> Dull with the ritual and records of death,
> That frost of fact by which our wisdom gives
> Correctly stated death to all that lives.'

X

ACADEMIC FREEDOM [1]

FREEDOM, in that sphere of politics in which we use the word most often, may be an attribute either of the individual, in his thought and action within the community, or of the community itself, in its relations and standing among other communities. It may be a right of the citizen, or it may be an attribute of the State. In the intellectual sphere, with which we are here concerned, freedom may similarly be an attribute either of the individual teacher, in his teaching and speaking and writing, or of the whole academic community, in its relation to the general environment of political authorities and economic interests in which it is set. These two freedoms of the mind are almost correlative. We may almost say that a free professoriate means a free academic community; and, conversely, that a free academic community means a free professoriate. But there are qualifications and limitations of this identity. A university which is free from control by the general social environment may seek to control unduly its own professors in the name of its own alleged freedom. We cannot, after all, treat academic freedom under a single head; and in any discussion of the subject we must distinguish the freedom of the teacher from that of the university.

I

THE freedom of the teacher, like all freedom that is other than mere licence and anarchy, must exist within

[1] A Paper read before the Education Section of the British Association at Toronto in 1924.

a framework of law, because it exists within the framework of an institution, and because any institution necessarily involves some system of law. The law of an academic institution is partly an unwritten code of professional conduct, and partly, it may be, a written set of principles and tenets. The unwritten code forbids a teacher to use his classroom as a place for the inculcation of partisan views. It may be difficult to draw a clear line of division between what is partisan and what is impartial ; but we should all agree that there *is* a line, and that, in his classroom, a professor is not free to wander on the farther side of that line. What he may do outside the classroom is another matter, which we must consider later. A written set of tenets and principles is comparatively rare ; but it may obviously exist, for example in a theological college or a general college founded on a confessional basis. A professor who has subscribed to these tenets has voluntarily limited his freedom by that subscription. The college to which I belong [1] at one time required from its teachers a written subscription to the Thirty-Nine Articles. When F. D. Maurice was deprived of his chair, in 1853, for his views on eternal punishment, it was not definitely stated in the resolution of the governing body that he had contravened those Articles. It was stated, in vaguer terms, that his opinions were ' of dangerous tendency . . . calculated to unsettle the minds of the theological students . . . detrimental to the usefulness of the college.' None the less, though the action taken by the governing body was not grounded, and perhaps could not have been grounded, on a definite contravention of the Thirty-Nine Articles, the existence of a rule of subscription to those Articles was the real basis of that action.

A much more difficult question arises when we turn to consider the action of a professor outside his classroom. Here, again, the case of F. D. Maurice occurs to the mind. He had already been attacked in 1851, and virtually cen-

[1] When the Paper was delivered, the writer was the Principal of King's College, London.

sured, though not deprived of his chair, for his connexion with the Christian Socialist movement. The case is curiously apposite to our modern difficulties, even though it occurred over seventy years ago. Croker had launched the attack in the Press, and besides attacking Maurice he had drawn the college into the issue, by stating that ' it added to his surprise to find the holder of such views occupying the professorial chair . . . in King's College, London.' Some general considerations of a large pertinence are suggested by Croker's action and words. The Press, in virtue of its own position as a natural champion of freedom in the expression of opinion, will always tend to defend, and may often actually defend, the freedom of a professor ; but just because it is necessarily set on publicity, it is also a danger to that freedom. It does not help the free course of thought that its delicate difficulties should be cried in the streets. The Press, again, will always attach the label ' professor,' and the name of his institution, when it chances to mention in any connexion an ordinary citizen who is also a professor at any institution. By such attachment a sad result is entailed. If the citizen who is also a professor speaks on a public issue, he is made to involve his institution in what he says. If what he says is unpopular, he may make his institution unpopular : it may lose students : it may lose benefactions.[1] What is the institution to do ? Should it make a rule, such as the Principal of King's College seemed to suggest in 1851, ' that you will do your utmost to bear in mind the duty and importance of not compromising the College ? ' If it makes such a rule, it will be bound to define what is compromising, and it will be bound in the last resort to enforce its definition. In order to prevent itself from being compromised, it will compromise itself terribly. A professor may compromise it in part : it will compromise itself as a whole. A wise president of a great American University—President Lowell of Harvard—

[1] This was stated, or implied, by the Principal and Council of King's College in 1851. See the *Life of F. D. Maurice*, by F. Maurice, ii. p. 80, p. 98, p. 101.

has put the point admirably in his annual report for the Session 1916–7 : ' If a University or College censors what its professors may say . . . it thereby assumes responsibility for that which it permits them to say. This is logical and inevitable, but it is a responsibility which an institution of learning would be very unwise in assuming.' A wise university will run any risk of being compromised by its members rather than compromise its entire self.

BUT if the university is wise to tolerate, the professor is wise to be severely moderate and master of himself. It is true that he is a citizen, and has every right of an ordinary citizen—engineer, lawyer, doctor, or banker— to express his opinions on civic affairs. It may even be urged that he has a special right to express himself, in virtue of the possession of special knowledge ; and it is possible to contend that he has even a duty to aid the judgment of the community by contributing his knowledge and his opinion on vexed questions which lie specially within the ambit of his chair. A professor of Spanish, for example, may hold himself bound to instruct the public opinion of his community on Spanish affairs, and even to suggest the adoption of a definite attitude by his fellow-countrymen in relation to such affairs, if they have become the question of the hour, pregnant with issues of peace or war, and if he has a knowledge which has not yet been attained by publicists, journalists, and other such guides of public thought. On the other hand, it is a pity that a professor should become a publicist except in the gravest emergency. It is difficult to be at once a publicist and a scholar ; and a professor is primarily a scholar. Here we touch a fundamental consideration. A professor is a citizen, with the general rights or obligations of a citizen : he is also a member of a profession, with the special obligations of that profession. Herein he is like the doctor or lawyer, who have also their special obligations, as, for example, the obligation of secrecy in regard to the affairs of their clients. The special obligations of the professor, which are contained in the unwritten code of which we have already spoken, are less definite than those of the doctor or lawyer ; but they are there. He has embraced a profession devoted to the dispassionate search for pure truth. He seeks truth for truth's sake by a rigorous method of inquiry. The temper of his mind must be steeled into a resolute disposition to see every side and to weigh every factor. He is training young minds ; what he is, and what he does, affects the growth of those minds, just because the attitude, the temper, and the method of the teacher are always a suggestive force to the young, and are always, however unconsciously, in virtue of that law of imitation which sways so strongly all our minds, the fountain and source of a like attitude, temper, and method among the taught. If there is a discipline which is a special obligation of the soldier, there is also a discipline which is a special obligation of the professor who serves under the banner of truth. To see, and to show to others, the six sides of a square question : to amass every relevant fact, and to leave no fact unverified : to shun the limelight of publicity, because it distorts and is not the clear light of truth : not to lend knowledge to the service of a one-sided cause, or to divulge research in aid of a journalistic ' scoop '—all these are parts of the discipline. At the same time, the professor must be a man, and not an automaton. He may become the latter, if he is purely and solely of the laboratory. Some measure of outside interest and outside work is a condition of vitality and even of balance. Without it he may be anæmically academic, and lose himself in an exaggerated sense of the sovereignty of his subject. F. D. Maurice was not in error when he said of his colleagues that ' their classes in the college, I believe, are infinitely the better for their labours and studies out of it.' [1]

THERE are certain subjects in which the freedom and the duty of a professor raise specially difficult problems. They are the subjects of history, government, and economics

[1] Op. cit., ii. p. 85.

—to which we may perhaps add the subject of modern languages, when the professor of such a subject concerns himself, as it is good that he should, not only with the language and literature, but also with the history and contemporary civilization of the nation with which he is concerned. If the cause of academic freedom was fought in the past on the ecclesiastical field, and in regard to chairs of divinity, it is likely to be fought in the future on the field of politics and economics, and in regard to the chairs which touch those subjects. A professor of such subjects cannot stop short of running into the actualities of the present. If he were required to do so, he would be stopped from reaching what we may almost call the point of fertilization, where his knowledge touches actual life. I would not say that the history of the past is the guide to the solution of the problems of the present; I would rather say, with Croce, that all history is contemporary history, and that the historian explains what we are by showing to us the living past which makes our present life. Even on that basis, the present is the concern of the historian, as it is also, for that matter, of the teacher of political theory, or of economics, or of modern languages. The teachers of all these subjects are handling and interpreting the present. They move in a region of very special difficulty and very special obligation. They handle the live stuff of which actual political and economic questions, national and international, are made. *Incedunt per ignes.* They may write to *The Times* on current questions, according to our English habit, which has no doubt its Canadian equivalent; they may publish pamphlets and books on current questions; they may even (and this raises its own difficulties) become parliamentary candidates. I cannot deprecate the trend of these subjects and of their teachers in modern universities towards what I may call actuality. At the same time, I cannot but register the difficulties to which it leads. Public attention may be drawn to a university which has become a live coal, and public criticism may fasten on its burning. What is more, a number of interests may concern themselves in controlling the manner of its burning. Universities are always in need of endowment. A benefactor, or a group of benefactors, may be very ready to found a chair—and that possibly a chair of a certain complexion—in a subject of history, or of politics, or of economics, or of the language, literature, and civilization of a given nation. If the professor is conformable to their expectations, all may be well—from one point of view. If he is not—*surgit quaestio*. But this difficulty belongs rather to the topic of the freedom of the whole academic community, and that belongs to another and later inquiry. Here we are concerned with the freedom of the individual professor. So far as that freedom is concerned, I can only repeat, with some qualification and extension, the conclusions I have already tried to state. My general principle is freedom, uncontrolled by any assumption of responsibility by the university, which is likely to run more danger thereby than can ever be involved in any possible indiscretion which a professor may commit in the use of such freedom. My qualification of that principle is two-fold. In the first place, the freedom of the professor is subject to the discipline of the profession, which commands him to seek the truth, the whole truth, and nothing but the truth. If he cannot submit himself with all his heart to that discipline, he had better quit the profession and become a politician or a journalist. In the second place, the freedom of the professor, while it is not subject to the control of the institution to which he belongs, must at any rate be qualified by the duties inherent in his membership of that institution. If it gives him freedom, he must not give it obloquy in return. He will be wise, in many cases, to say, and to say very clearly, that he speaks in his own name, as a private citizen, without any warrant from his institution, or any power to bind or conclude his institution in any way by what he says. But I do not think that a professor will ever go far wrong if he submits himself to the discipline of the profession. The great safeguard of true professorial liberty is simply a stern sense of the sanctity of the academic vocation, cherished among all its members, and enforced by all its members through the sanction of disapproval against an erring colleague. What we need is the elaboration by the professors themselves, and the enforcement by the professors themselves, of a code of professional conduct. But it is not exactly an easy thing. Some professors, of a conservative cast of mind, will always frown upon their colleagues who are hardier, even when they walk within just limits. Others, of more radical propensities, will always smile upon a bold colleague, even when he has obviously overshot any conceivable mark. But if the thing be difficult, it is none the less needful.

II

I TURN from the theme of the teacher's freedom to the broader theme of the freedom of the whole academic community. The mediaeval university, as its very name implies, was a free guild of teachers, or sometimes of teachers and scholars. It was not subject to any local authorities (there were none, and anyhow it was not local) ; it was hardly subject to the State, for the State was a loose federal sort of body, which left all guilds pretty much to their own devices ; it *might* be subject to the Pope, because its members were clerks, but it could be turbulently independent even in the face of the Pope. There were benefactors—munificent benefactors—who founded great colleges within the universities ; but though they were fond of making statutes for the government of their colleges, they left opinion alone, for the simple reason that there was no need for any sort of control. The curriculum was largely a traditional curriculum in the arts ; and if theology was sometimes fertile of heresies, there was, at any rate, only a single Catholic Church, and all men were members of one communion. The modern university is set in a far more tangled web of environment. It is an object of lively interest to the State, which may sometimes exert, or seek to exert, a control of its teachers and its teaching, and may at any rate (I speak of Great Britain)

appoint Royal Commissions to inspect and statutory commissions to reform its organization. Local authorities—
a province in Canada ; a county or city in England—may
interest themselves deeply in what they regard as a local
university. Benefactions and endowments from private
sources may play a large part in determining the extent
and the direction of university development. A Labour
party may demand that the universities shall undertake
extra-mural work among the working classes ; an organization such as our National Union of Teachers may ask that
the universities shall make it their policy to accept and
train as graduates all the members of the teaching profession
in the country. What has become of the free guild of the
Middle Ages ? And should the free guild of the Middle
Ages be our modern ideal ?

No modern university can have anything of the freedom
of a mediaeval university. The mediaeval university
stood alone ; the modern university is part of a great
educational system which embraces the whole community.
It cannot control the lower ranges of this system—the
elementary and secondary schools—or demand that the
work done in those ranges shall be simply preparatory to
its own work as conceived and determined by itself ; for a
majority of the students in the lower ranges will never
come to the universities, and their studies must be organized
as ends in themselves, and not as means or propaedeutics
to work in the university. The university has to adjust
itself to the educational system, and not the educational
system to itself. That educational system is the result
of a social ideal, and that social ideal is in the last resort
defined by Parliament. The university is therefore bound
to conform to the social ideal adopted by Parliament and
expressed in the national system of education. It has the
one consolation of hoping that by its thinking and teaching
it is a great force in forming the social ideal by which it is
itself controlled. In English-speaking countries, at any
rate, the final authority of the State is not an enemy to the
freedom of the university. A much more dangerous enemy

is social interests, especially when they are backed by the power of money. We may not believe in more than five-eighths of the argument of *The Goose Step*, in which Mr. Upton Sinclair draws his lurid picture of the bogy of social interests, and seeks to terrify his readers into a feverish concern for the future of American universities. But even with a discount of three-eighths, or more, he is alarming.

It is a saying current in universities—and, I dare say, everywhere else—that finance determines policy. It is certainly true that the methods by which a university secures its revenue cannot be without effect on the freedom with which it develops its policy of education. In no university—not even in Oxford and Cambridge—does the student pay the whole, or anything like the whole, of the cost of his education. In the newer English universities we may say that, on the average, the student provides three-tenths of the cost of the running of his university. The remaining seven-tenths has to be found from other sources. Before we look at those other sources, we may venture on a general observation. The persons or bodies who provide the required seven-tenths may be inspired by a variety of motives. We may put first the motive of advancing the cause of truth and promoting the higher education of the best minds of the community. But we must allow for the entry of other motives. A university is, we may say, a great pulpit ; and there will also be some who desire to ' tune the pulpits' and to make the preachers say acceptable things. It is another current saying that those who pay the piper call the tune. We should be shutting our eyes to a genuine danger if we did not admit the possibility of ' tuning.' And if we regard it as an un-desirable possibility, we must be ready with suggestions for its avoidance or, at any rate, its diminution.

THERE are three possible sources of university revenues. One is the fees of students : a second is private benefac-tion : a third is public assistance, whether from the national or the local authority. It is a desirable thing that universities should continue to draw an income from the fees of their students.   It is earned income : it is independent money. It is good both for the university and the student, making the one feel that it earns as well as spends, and the other that he gives as well as receives.   It is indeed a pity that any system of fees should exclude a single student of promise from a university.   But a proper system of national and local scholarships (which should include maintenance, where it is necessary, as well as fees) will prevent any such exclusion.   Granted, therefore, such a system of scholarships, there seems to be every reason for maintaining university fees which provide from three-tenths to two-fifths of the income of a university.   They help to give the university self-respect and independence ; they may help to give the same qualities to students.

The second source of income, which takes the form of private benefaction, has its fine and attractive side.   When one listens, in the Bidding Prayers of the old English universities, to the names of the benefactors of dead and bygone centuries, one cannot but be proud of a great tradition long and truly maintained.   And again, when one thinks of the paucity of private benefaction to universities in England to-day, and contrasts the abounding munificence of many cheerful givers in the United States, one cannot but feel abashed.   Yet there is some reason for feeling that, in modern democratic communities, there is a limit to the extent to which private benefaction can safely endow universities.   Universities are great public institutions. They belong to the general commonwealth.   They cannot be proprietary.   They cannot be sectarian.   They must be above even the suspicion of belonging to one or other side in our social cleavage. They belong to both.   A university which relies to any great extent on private benefaction may tend, however unconsciously, to teach and to preach acceptable things ; and that is the greatest offence which it can commit against the spirit of truth.   To take benefaction if it comes, but not to go out to seek it ; to look even a gift-horse in the mouth with a modest and discreet inquiry ; to be sure that no endowment contravenes by one jot or tittle freedom of inquiry or freedom of expression—these are the natural policies of a university which respects its own genius of academic freedom. I would not exaggerate the dangers of private benefaction to universities. Often and often it is the fruit of plain and unconditioned generosity. But I would not be blind to the possible dangers. And it is always possible that private benefactions may have their tacit implications— a form of capitalism ; a particular kind of nationalism ; some brand of confessionalism—which may make them enemies of academic freedom.

I come, in conclusion, to the third source of university revenue, which is that of public assistance from the local or national authority. If our universities are truly great public institutions, subject (as they are in England) to visitation by the State and to reformation by the State, they must be a charge on the public revenues for that part of their expenditure which they cannot earn by fees from their students or receive in gifts from private endowments. In our English system the aid given to education from public funds (whether the education be elementary, or secondary, or university) is always two-fold. Part comes from the local authority—the county or borough council : part comes from the national exchequer. The two co-operate : they bargain, and often dispute, about their respective shares. Sometimes education suffers from their disputes ; but in many ways (and not least in universities) it gains from the presence and joint action of the two authorities. The national authority may stimulate a local authority to increase its contribution ; the local authority may attach such conditions to its contributions as will prevent the national authority from decreasing its quota of support. There is a certain gain in the system of check and counter-check between local and national authorities. It is more favourable to universities than a system in which there is only a single public authority. It is sometimes a little of a trouble (and in a moment of irritation one might even describe it as a nuisance) that both authorities are apt to crave information about the same point on different schedules. But the gain is much greater than the loss.

The aid which is given by the national authority to universities in Great Britain is at the present time much greater than that which is given by the local authority.[1] And it is given on a singularly liberal scheme. An annual sum of a given amount is distributed by a Treasury Committee of independent scholars among the universities in the shape of block grants, which each university is free to spend along the lines of its own policy. Only in the sphere of medical education, and in respect of the grants made to medical schools, has any specific educational condition been attached. Here the policy of favouring the system of clinical units has been adopted by the Committee, and that policy has its critics. That, however, is the only action which even smacks of interference. The aid given by local authorities is hardly given on so liberal a scheme. Local authorities are apt to regard universities as their own local institutions which they should control to a greater or less degree ; and they sometimes allocate their aid to specific purposes only, or attach very definite conditions to their grants. So long as their grants are decidedly less than those of the national authority, and so long as there is the dualism of the local and the national authorities, no serious alarm need be felt. At the same time one cannot but feel that the local authorities are inclined to press too far the idea that ' democratic control ' of university education means its control by elected local representatives assembled in county or borough council. We may rejoin that democratic control of a university is control by its own governing body, provided that that body is democratically constituted, and that its action is publicly conducted and amenable to public criticism. The Treasury Committee, which virtually proceeds on that conception, seems closest to genuine democratic principles.

[1] In England and Wales, during the academic year 1922–3, the percentage of the total income of universities due to grants from Parliament was 38·1 : that of total income arising from grants made by local authorities was 14.4.

ON the whole, there is no serious menace to academic freedom in Great Britain from a system of university finance which relies, as our system does, on a balanced mixture of income from fees, public assistance, and private benefaction, with the balance perhaps inclining more and more to a preponderance of public assistance. Much, however, depends on the dualism of our system of public assistance, and much too on our habit of leaving institutions alone, to go their own way, as far as possible. The present position is very tolerably good, and the general English notion of self-government leaves our universities as free as it is good for them to be. There might conceivably arise a government, strongly wedded to definite principles, which refused to give aid to universities unless those principles were taught, or were not, at any rate, neglected in the instruction given by the universities. An advanced Labour Government, for instance, might possibly take objection to the teaching by a university of what, in its view, were ' capitalistic ' economics, and the omission of the economics of Socialism. But the possibility is most exceedingly improbable—unless the professors of economics are exceedingly injudicious. We may safely conceive our universities as already, and likely to be more and more, great public institutions, deriving their income in increasing measure, and yet without any diminution of freedom, from the State and the local authorities. It is to be hoped that the teachers of our universities will *pari passu* conceive themselves (as I believe they increasingly do) as lovers, seekers, and preachers of pure knowledge for its own sake, vowed to no party when they speak from the chair, and rising above party so far as they can in all that they say or do in civic affairs outside.

XI

UNTIL TEACHERS ARE KINGS [1]

' A big subject which I have thought about a great deal is a possible
change in the form of Western civilization from a political to a cultural
basis, in which the dominant relation would no longer be that of ruler
and subject, or " government " and citizen, but that between teacher
and taught. . . . There seem to be signs that political civilization is
nearing its end, and that the other thing is coming to birth—very slowly
of course. Does this signify anything to you ? ' (Extract from a corre-
spondent's letter.)

THE sociable and quarrelsome being called man—who
is often quarrelsome because he is sociable, and
because his passion for his own society leads him to
challenge the principles and the claims of another—has built
for himself societies of an admirable complexity. In the
beginning of time he wrought a small society, curiously composed of men and beasts (for alone of living things he can
give a sort of citizenship in his own polity to beings of
another order)—a society of his women, and the children of
his women ; his dog, and the animal pets of his women ;
his horse, and the cows which, once the pets of his women,
he annexed at an early stage and made his own private
property. To the end of time he will be weaving some social
texture—broad, it may be, as the world he inhabits ; as
fine and as delicate as the subtlest threads of his intelligence
when they have been spun to their finest count after thousands of experimental years. By his very nature he is a
society-making animal ; and there are many factors in his
being which urge him to perpetual creation. There is
common blood, issuing in family and clan, and helping to
make (but not in itself making) the nation. There is

[1] The substance of a Paper contributed to the *Hibbert Journal*, April
1923.

common speech, with its images, its intimacies, its glimpses into the life of things, which are peculiar to some group and all but incommunicable to others. There is common faith, which makes the Church, and a common longing for an ordered life of peaceable exchange, quiet law, and calm security, which creates the State. There is common occupation, the mother of guilds, trade unions, and all professional associations ; there is contiguity, which has always knit neighbours together, and knits them more than ever to-day, as human communications are multiplied and accelerated by the progress of invention. Last of all (but last only in this enumeration, which is very far from ex-haustive) there is common culture—the common heritage of thought and morals ; the sum of intellectual and moral conquest from the wilderness into which man was born ; the slow-bought gain of the long ages, into which each of us is gradually inducted from birth by the process called education.

None of these factors works in isolation. They blend : they cross : they intertwine : they interact. Common blood and common speech, contiguity and a common culture, are all blended with some measure of common faith in the society which we call the State. It is difficult to think of any society which has been, or could be, based only and solely on community of culture. A university may seem to be such ; but a university, as its very name in-dicates (for a university is an *Academia Communitas et Incorporatio* of masters and scholars organized as a guild), is primarily based on a common occupation. Yet if a common culture does not in itself constitute a society, it may be the brightest and most essential star in the con-stellation of which it is part. It may be set, and may shine, either in the State or the Church. The society based primarily on the needs of an ordered life may seek to crown itself with the new lustre of a teacher of men : the society based primarily on a common faith may strive (and this is a thing very natural in such a society) to make itself the expounder not only of its own divine tradition, but also of

all human culture and ' civility.' In the same country, at
the same time, it is difficult to imagine the two separate
societies—if, indeed, they are separate (as perhaps they
need not be, and at times have not been)—both attempting,
whether in union or in rivalry, to perform an identical task.
It is equally difficult in any country, and at any time, to
imagine the task unattempted by either. Society, in one
or other of its forms, cannot escape the burden of enabling
its youth to recapture and recapitulate, by the process of
education, the spiritual experience and the spiritual gains
of all its long ancestry. Just as the embryo in the womb
must pass, in a period of months, through the process of
evolution at which animate nature toiled for æons, so
must the growing mind, in a short period of years, pass
through the spiritual process of development at which
humanity has laboured for untold centuries. And since the
spiritual process has been achieved in society, and by the
stimulus and aid of society, it is by society that its gains
must also be transmitted. We cannot enter into ' our
social heritage ' unless society adopts us as heirs and trains
us for our inheritance.

IS there any record in history of societies which, whatever their other aims, have regarded themselves, or have
been regarded by contemporary thinkers, as primarily concerned with education, the pursuit of a way of life, and the
training of their members to walk in that way ?   In a sense
every Church is such a society—a society of teachers and
taught, of catechists and catechumens.   But many Churches
have dwelt more on the performance of ritual (and they have
made that ritual a priestly mystery, to be witnessed without
being understood) than on the teaching of tradition and truth ;
and even some Churches which have sought to be teachers of
men have preferred the teaching of a peculiar tradition to
the education of the whole man in the whole human inheritance.   There are only two societies which occur to the
retrospective mind as societies which were primarily and
generally educational.   One is the Greek city-state, and

even this rather as it was seen and idealized by Plato than as it actually was—the teacher and the trainer of men which led them to righteousness through the beauty of ' music ' and the austerity of what we call ' science.' The other was the mediaeval Church, and this again as it was seen and sublimated by Hildebrand and his followers, rather than as it actually was—the great mother who reconciled divine tradition with the inherited wisdom of antiquity, and sought to make the concordance thus achieved into the general guide and discipline of life for a universal society. The great didactic of Plato, and the great didactic of Hildebrand (curiously congruous in many ways with that of Plato)—these are the two precedents, and perhaps the only two, on which we can count.

TO Plato, as also to Aristotle, the constitution of the Greek city-state—the scheme which united and incorporated its members in a society—was fundamentally a ' way of life ' (βίος τις). The laws (written and unwritten, but especially the unwritten) were a social code for the making of righteousness. The magistrates were teachers, set to educate the citizens in the knowledge of things good and true and beautiful. In the *Crito* Plato makes the laws of Athens, which he personifies, admonish Socratés as he lies in prison : ' It is we who begat thee, nurtured thee, educated thee, gave thee and all other citizens a share in all that we could.' [1] In the *Protagoras* he makes the sophist Protagoras argue: ' It is the city which compels us to learn the laws and live according to them as our example ' ; [2] for the city is, as it were, a school, and all its members are in a measure teachers, according to their ability. The trend of Plato's thought reaches its culmination in the *Republic*. Here he handles the problems of ' polity ' ; but he finds the supreme concern of polity in the problem of education. He treats, indeed, of those economic and social problems which enter into the foreground of our thought—the problem of property and its distribution ; the problem of the family and its

[1] *Crito*, 51 C.   [2] *Protagoras*, 326 I–E.

social value ; but he regards these as secondary and relative matters, to be determined by reference to the sovereign and absolute standard of education. He would crown the teacher, rigorously trained for his high vocation, as King and Sovereign Lord : he would make the work of kingship consist in the moulding of men's minds, ' until they are god-like,' according to the example of the ideal Good, the ideal Beauty, the ideal Truth, which the king-teacher has come to know. ' Instead of conceiving education as a con-sequence of the existence of government, and as one of the functions of government, he conceives government as the consequence of education ; and he finds his rulers in the course and as the result of the creation of an educational system.' Even in the State which he constructs in his old age in the *Laws*—the State which is only sub-ideal or second best—he clings to the primacy of education. The teacher is no longer sole monarch ; but the Minister of Education (ἐπιμελητής τῆς παιδείας) is the president of the whole college of magistrates. ' He must be the best of all citizens in all respects ; his office is far the greatest among the highest offices of the State.' [1] The Prime Minister of the State of the *Laws* is the President of the Board of Education.

We must not regard this line of thought as confined to Plato. It runs through the sober thought of Aristotle. ' Nobody,' he says, ' could possibly doubt that the chief concern of the law-giver must be the education of the young.' [2] His whole theory of ethics demands a process of ' habituation,' or training in moral habits, as a necessary propaedeutic to virtue ; and he regards the city-state and its authorities as alone competent to furnish this training. Nor were Plato and Aristotle, in entertaining such opinions, walking on clouds, far above the actual practice of the cities of their day. It is true enough that there was very little of what we should call public education in contemporary Athens ; it is true that parents ' saw to their children them-selves, privately, giving such private instruction as they saw fit.' [3] But Pericles could claim for Athens : ' Our city as a

[1] *Laws*, 766 A ; 765 E.   [2] *Politics*, 1337*a* 11.   [3] Ibid., 1337*a* 25.

whole is an education to Greece ' ; and the city which was a school for other cities was also a school of taste and conduct and character for its own members. It taught its citizens by a spontaneous didactic ' to be lovers of beauty without extravagance and lovers of wisdom without unmanliness ' ; it provided, above all other cities, ' recreations from toil for the spirit—contests (in tragedy and in comedy and in lyric poetry) all the year round, and beauty in public buildings to delight the eye day by day.' [1] The Athens of Pericles, after all, was an educational State.

THE parallel between the *Republic* of Plato and the Church of the Middle Ages is one which always fascinates the mind. There are many factors in the parallel (the Seven Liberal Arts and the Three Estates of the Middle Ages are Platonic) ; but there is one which is fundamental. The Mediaeval Church, like the Platonic State, was essentially an educational society—educational not only in the sense of teaching the absolute Truth, but also in shaping the minds of men into a ' god-like ' conformity with it by the discipline and habit of a social organization. The priest-teacher, like the philosopher-teacher of Plato, was a sovereign king. He held in his hands the divine and eternal Essences of whatsoever things were true, or just, or lovely. By the triple power of his holy orders, which made him at once teacher and judge and dispenser of sacraments, he led men from the cave of this world into the Light. ' Perfect guardian ' of the Faith, trained by the University in all its wisdom, he trained in his turn, from pulpit and confessional and altar, all the ranks of the faithful—instructing the military classes when, and for what just cause of crusade or chivalry, they might draw the sword ; and showing the producing classes how, and under what rules of just price and fair wage and abstention from usury, they should discharge their function of making and exchanging commodities in the service of society.

In diminished form, and with fading splendour, the

[1] *Thucydides*, ii. c. 40 ; c. 36.

educational conception of the Church lingered still in early Anglicanism and in early Calvinism. Laud, who acknowledged Aristotle as his ' master *in humanis*,' would gladly have habituated all Englishmen by a decent and orderly ritual into the ' Beauty of Holiness ' which he revered.[1] But his thought moved in a narrow circle of vestment and canon ; and in England neither the Church, nor the State which had encroached on the Church, was for many centuries to be concerned in any serious way with the problem of social education. Calvin furnished his followers with logic and a moral code. A system of ' holy discipline ' enforced the code with the rigour of an austere drill. But the social note of Calvinism grew faint and thin as emphasis came to be laid more and more on the lonely individual, and the holy discipline of the congregation passed into the private duty of a stoical self-conquest and self-mastery. Formal as Anglicanism and solitary as Calvinism became, the parish churches and the dissenting chapels of our country have none the less continued, each within its range, to be centres of social life and training. Even to-day, when the hold of church and chapel seems to ourselves more and more loose, the foreign observer will tell us that one of the most salient factors in our national life is the training which, by preaching and by social teaching, both seek to give to their members.[2]

BUT we have to confess—and not only to confess, but to cry aloud, lest the State should forget its duty—that since the Reformation the State has taken over from the Church the mission of culture which the Church had hitherto assumed, and made education henceforth a lay concern and a lay prerogative. What has the State done with its mission ? In our own country, at any rate, we must admit that for many centuries it made default. Neither in the practice, nor even in the theory, of the English State was there any real recognition of its educational duty. Burke,

[1] Gardiner, *History of England*, vii. p. 125.
[2] The observation was made to the writer by Professor Salvemini of Florence.

indeed, could think of the State as a partnership in every art and in every virtue. This was a noble idealism. But it was an idealism more remote from the facts of English life than was Plato's dream of his heavenly city from the facts of the life of Athens. Perhaps there was no time, and no country, in which education was so much the duty of the State, and so little its actual concern, as in England during the reign of George III.

The old England, of the quiet stationary days before the Industrial Revolution, was a home of agriculture, but of agriculture which was combined, in a greater or less degree, with domestic industry. In itself the combination of the two was something of a training, and served to elicit and develop general faculty. It belonged to a stage of mental growth—' the stage,' as it has been said, ' during which education springs naturally from the experiences of daily life.' [1] The village, too, was still a society, with a life and order of its own ; and village opinion combined with squire and parson to exact standards of conduct and to give a training in the decencies and courtesies of life. There was no general national culture, but there was at any rate a culture of the village ; and even if it was rude, vernacular, and stolid, it was a way of life and a discipline.

Then there came—first for thousands, and in time for hundreds of thousands, and in time for millions—a period of uprooting ; a period of bare and squalid isolation, when life was lived in the moral loneliness of the crowded slum. The Industrial Revolution took men and women from the old order of the village ; it planted them in a new environment, with no principle of order or system or life. They lost the fullness of occupation, which in itself had been a training of faculties : they were set to a single process in a single occupation. There were advantages in the Revolution for those who had a quick eye and a ready initiative : there were some working men who became great inventors, and many who became small capitalists, in the new age. For the mass of men there was a double loss—the loss of the general training

[1] A. E. Dobbs, *Education and Social Movements*, p. 15.

of faculty which the old order had in its measure provided, and the loss of the social environment and the social discipline which the old order had to some extent given.

The national volume and the national character of the great dislocation involved a national remedy. The industrialized State, to save its soul, must also become an educational State. Society at large must give that general training of faculty and provide that social environment and discipline which were now a general social need. It was a hundred years before the problem was fully faced. Even to-day, more than a century and a half after the beginning of the greatest revolution which has happened in our history, we are still confronted by the problem, which we not only have not solved, but have not even yet entirely understood.

THERE are three absolute and sovereign Ideas, or values, which a society should ensue as the standards of its life. There is the True ; there is the Beautiful ; there is the Good. The apprehension of these three involves a corresponding group of spiritual powers—knowledge, taste, and the faculty of moral judgment which issues in right conduct. The acquisition of knowledge, and of taste, and of the faculty of moral judgment, is a social process. It must be pursued in a social environment : it can only be attained by social organization and a social discipline. Knowledge is not only concerned with what *I* think to be true ; taste is not only concerned with what *I* think to be beautiful ; moral judgment is not only concerned with what *I* think to be good. No one need decry the healthy salt of individualism in the English temper, which made ' self-help ' a word of magic and a principle of conduct, from the days of the Puritans to the days of the modern man of business, and impelled English working men, when they were left destitute by society, to seek what was true and lovely and of good report for themselves, by their own mechanics' institutes, their own mutual improvement societies, their own educational associations. The fact remains that without the co-operation of the general society, which alone can supply adequate means, a full environment, and a broad and dispassionate spirit, self-help must labour in vain. It will be weak for want of means ; it will be thin and meagre for lack of compass ; it will be one-sided and sectarian for lack of correction. Only the whole society can educate the whole man in the whole of his powers. However averse we may be in England from the old Greek conception of a social discipline, we must conquer our aversion.

We began to conquer our aversion when, in the nineteenth century, we recognized that the State must undertake elementary education : we conquered it still further when, in the beginning of the twentieth century, we recognized that it must also undertake secondary education. A technical and utilitarian bias, as was natural in England, deflected our first beginnings. Knowledge, regarded as a practical power making for self-advancement, was the only power which the State sought to give, and truth, of the sort which helped the industrial wheels to revolve, was the only value which it recognized. It was not so in the private secondary schools which multiplied apace in the nineteenth century. Here, under the influence of great headmasters and headmistresses, a wider and deeper conception held the field. The school attempted and achieved for its pupils, in something of the old Greek way, a general training of mind and taste and character. This was the privilege of a class ; but in the twentieth century the privilege of a class began to be vindicated as the right of the nation. The men charged with the care of national education had come from the great private secondary schools (which we paradoxically call ' public schools '), and they had learned their lesson. They had been trained at the older universities (and especially at Oxford) in an understanding of the Greek ideal. The consequences may be seen in the Introduction to the Code of Regulations for public elementary schools, as it was framed in the days of Sir Robert Morant : [1]

[1] Now printed in Section 1 of the *Handbook of Suggestions* issued by the Board of Education.

'The purpose of the public elementary school is to form and strengthen the character, and to develop the intelligence of the children entrusted to it. . . . With this purpose in view it will be the aim of the school to train the children carefully in habits of observation and clear reasoning, so that they may gain an intelligent acquaintance with some of the facts and laws of nature ; to arouse in them a living interest in the ideals and achievements of mankind ; . . . to give some power over language as an instrument of thought and expression.[1] . . . And though their opportunities are but brief, the teachers can yet do much to lay the foundations of conduct. They can endeavour, by example and influence, aided by the sense of discipline which should pervade the school, to plant in the children habits of industry, self-control, and courageous perseverance in the face of difficulties : they can teach them to reverence what is noble, to be ready for self-sacrifice, and to strive their utmost after purity and truth ; they can foster a strong sense of duty, and instil in them that consideration and respect for others which must be the foundation of unselfishness and the true basis of all good manners.'

Here is an ideal, and a noble ideal. How can it be translated into the substance of our social life ? Let us remember, in the first place, that we are mainly concerned with the problem of primary education. Primary education is the primary duty of the State. Secondary education will not solve, and is not meant to solve, the problem of the training of the mass of our population. It is easy to think of free secondary education for all. Free secondary education for all, if it were actually given and actually taken, would raise an insoluble problem in its turn. How could society ever find for its members sufficient work, of what we may call the professional order, if there were added to the natural and general passion of all men to find such work a training which must always be interpreted as leading directly to it ? An educated nation is a good thing ; but a nation in which all were educated alike would be a poor thing. It would be a fantastic society in which every member went

[1] One might add : ' To give some command of drawing and music as instruments of the appreciation and expression of beauty.'

each morning to a business which did not exist by a train which there was nobody to drive. There is no good reason, if there is any, for the existence of different classes based on differences of descent or wealth, or for different systems of education to suit those differences. There is a reason deep in the constitution of human nature for different aptitudes and for different systems of education to suit those differences of aptitude. There must be an independent and complete system of education—begun in elementary schools, maintained in senior schools, and continued in adult schools and classes—for that great part of our people which maintains the state of the world by the work of its hands. Such a system is an end in itself, and not a means to secondary education, which is, in comparison, a secondary thing. It is the greatest and most important of educational systems, because it affects the greatest part of society, and because it needs for its working a genius of comprehension and a wealth of character. It is its task to give to all (what for some will be further polished and refined) a knowledge of fundamental truths and a taste for essential beauties and a grasp of vital duties, so that all may realize the same values, and all may meet in a common understanding of the same terms. There can be no greater task.[1]

In the second place, the realization by a society of an educational ideal is a matter that goes beyond schools. No society can devolve this work altogether upon its schools. Every society must also shoulder the burden itself. The houses in which men live ; the public buildings by which they are surrounded ; the amusements with which they are provided—all these affect education, and are part of education. Ugly and crowded homes ; mean or flamboyant public buildings ; places and modes of amusement provided by dealers ready to make profits by playing on men's meaner tastes—all these are teachers, and bad teachers. It is a

---

[1] The ideas which are here dimly expressed were clarified for me by my membership of the Consultative Committee of the Board of Education, and by the report on *The Education of the Adolescent*, which that Committee issued in 1926.

lesson of Plato, and a very true lesson, that youth should
' dwell in a land of health, amid fair sights and sounds, and
receive the good in everything ; and beauty, the effluence
of fair works, should flow into the eye and ear, like a health-
giving breeze from a purer region, and insensibly draw the
soul into likeness and sympathy.' [1]   It is not a fantastic
folly of the artist to demand beautiful buildings for the eye
to feed upon : it is not an aesthetic pose to claim that the
State should support good music and good plays.   These
things are teachers of us all.   They are part of the social
influence ' which flows into the eye and ear.'   The teaching
should be clean : the influence should be pure.   It is more
than a matter of the education of taste.   If cleanliness is
next to godliness, taste is a still nearer neighbour to goodness.   We are taking out an insurance for right conduct as
well as for good taste when we set beauty in our public places.

BUT if the education of a community is wider than
schools, it is deepest in schools.   They are the pivot of
everything else.   Unless we train taste and bestow the gift
of appreciation in schools, it will avail us little to create
beauty outside.   And the essence of the school is the
teacher, and his personal influence, and the suggestion which
that influence carries to his students.   This may seem
obvious.   But do we really apprehend the obvious ?
Besides education, there is a thing called educational
administration.   Under present conditions it is the educational administrator, and not the teacher, who is climbing
the throne and clutching the crown.   In the capital there
are the officers of the Board of Education : in the counties
and county boroughs there are directors and secretaries
of education.   They administer the funds which support
education ; they determine (subject to the control of the
elected members of Parliament or Council, which may be
effective, or may be complacent) the methods of expenditure of these funds ; they issue regulations and circulars ;
they inspect and criticize.   On the ground that public

[1] *Republic,* 401 C–D.

moneys must be expended by public officials subject to the control of public elected bodies, the process of education, which is a spiritual process, is regulated by administrative exigencies and political machinery. This is not democracy, which should surely mean that the essential agents of the process of education are at least partners in its direction. Yet in the name of democracy the negation of democracy is practised ; and the ideal of the educational State is dimmed by a heavy cloud. However popular, in its ultimate basis, a system of ' public control ' of education may appear to be, there is something wanting in such a system if it leaves the teacher as an official, controlled by officials, who in turn are controlled by public bodies. The State political triumphs over the State educational ; and education is guided not by its apostles, but by the organizers who stand behind the apostles. But if the State, in one of the greatest of its aspects, is an educational institution for the civilization (which literally means the induction into citizenship) of all its members, we must count its teachers among its ministers rather than among its officials. They are the mediators in that process of harmonizing the mind with things good and true and beautiful, which is education ; they carry the torch and tip with flame the outstretched unlit torches of the young. Administrators exist to secure the conditions which are necessary for this service of ministration. But ministration is prior to administration.

Yet we need not, upon this basis, assume that a guild of teachers should manage the profession of teaching as its own particular concern, on the lines of syndicalism. Education is the concern of the whole community (as indeed are all professions and occupations in their degree), and its care is the care of the whole community. But the community includes teachers ; and the only way in which the community can control education democratically is by the association of the teacher with its control. The University, as it is organized in England, is a model. Each University has its senate of teachers for academic matters ; each has also its court or council for general affairs, and a certain number of teachers are always members of that court. One need not urge that every secondary and primary school should have its senate ; but it is hardly a wild dream that every type of school should have a governing body of its own, on which a certain number of teachers might always sit. There might well be difficulties in the inclusion of teachers on governing bodies which regulated the pay of teachers ; but anyone who has been accustomed to the methods of university government knows that such difficulties can be surmounted. Nor is it enough to associate teachers with the governing bodies of particular schools. They should also be associated with the county and county borough educational authorities ; and they should be associated, too, with the Board of Education. There is a model for this latter association in the Consultative Committee, which is a body of teachers, and of men and women of experience in education, connected (only, as yet, in a small way, but the connexion may well be extended) with the officers of the Board. One would like to see similar consultative committees attached to the local educational staffs which in London, Manchester, the West Riding, and other cities and counties, have assumed so large dimensions.

It may seem a far cry from Plato and the Mediaeval Church to things such as these. We started by desiring an educational society, which placed first among its duties that of handing to each generation the accumulated tradition of beauty and truth and goodness : we end by desiring that teachers should sit on the governing bodies of schools, and be associated through consultative committees with the local and national administration of education. But perhaps the first step towards the ideal is this modest recognition of the teacher. Not that we need despair of a future in which we shall go still farther. The Minister of Education of whom Plato wrote in the *Laws* was the Prime Minister of the State. We have known in England a Prime Minister who was also Foreign Secretary ; we may yet know a Prime Minister who shall also be President of the Board of Education. If that should come, it may well

17

be interpreted as a sign and a symbol of the primacy of the educational function of the State. ` In those days there may also be a Minister of the Fine Arts ; and then ' beauty, the effluence of fair works, may flow into the eye and ear . . . and insensibly draw the soul.'

WE have dreamed enough of the organization of education in a future England—the position of the teacher, the action of ' authorities ' and ministries, the system and the machinery of an educational society. It is time to turn to the inward life and the essential process of such a society. What can it give to its members ? First, perhaps, and foremost, a gift which we all desire, and few of us ever obtain —the gift of ' redeeming the time.' We all desire energy of life—the quick beat of the pulse and the eager sweep of the spirit ; but what dusty answers most of us get to our desires ! The poet wrote :

'Getting and spending we lay waste our powers.'

But it is not so much in getting and spending, as in the intervals of leisure which lie between the spaces of our work, that we are guilty of waste. Leisure can be a noble thing, but how few can spend their leisure nobly ; how few have had the training which alone can give men ' the harvest of a quiet eye.' A community has to be trained not only to do its work, but also to enjoy its leisure ; and there is a sense in which leisure, in the fine Aristotelian sense of the word, is more important than work. One might almost say that the greatest aim of any training of the mind is to ensure, or at any rate to promote, the right enjoyment of leisure.

But it is not only the gift of enjoying leisure which an educational society might bring to all of its members. There is another thing, which is closely allied ; and that is the gift of social homogeneity. A good community should be homogeneous, in the sense that its members have been trained together, can enjoy their leisure together, are able

to discuss things together, and have learned to meet together in all things on a common ground. Education
should unite ; but it can also be made to divide. When
there is one system and scheme for one class, and another
for another, education creates ' two nations ' and two
States, where there should be one nation and one State.
It ought to be the initiation of all into the total civilized
achievement of the centuries. It fails if some are initiated
into the achievement as it stands to-day, and some are
left on the level of *panis et circenses* attained in the first
century A.D.

If we could create, through education, a homogeneous
community, thinking in the same terms, and therefore
capable of bringing all things to the arbitrament of discussion, we should have gone far to solve the general social
problem. There is a momentous choice before us at the
present time. Which is to be our conception — the State
socialistic, or the State educational ? If we reflect that
what is wrong with our economic life is less the unfair distribution of the product than the inadequate volume and the
unsatisfactory organization of production, we shall realize
that our chief material need is an increase in the energy
and the mass of production ; and if we realize that, we
shall conclude, simply on material grounds, that the right
conception of the function of the State is the conception
which makes most for energy and increase of production.
But production depends fundamentally on the two factors
of knowledge and goodwill. The State can do most to
ensure the presence of these factors by educating its members
in knowledge, and in that mutual understanding which is
the foundation and the condition of goodwill. It may do
more, and go further, if it seeks to create the conditions in
which the social problem (I would rather call it the economic
problem ; the social problem is something greater) can be
solved by its citizens, than if it attempts to solve the problem
itself. It can solve the true social problem which belongs to
its sphere if it educates employers and employed to the height
at which, by free discussion with one another, they can

solve for themselves the economic problems which belong to their sphere. The State is not an economic society, at any rate primarily ; nor is it primarily concerned with economic problems. It is a society of minds, and it is primarily concerned with educational problems. It is as Plato said in the *Republic* : ' If our citizens are well educated, they will readily see their way through other matters : . . . a good education is the best safeguard.'[1]

THE danger of the conception of the educational State is that it may mean in practice the dogmatic State. The Platonic State has its dogmatic side. In the *Republic* wisdom proscribes the dramatist and almost expels the poet ; in the *Laws* a State theology issues in the persecution of heretics. The Mediaeval Church also showed its dogmatic side. *Ex cathedra,* the visible Head of the Church issued his bulls, launched his excommunications, declared and stereotyped the truth. He who would assign to the modern State the inculcation of truth and beauty and goodness may find, if he succeeds, that truth may harden, and beauty freeze, and goodness become a dead form. The shadow of an academy may cover the land ; government may become a government of mandarins ; a correct and stiff prudery may usurp upon the free play of taste ; the initiative of heretics, which is the life-force of the mind, may take wings to itself and fly. The educated, disciplined community may show (as Plato desired that the community of his *Laws* should show) the stiff invariability of ancient Egypt.

But the ' fastidious or pedantocratic school of government,' of which Lord Morley once wrote, is too far removed from the scope of modern ideas, especially in England, to gain any footing among us. Discipline is a word that has lost its savour. . . . And yet it is a good word, which might well be more on our lips. You cannot acquire the things which really matter save by discipline. We may decry the discipline of imperial Germany in the years between 1870 and 1914 : we may doubt the discipline which the Roman

---

[1] *Republic,* 416 D ; 423 D–E.

Church has always exercised.   But no community is possible without discipline.   Plato's *Republic* has its place by the side of Mill's Essay on *Liberty*.   Even in matters of taste and conduct, where discipline is more delicate than in the sphere of knowledge, there are some rules and canons which are indisputable.   And we may go far in the way of making an educational State without infringing on liberty. Teachers to-day are not the autocrats of any finite system of knowledge.   They are researchers who see that the boundaries of their subject stretch out to the infinite.   The academic mind knows the value of liberty for its own work ; it will not readily subject the work of others to mere authority.

PERHAPS England is not very likely to become an educational State.   A State, Plato suggested in the *Republic*, has three aspects.   There is the State economic ; the State military ; and the State educational.   There will always be many—perhaps a majority—who see the State in economic terms as an insurance society making its profit and distributing a bonus.   There may always be some who see the State in terms of power, and believe that it must defend and extend its power by war.   There will always be a few who see the State in terms of the abiding standards, and think that it must train and perfect the faculties and the sensibilities of its members.   If we are not very military in England, we tend to be mainly economic.   Even our idealists to-day are concerned, if you hear them engaged in debate, with wage-systems, insurances, and the organization of industry. Education, they will tell you, does not interest the electorate : it does not excite opinion : it does not glow as a live issue. But there is an old Greek saying—

'Mind, it seeth : mind, it heareth : all things else are dumb and
    blind.'

And the concern of a community which is a community of minds is essentially a concern with the mind.

XII

THE USES OF LEISURE [1]

'The wisdom of a learned man cometh by opportunity of leisure :
and he that hath little business shall become wise.

'How can he get wisdom that holdeth the plough, and that glorieth
in the goad, that driveth oxen, and is occupied in their labours, and whose
talk is of bullocks ?

'He giveth his mind to make furrows ; and is diligent to give the kine
fodder.

'So every carpenter and workmaster, that laboureth night and day :
and they that cut and grave seals, and are diligent to make great variety,
and give themselves to counterfeit imagery, and watch to finish a work :

'The smith also sitting by the anvil, and considering the iron work,
the vapour of the fire wasteth his flesh, and he fighteth with the heat of
the furnace : the noise of the hammer and the anvil is ever in his ears,
and his eyes look still upon the pattern of the thing that he maketh ; he
setteth his mind to finish his work and watcheth to polish it perfectly :

'So doth the potter sitting at his work, and turning the wheel about
with his feet, who is alway carefully set at his work, and maketh all his
work by number ;

'He fashioneth the clay with his arm, and boweth down his strength
before his feet, he applieth himself to lead it over, and he is diligent to
make clean the furnace :

'All these trust to their hands : and every one is wise in his work.

'Without these cannot a city be inhabited : and they shall not dwell
where they will, nor go up and down :

'They shall not be sought for in publick counsel, nor sit high in the
congregation : they shall not sit on the judges' seat, nor understand the
sentence of judgment : they cannot declare justice and judgment : and
they shall not be found where parables are spoken.

'But they will maintain the state of the world, and all their desire
is in the work of their craft' (Ecclus. xxxviii. 24–34).

THESE sentences were written about two hundred
years before our era, under the influence of antique
ideas, common alike to Hebrew and Greek, concerning
knowledge and government and manual work. According

[1] An Address delivered in the Chapel of Trinity College, Cambridge,
on the occasion of the Second Annual Conference of the British Institute
of Adult Education, in 1923.

to those ideas, knowledge and government belonged to the few who had little business and sufficient leisure ; manual work was incompatible with the acquisition of the one or participation in the other ; and yet it had its advantages, for it gave the worker a technique, so that he was ' wise in his work,' and again it satisfied his longings, so that ' all his desire was in the work of his craft.' I have called these ideas antique ; but you may find them in modern history. In 1541, for instance, a body of Commissioners was proposing to confine a school at Canterbury to the children of the gentry, on the ground that it was ' meet for the ploughman's son to go to the plough, and the artificer's son to apply the trade of his parent's vocation ; and the gentlemen's children are meet to have the knowledge of government and rule in the Commonwealth.' Antique or modern, these ideas are contrary to the Christian spirit, as Archbishop Cranmer roundly told the Commissioners. ' Utterly to exclude the ploughman's son and the poor man's son from the benefits of learning,' he said, ' is as much as to say that Almighty God should not be at liberty to bestow His great gifts of grace upon any person . . . Who giveth His gifts . . . unto all kinds and states of people indiffer-ently.' [1] Challenged by the Christian spirit, the old ideas have also been undermined by the spread of democratic principles, which have vindicated the right of the suffrage and, as a corollary, the right of education, for all the mem-bers of the community. Finally, the great change in the nature of manual work which we call the industrial revolu-tion has abolished the advantages which might before be claimed for manual work, and it has thus completed the overthrow of the old ideas. Under the conditions of pro-duction by the machine in the factory it cannot be said that the worker, engaged in the repetition of some mechanical process, either becomes ' wise in his work ' or finds that ' all his desire is in the work of his craft.' And just because he cannot get wisdom or the satisfaction of his longings in the course of his work, he too must somehow find leisure and

[1] Strype's *Cranmer*, quoted by A. E. Dobbs, op. cit., pp. 83 *n.* 1, 104 *n.* 3.

release from business, and out of his leisure gain both wisdom and satisfaction.

We may thus vindicate a right of knowledge for all on three grounds—the ground that it is implied in the spirit of Christianity : the ground that it is a necessary corollary to democracy : the ground that it is a necessary corrective to the conditions of our present system of industrial production. The last of these grounds has been emphasized by Mr. Dobbs, in a work on *Education and Social Movements.* He shows how, in the old society before 1760, the manual worker, often engaged partly in farm-work, partly in domestic industry, and partly in the care of the animals which he pastured on the commons, drew a large experience from the variety of his daily life, and might find in that experience an education of faculty and a satisfaction of the longings of the mind. In the society which shaped itself after 1760—the society in which we now live—the old justifications, such as they were, for a life spent solely in doing manual work have dwindled. Such work is not a satisfaction, and it is not an education. Because it is not a satisfaction, but a drudgery, the workers have demanded, and the conscience of the community has agreed with the demand, that there should be a limitation of their hours, and that periods of leisure should be guaranteed to all who work in factories, shops, and places of business. It is now part of the policy of England to guarantee a weekly half-holiday and otherwise to limit the hours of work ; and we have gone beyond the other countries of Europe in this respect. Because, again, manual work has ceased to be an education—at any rate to the extent to which it once was so—the braver and more adventurous spirits among the workers, a chosen band, have been steadily seeking, for the last hundred years, to find a new education for themselves. More than a century ago the first Mechanics' Institute was started by London working men, in November 1823. Nearly thirty years ago the first conference of a national association for the education of workers—the Workers' Educational Association—was held at Oxford, in August 1903. There is a paragraph in one of the novels of one of the greatest of English writers which puts admirably the ideals of the sort of man who has been a leader of this movement. ' He loved his kind. He had a conviction that the want of most men was knowledge of a sort which brings wisdom rather than affluence. He wished to raise the class at the expense of individuals rather than individuals at the expense of the class. What was more, he was ready at once to be the first unit sacrificed.' [1]

Our modern economic society, we have seen, requires leisure and education as its complements and its correctives. They are two things which should go together. Leisure is a time to be devoted — not wholly, for the body has its claims to relaxation, and the mind too needs its gentle indulgences ; not wholly, but at any rate largely — to the purposes of education and the gaining of that knowledge, not to be acquired in the course of work, ' which brings wisdom rather than affluence.' Education, on the other hand, should be a training—not again wholly, but at any rate largely—in the right way of using leisure, which without education may be misspent and frittered away. This vital connexion between leisure and education is a fundamental thing. Unless we grasp it, we are in danger of abusing leisure and misusing education. And in order that we may grasp it, it is necessary that we should have a right conception of the meaning of leisure.

One of the old Greek philosophers made a distinction which may help us here. He thought that we ought not merely to distinguish between work and leisure, but also to distinguish between leisure and recreation. Work, he thought, was something done not for its own sake, but as a means to something else—affluence, let us say, or at any rate subsistence ; recreation was rest from work, which took the form of play, and issued in the recovery of the poise of body and mind, disturbed and unbalanced by work ; but leisure was a noble thing, and indeed the noblest thing in life ; it was employment in some activity (we may almost

[1] Hardy, *Return of the Native*, Book III., c. ii., *ad initium*.

say some form of work) which was desirable for its own sake,[1] such as the hearing of noble music and poetry, intercourse with friends chosen for their worth, or the exercise of the speculative faculty. In this fine sense of the word, we may say that we live for leisure ; that it is the end of our being, which transcends work and far transcends recreation ; that it is the growing time of the human spirit, which in its leisure from necessary toils, and the necessary recreations they entail as their counterpoise, can expand in communion with its own thoughts and with the thoughts of others and with the Grace of God. The sad thing about modern English society is that there is so little leisure in this higher sense. It is not only that we work so hard : it is also that we play so hard. Perhaps the monotony and uniformity of work sends us in reaction to the hazards of games, or the excitement of watching them, or the still greater excitement of betting upon them : perhaps the urban aggregations in which men now live make them unhappy unless they are crowding together to some common game or spectacle. Whatever the reason, poor leisure is far too often out in the cold, while recreation is romping about all the rooms in the house. One need be no kill-joy or Puritan to think or talk in this strain. Life is something more than a series of alternate layers of lean work and fat hearty play. It is meant for the growth and development of the human spirit. And that growth needs its growing time, which is leisure.

If leisure be largely for education, education is also largely for leisure. We too often think and speak of education as something intended to fit us for life's work. Ideally, it should rather be intended to fit us for life's leisure. I do not mean that education should be humane rather than vocational. Education may be humane, and yet directed to work and the better doing of work. I mean something more—that education should mean the filling of our mind with interests and possibilities of high delight, which we can develop for ourselves in all our leisure hours ; that it should be an initiation in the tastes and pursuits which will

[1] Newman's edition of Aristotle's *Politics*, III. p. 422.

crown our leisure with fulfilment ; in a word, that it should
be a training and a preparation for the right use of the
time of the spirit's freedom. Perhaps education has not
hitherto been sufficiently adjusted to this end. Perhaps,
if it had been, it would have been directed more to the
awakening of a taste for art and music, in order that they
might become the permanent possession and the abiding
joy of later years. Be that as it may, it is surely true that
education is a necessity if men are to gain the faculty of
using leisure easily, happily, and fruitfully.

The use of leisure is a difficult thing. The majority of
us, when freedom is given into our hands, fly to the excitement of some form of recreation. We must be ' doing '
something—preferably something physical : if we are not,
we are lost and without resource. We know the routine of
work : we know the rules and the routine of different forms
of play ; but we do not know how to move freely, originally,
and by our own choice in the world that lies above work and
play—the world of leisure. This is why holidays sometimes
pall, and leave us at a loss : it is why men who have retired
from work sometimes fall into melancholy, and find their
reason for living gone. Leisure without faculty for its use
may even be a mother of mischief ; men may dissipate
themselves in frivolities, and worse than frivolities, because
they do not know how to concentrate themselves upon
better things. A society which guarantees leisure is guar-
anteeing something which may be useless, and even dangerous, unless it adds, or at any rate encourages its members
to add, the one thing which will enable the gift to be used—
a continuous process of education.

The world offers to the mind of man many noble joys.
There is a joy in knowing the flowers of the field, and calling
them by their names. There is a joy in knowing the heavenly
bodies which move above us, and in understanding the
rhythm and the rules of their motions. There is a joy in
knowing the past of our kind, and in unrolling the long
record of human history which explains what we are to-day.
There is a joy in entering into the vision of the poet and

painter, who have seen the ideal beauty which lies hidden from ordinary eyes. There is a joy in wrestling with the thought of great philosophers, who have pondered about the why and wherefore of this mortal world and our mortal existence in it. These are the joys of leisure ; and leisure is the growing time of the spirit because it is the time of these joys. But it needs an effort to catch these joys ; and you cannot catch them without hooks of apprehension. You must know a little in order to want to know more. Blank ignorance is blank incuriousness, but a little knowledge may be the opportunity and the incentive for more knowledge. The facts presented to mere ignorance are facts which there are no hooks to catch ; but when a mind has had some little training, it develops tentacles of apprehension ; it is anxious to seize new stuff, to arrange it and co-ordinate it with the old stuff which is already there, and so to make a little systematic world of its own for its own high delectation. The mind which is furnished with these tentacles and hooks of apprehension is a mind which will never be embarrassed or dumbfounded by leisure. It will begin to play at once, in the nobler sense of the word play : the hooks will grip more and more of things seen and unseen into its consciousness ; and in the growing time there will be growth. When we say, therefore, that education is a preparation for the enjoyment of leisure, we mean that it is an equipment of the mind with these hooks and tentacles, these curiosities and appetites. And from this point of view we may see that there is a large sphere for the education of the adult, and that education is in no sense only the concern of childhood. The child learns at school ; but the child learns at a time when real experience of life has not yet begun. He learns, and is often curious to learn ; but what he learns cannot be co-ordinated with, or grappled into, a first-hand experience, because such experience has not yet begun to be gathered. When he goes out into the world, and begins to gather experience, that experience may seem to him the one essential thing, and the schooltime lessons may fade away into the outgrown occupations of a vanished childhood. It is at this age—the age of adolescence, young manhood and young womanhood—that everything turns on the rescue of young minds from being immersed in mere experience. It is now that they need to recover curiosities, and to be furnished with hooks and tentacles of apprehension, by which they can capture a knowledge which can now be co-ordinated with experience. History, for example, is one thing to a child—a record of exciting events which satisfies curiosity : it is another thing to an adult—a record of the moral experience of men and nations which can be compared with and interpreted by the moral experience which the adult has himself gone through. But unless, in adolescent and adult years, the curiosity be reawakened and recovered, the adult mind may remain immersed in its own more immediate experience ; and the high contemplation which lifts it above such experience, and yet explains and interprets that experience, may never be attained. Adolescent and adult education are in this way of primary importance, if man is to rise to that height of his being in which he uses leisure for the purpose of contemplation of the world, in order to explain it, and his own experience of it, and to attain to the justification of faith in its purpose and operation.

TO the Hebrews, as to the Greeks, the end and the height of life was wisdom—' knowledge of the sort which brings wisdom.' The interest of the Hebrew was in the moral order of the world, and his passion was for a God of righteousness, a strength and stay of justice upholding all creation. ' Behold,' it is written in the Book of Job, ' the fear of the Lord, that is wisdom, and to depart from evil is understanding.' To the Greek the problem of understanding was intellectual : he sought to see the world in the guise of eternity, and to be a spectator of all time and all existence. But he knew that wisdom was not to be had except through a rigorous moral self-discipline. ' Wisdom is not to be won,' said Plato, ' unless a man make himself a slave to its winning.' The Hebrew and the Greek strains were transmitted

together to the Middle Ages ; and the men of the Middle
Ages, from St. Augustine to St. Bernard, from St. Bernard
to Thomas à Kempis, set their minds upon the life of contemplation, the entry into the divine wisdom, the enjoyment
of God. What Job sought, and Plato sought, and the saints
of the Middle Ages sought, is still the goal of our seeking.
Leisure used in contemplation—leisure prepared and trained
for that high vocation—this is the ideal we have to pursue,
because this is the way we go to find our souls, and to find
our God. Action is a natural ideal to a stock like ours, set
in a northern climate, and inured to physical activity ; but
contemplation, though it may be more difficult for us than
it was for Job among his flocks and herds, or for Plato in
the academy, or for St. Bernard in the cloister, is still the
appointed way. We have all, indeed, to play our social
part—to work for our community or class (I would rather
say community than class)—but even to do that properly
we have to retire into ourselves whenever we can, and to
contemplate the why and the wherefore•of what we are
doing, and to think of the ends of being and of grace.

But the contemplation which in this age we have to seek
is a contemplation in which all the community shares.
That is where we must transcend antiquity. Not a lonely
and stricken master of flocks and herds, not a philosopher
among his disciples, not an abbot among his monks—not
these only, but a whole society, is what must somehow come
into the light and life of thought. We must dream a dream,
and we must dream it until it is not a dream. It is a dream
of an England which is not a power that makes war : not
an industrial organization that makes wealth ; but an
educational society, which makes and diffuses wisdom among
all its members. The State which began in war and continued in wealth must one day live for wisdom. It will
guarantee leisure, for 'wisdom cometh by opportunity of
leisure' ; but it will also guarantee that training, and that
furnishing of the mind with curiosity and capacity for
learning, which are necessary for the right employment of
leisure. And the wisdom and understanding for which men

will be curious and passionate in those days will be the knowledge of the Lord, which comes from contemplation of all His works and ways. For the Lord is a God of Knowledge ; and to know Him is our peace. We have each, indeed, an assigned business in this world, and we must each of us be about our business. But the end of our life is not doing : it is knowing—to know, even as we are known. In this age we may pray to be delivered from over-much doing, from the restlessness of action, from the passion of practical energy which is at once the quality and the defect of our nation. The prophets and teachers of Israel pointed to a higher thing. Their prayer was, ' Make me of quick understanding in the fear of the Lord.' ' Give me the spirit of wisdom and understanding, the spirit of knowledge and of the fear of the Lord ! ' ' O, send her out of thy holy heavens, and from the throne of thy glory, that being present she may labour with me, that I may know what is pleasing unto Thee.' ' O God of my fathers, and Lord of mercy, who hast made all things with thy word . . . give me wisdom, that sitteth by thy throne ; and reject me not from among thy children. . . . For wisdom is more moving than any motion : she passeth and goeth through all things by reason of her pureness. For she is the breath of the power of God, and a pure influence flowing from the glory of the Almighty : therefore can no defiled thing fall into her. For she is the brightness of the everlasting light, the unspotted mirror of the power of God, and the image of his goodness.'

NOTE

I have quoted a number of passages from the Apocrypha in this Address. I cannot refrain from expressing my regret that the Apocrypha should have disappeared from almost all the current copies of our English Bible.

May I add that Burke, in his *Reflections on the Revolution in France* (vol. iv. pp. 53–4, of the edition in the ' World's Classics '), quotes the passage from Ecclesiasticus which is quoted at the beginning of this address ? Unlike Cranmer, he accepts the philosophy of the passage. ' The occupation of a hairdresser or of a working tallow-chandler cannot be a matter of honour to any person—to say nothing of a number of other more servile employments. Such descriptions of men ought not to suffer oppression from the State ; but the State suffers oppression if such as they, either individually or collectively, are permitted to rule.'   But it is only fair to say that he adds a proviso : ' There is no qualification for government but virtue and wisdom, actual or presumptive.   Wherever they are actually found, they have, in whatever state, condition, profession or trade, the passport of heaven to human place and honour.'

APPENDIX

LORD BRYCE [1]

IT may be said of Lord Bryce *multis ille bonis flebilis occidit.* In the pages of this Review we may justly, and with a natural piety, add *nullis flebilior quam historicis.* He was a man 'universal in all things,' touching life at many points, and adorning what he touched : he was traveller, jurisprudent, statesman, and publicist ; but there are many to whom he will always be remembered most especially as a lover of history and historical knowledge. It may almost seem that it was by an accident— the winning of the Arnold Prize, nearly sixty years ago, by an essay on the Holy Roman Empire—that his thoughts were turned to history. If it were so, it was a most fortunate and auspicious accident ; for through all the course of a long life history was henceforward to be an abiding possession and a perennial interest in his mind. Busily occupied as he was in multifarious activities, historical studies were rather the occupation of his leisure than the business of his working day. But the occupations of leisure can be the noblest of occupations ; and the pursuits to which the mind turns in moments of freedom may be followed with a zest and a fervour which it is hard to maintain in the dull recurrence of daily routine. It is certain, at any rate, that Lord Bryce always brought an eager and alert vitality to the study of historical problems, and always found a genuine delight in the company of historians. Two instances occur to the mind which deserve to be recorded. Some eighteen years ago Lord Bryce was engaged in the preparation of a new edition of the *Holy Roman Empire,*

[1] An article contributed to the *English Historical Review* in April 1922.

and it was the good fortune of the present writer to be associated with him as his assistant. At the end of August 1904 he was just about to leave London for the United States, but his mind was running with unabated energy on mediaeval questions. A letter of 19th August, written on the eve of his departure, raises a crop of *quaestiones*— the date of Nicolaus Burgundus ; what is to be said about Isaac Angelus and Bonaventura ; what is the best edition of Gerhoh ; what manner of bibliography should be appended ; whether a chronological table of events is desirable, and how it should be constructed. The second instance is curiously analogous, and even more striking. A dinner was being arranged at the end of 1905, in honour of Mr. R. L. Poole, who had been for many years its editor, to celebrate the completion of twenty years of the Review. Bryce was to take the chair. Sir Henry Campbell-Bannerman was forming a ministry ; he had asked Bryce to become Irish Secretary ; and he was forced to pay a flying visit to Ireland two days before the date fixed for the dinner. Just as he was about to leave England he wrote a postcard from Holyhead : ' I have had to cross over to Ireland, but hope to return on Thursday night and to be at the dinner on Friday. Should anything occur to prevent my arriving, I will telegraph ; but I have done everything in my power to secure my being free to come.' He came.

Sixty years of unflagging and versatile work lay between the date at which he took his Oxford Degree, in 1862, and the date of his death. He was called to the bar in 1867, and practised for the next fifteen years. Busy as he was in London, he still maintained a close connexion with Oxford. He had been scholar of Trinity and fellow of Oriel ; in 1870 he became Regius Professor of Civil Law, and he held the chair, though without residing in Oxford, till 1893. But by 1880, when he became Member of Parliament for Tower Hamlets, he had already turned to politics. He was Under-Secretary of State for Foreign Affairs in Mr. Gladstone's brief ministry in 1886 : he was successively Chancellor for the Duchy of Lancaster and President of the

Board of Trade in the Liberal Ministry of 1892–5 ; he was Chief Secretary for Ireland under Sir Henry Campbell-Bannerman from 1905 to 1907. A new epoch of his life began in 1907. Recognized as a foremost authority on the affairs of the United States after 1888, when he published his *American Commonwealth,* he was appointed ambassador at Washington ; and he held that office, with unqualified success and universal approbation, till 1913. The last nine years of his life he divided between his house at Forest Row and his flat in Buckingham Gate. They were in no sense years of retirement. He served as chairman of the committee on Belgian atrocities ; he advocated the cause of Armenia ; he played no small part in the thinking and the discussions which helped to bring into life the League of Nations. He was often to be seen, and he often spoke, at public gatherings in London—at the opening of the Institute of Historical Research ; at the unveiling of the bust of George Washington in St. Paul's ; at any gathering which touched the many interests he cherished. Only a fortnight before he died he delivered the inaugural address at the annual meeting of the Historical Association in King's College, London.

It was a busy life of action ; but he found abundant time for the life of contemplation also. The list of his published works embraces some fifteen different items. He ranged from the flora of the Island of Arran, on which he published a chapter in 1859, at the age of twenty-one, to Modern Democracies, on which he published two volumes in 1921, when he was eighty-three. He wrote books of travel ; books of descriptive politics (with which his name will perhaps be specially associated) ; studies in law ; and studies in history. Two of his books—the *Holy Roman Empire* and the *American Commonwealth*—are permanent classics ; two others—his *Studies in History and Jurisprudence* and his *Modern Democracies*—are mines of solid learning and searching observation. If he did not write on the classics, he was a sound classical scholar, with a classical scholar's gift of happy quotation. If he was a politician, he was also an educationalist. One of his early writings was a report on the condition of education in Lancashire, published in 1867 ; and he rendered an even greater service when he acted as chairman of a Royal Commission on Secondary Education in 1894. If any man ever did, he may seem to have filled his life and fulfilled his plans. Yet he had his unachieved ambitions. The work on Modern Democracies was originally planned as a History of Democracy ; but the mass of material proved too abundant for the potter's hand. And there was a work on Justinian of which he sometimes spoke, and of which, it may be, some portions are to be found among his unpublished papers.

HE was a spare figure, with eyes that you could not but associate with a rapid and piercing vision, set deep under bushy brows. His voice was not resonant, and it had no large compass ; but he persuaded and convinced by the weight of what he said. He had a great discourse in conversation. He had seen many countries, and lived through many years ; and his retentive memory gave him a rich material on which he readily drew. There were times when his wealth was his own embarrassment ; and discursiveness might on occasion be the penalty of his width of range. But he had a shrewd judgment : he never missed the point, even if he turned aside for the moment to follow the many suggestions of association which his memory conjured before him ; and you could trust him to reach with a just precision the conclusion of the whole matter. He had the encyclopaedic mind which is vouchsafed to a chosen few among scholars. He could readily have joined the company of Scaliger or Casaubon or Grotius. Perhaps he was not, in the strict modern sense, a researcher ; but he was, to a very high degree, an inquirer. He was an eager traveller in many lands, with a zest for climbing ; and he travelled in the mind as he travelled in the body, with no less zest for reaching peaks and points of vantage. He had that abundant curiosity which is the mother of observation and wisdom ; and it was joined with an unassuming and natural simplicity of manner, which enabled him to talk easily and associate readily with all the men whom he met. All the qualities of his mind conspired to win him instant and lasting success in the years in which he was ambassador at Washington. Americans honoured the encyclopaedic range of the scholar ; they admired the observer who had written the classical work on their own commonwealth ; they had an affection for the man himself, with whom it was so easy to talk, on a footing of simple equality, whether at receptions, or in clubs, or in the Pullman car of a railway train, or in any other place where men were gathered together. He was simple in a land that loved simplicity ; and of all the phases of his political activity that of his embassy was perhaps the one in which all his gifts worked most harmoniously together to achieve an unparalleled success.

IN the pages of this Review it is fitting that Lord Bryce should be more especially mentioned as a political observer and as an historian. As a political observer he had for his forerunners Montesquieu and Tocqueville, as he has for his successor (if we may speak of a successor) Mr. Lawrence Lowell, the author of a work on the *Government of England* which gives back to England in good measure what Lord Bryce gave to America in his volumes on the *American Commonwealth*. The cultivation of this field of descriptive politics is a matter of no small moment in the modern world. To explain to one country the genius of the institutions of another is to act as an intellectual ambassador, and to lay the foundations of international understanding. There is an internal logic which connects the work of Lord Bryce as a master of descriptive politics both with his embassy at Washington and with his labours in later years in the cause of a League of Nations. He was, indeed, following the most native and the most strongly marked of all his inclinations when he wrote on the institutions of other lands— the United States, France, Switzerland, South Africa, and South America ; for here the traveller was at one with the scholar, as the scholar was at one with the statesman. Not only had he, as a traveller, seèn what he described face to face ; not only did he, as a scholar, know the past of what he described, and the past of other things similar : he had also, as a statesman, played his part in active politics, and he knew with an internal knowledge the actual working of institutions. His books in this field must remain for long years original and authoritative sources from which scholars will draw their accounts of the nature of the political institutions of a large part of the world at the end of the nineteenth and the beginning of the twentieth century.

In political theory, as distinct from political institutions, he was less interested and less versed. There are pregnant passages in the *Holy Roman Empire* on the mediaeval theory of the empire ; there are essays in the *Studies in History and Jurisprudence* on matters of political theory such as Obedience, the Nature of Sovereignty, and the Law of Nature. But his mind inclined to the concrete rather than to the abstract ; he had not that passion for ' seeing things together ' which makes the philosopher. He was less interested in what the state should be than in what it was ; he wished to know what it did rather than what it should do. He believed, indeed, that a knowledge of the past and the present was a guide to the future ; but he did not, perhaps, investigate the implications or the validity of that belief, nor did he reckon very greatly with the part which ideals—ideals that stand above time and experience—may play in the lives of men. He was an Aristotelian rather than a Platonist ; he turned to the ' polity of the Athenians ' more than to ' the polity which is laid up in the heavens.'

A S an historian he gave to his fellows a book which has been a profound influence for nearly sixty years and will be a profound influence for many more ; an essay on the Life of Justinian by Theophilus, which appeared in the second volume of this Review ; and a number of historical addresses and studies which range from the ancient Roman empire to primitive Iceland. His book on the *Holy Roman Empire* appeared in 1864, with a motto on the front page, which disappeared in later editions, *verso Tiberim regit ordine Rhenus*. It was a slim volume of 176 pages ; but already, as is stated in its preface, it had been ' greatly changed and enlarged since it was composed for the Arnold Prize at Oxford.' It continued to be greatly changed and enlarged. In forty years there were four new editions (one of which—that of 1875—was reprinted no fewer than fourteen times), as well as translations into French, German, and Italian. It is curious to compare the edition of 1904 with that of 1864. It contains 571 pages in place of 176 ; and it contains in addition some 70 pages of prefatory matter. New chapters have been added, especially the fine chapter on the theory of the mediaeval empire ; a profounder learning has given a new substance, and a deeper understanding has informed the whole theme. Yet we must not undervalue the original edition. Appearing in the same decade as Maine's *Ancient Law* (1861), it was no less of a landmark and perhaps even more of an influence. It suggested a new interpretation of the course of the development of the modern world ; and instead of tracing, like Gibbon, the decline and fall of civilization from the happy age of the Antonines, scholars were henceforward able to regard the imperial scheme as something which survived, as a living idea and an active force, through all barbarian invasions and dark ages and tumults, and maintained the conception of an ordered polity until the days in which Europe was able to organize itself on new and original lines of its own.

The author of the *Holy Roman Empire* was pledged to history by his own first fruits, and he never failed to redeem the pledge. He was always prepared to take any pains which might advance the cause of historical study. Of the *English Historical Review* itself, as Mr. Poole has testified in a recent number, he was, if not the father, at any rate the godfather. As early as 1867 he had been planning a purely Historical Review ; and when in 1885 the foundation of this Review was taken in hand by a group of scholars at Oxford—acting, Mr. Poole believes, under the inspiration of York Powell, who had talked the matter over with Bryce —he was invited to become its editor. Already immersed in politics, he was unable to accept the invitation ; but it was through him that Creighton became the first editor ; it was he who gave a dinner-party at which the policy of the Review was settled ; and it was he who wrote the preface for the first number. One of the articles which he contributed has already been mentioned ; another, which appeared in volume vii, was a memorial notice of Freeman. And now, thirty years afterwards, in this thirty-seventh volume, it is of Bryce himself that a memorial notice falls to be written. Few as are the titles of the present writer to compose that notice, he has at any rate one—which he shares with many others—that he found in Bryce a generous inspiration and encouragement. For he was kind with a great kindness to young students : he would write to welcome their 'prentice efforts ; he would gather them round his table, and encourage them by his suggestion and advice. He has left many monuments behind him. His books are possessions for ever in the student's library ; the work which he did in politics is a permanent part of national, and indeed of international, history. Among other monuments there stands the remembrance and the affection of those whom he helped and encouraged. There are nations which call him benefactor (*testis Armenia*) ; but among other and larger cares he always remembered the service of scholarship, and he was always ready to aid any student concerned with those studies of history and politics of which he was so eminent a master.